Lecture Notes in Computer Science 9397

Commenced Publication in 1973
Founding and Former Series Editors:
Gerhard Goos, Juris Hartmanis, and Jan van Leeuwen

More information about this series at http://www.springer.com/series/7408

Manjunath Gorentla Venkata · Pavel Shamis
Neena Imam · M. Graham Lopez (Eds.)

OpenSHMEM and Related Technologies

Experiences, Implementations, and Technologies

Second Workshop, OpenSHMEM 2015
Annapolis, MD, USA, August 4–6, 2015
Revised Selected Papers

 Springer

Editors

Manjunath Gorentla Venkata
Oak Ridge National Laboratory
Oak Ridge, TN
USA

Neena Imam
Oak Ridge National Laboratory
Oak Ridge, TN
USA

Pavel Shamis
Oak Ridge National Laboratory
Oak Ridge, TN
USA

M. Graham Lopez
Oak Ridge National Laboratory
Oak Ridge, TN
USA

ISSN 0302-9743   ISSN 1611-3349 (electronic)
Lecture Notes in Computer Science
ISBN 978-3-319-26427-1   ISBN 978-3-319-26428-8 (eBook)
DOI 10.1007/978-3-319-26428-8

Library of Congress Control Number: 2015955859

LNCS Sublibrary: SL2 – Programming and Software Engineering

Springer Cham Heidelberg New York Dordrecht London

Printed on acid-free paper

Springer International Publishing AG Switzerland is part of Springer Science+Business Media
(www.springer.com)

Preface

OpenSHMEM 2015 was the second event in the OpenSHMEM and Related Technologies workshop series. The workshop was organized by Oak Ridge National Laboratory and held in Annapolis, Maryland, USA, and it was and sponsored by ORNL, DoD, Mellanox, NVIDIA, Intel, and SGI.

The OpenSHMEM Workshop is the premier venue for exhibiting and presenting research on partitioned global address space (PGAS), particularly as it relates to OpenSHMEM. The workshop was attended by participants from across academia, industry, and private and federal research organizations. The topics for the workshop included extensions to the OpenSHMEM API, implementation of the API for current and emerging architectures, tools to debug and profile OpenSHMEM programs, experience porting applications to the OpenSHMEM programming model, and changes to the OpenSHMEM specification to address the needs of programming exascale systems.

The response to the OpenSHMEM Workshop call for papers was very encouraging. The Program Committee members reviewed the papers with a very short turnaround. Despite the short turnaround, each paper was reviewed by more than three reviewers, and 12 papers were selected to be presented at the workshop.

This proceedings volume is a collection of papers presented at the second workshop, during August 4–6, 2015. The technical papers provided a multitude of ideas for extending the OpenSHMEM specification and making it efficient for current and next-generation systems. This included non-blocking APIs, teams (similar to "communicators" in the message-passing paradigm), extended capabilities for collective operations, and considerations for additional memory architectures such as accelerators. OpenSHMEM is now being used to explore new parallel algorithms for applications, and those experiences from the developers were also an integral part of the technical program at the OpenSHMEM Workshop this year.

Besides contributed papers, the technical program consisted of tutorials, invited talks, and specification discussion. The tutorials were presented by speakers from NVIDIA, Mellanox, Oak Ridge National Laboratory, Allinea, ParaTools, University of Houston, and TU Dresden. The invited talk from NVIDIA discussed the role of OpenSHMEM in programming GPUs, the talk from Mellanox discussed the effectiveness of using InfiniBand hardware for OpenSHMEM, and the talk from Intel provided an overview of OpenSHMEM activities in Intel.

The third day of the workshop was focused on developing the OpenSHMEM specification. This was a very exciting year in the OpenSHMEM community since the first OpenSHMEM Workshop in March 2014. Two updates to the OpenSHMEM specification have been introduced in the meantime: version 1.1 was released during summer 2014 and version 1.2 in spring 2015. The discussion in this workshop focused on features for the upcoming 1.3 version and future versions.

The general and program chairs would like to thank everyone who contributed to the organization of the workshop. Particularly, we would to thank the authors, Program Committee members, reviewers, session chairs, participants, and sponsors. We are grateful for the excellent support we received from our ORNL administrative staff and Daniel Pack, who maintained our workshop website.

August 2015

Manjunath Gorentla Venkata
Pavel Shamis
Neena Imam
M. Graham Lopez

Organization

Program Committee

General Co-chairs

Neena Imam	Oak Ridge National Laboratory, USA
Pavel Shamis	Oak Ridge National Laboratory, USA
Manjunath Gorentla Venkata	Oak Ridge National Laboratory, USA

Steering Committee

Steve Poole (Chair)	Open Source Software Solutions, USA
William W. Carlson	IDA, USA
Janice Elliott	Department of Defense, USA
Oscar Hernandez	Oak Ridge National Laboratory, USA
Neena Imam	Oak Ridge National Laboratory, USA
Barney Maccabe	Oak Ridge National Laboratory, USA
Nicholas Park	Department of Defense, USA
Lauren Smith	Department of Defense, USA

Tutorial Chair

Nicholas Park	Department of Defense, USA

Technical Program Chair

M. Graham Lopez	Oak Ridge National Laboratory, USA

Technical Program Committee

George Bosilca	University of Tennessee, USA
Barbara Chapman	University of Houston, USA
Tony Curtis	University of Houston, USA
James Dinan	Intel, USA
Manjunath Gorentla Venkata	Oak Ridge National Laboratory, USA
Richard Graham	Mellanox Technologies, USA
Gary Grider	Los Alamos National Laboratory, USA
Jeff Hammond	Intel, USA
Chung-Hsing Hsu	Oak Ridge National Laboratory, USA
Dounia Khaldi	University of Houston, USA
David Knaak	Cray Inc., USA
Andreas Knuepfer	TU-Dresden, Germany

Contents

Poster

API Extensions

Extending the Strided Communication Interface in OpenSHMEM

Naveen Namashivayam$^{(\boxtimes)}$, Dounia Khaldi, Deepak Eachempati,
and Barbara Chapman

Department of Computer Science, University of Houston, Houston, TX, USA
{nravi,dounia,dreachem,chapman}@cs.uh.edu

Abstract. OpenSHMEM is a library interface specification which has resulted from a unification effort among various vendors and users of SHMEM libraries. OpenSHMEM includes routines which aim to support a PGAS programming model, encompassing data management, one-sided communication, atomics, synchronization, collectives, and mutual exclusion. In the work described in this paper, we investigated the usage and performance of strided communication routines. Moreover, we propose and describe an implementation for new strided communication routines, shmem_iputmem and shmem_igetmem, which enable a more general means for expressing communications entailing data transfers for two-dimensional subarrays or for arrays of structures. We demonstrate the use of these routines on a halo exchange benchmark for which we achieved, on average, a 64.27 % improvement compared to the baseline implementation using non-strided communication routines and also 63.37 % improvement compared to the one using existing strided communication routines.

1 Introduction

Partitioned Global Address Space (PGAS) [7] refers to a class of parallel programming models which is characterized by a logically partitioned global memory space, where the partitions have affinity to the processes/threads executing the program. OpenSHMEM [9] is an evolving API standardization for SHMEM which provides a PGAS programming model. OpenSHMEM provides users with the support for explicit data transfers, similar to the message passing model, and explicit data synchronizations, similar to the shared memory model. Through its remote memory access (RMA) interfaces, OpenSHMEM permits a global access to memory partitions across processing elements (PEs) which may reside within or across physically distinct compute nodes.

OpenSHMEM is designed to be suitable for asynchronous, scalable software systems. Typically the data transfers in these software systems are contiguous in nature. However, there are software systems that require non-contiguous data transfers. OpenSHMEM is currently limited in its ability to express such data transfers. Moreover, the strided data transfers which are available are typically

© Springer International Publishing Switzerland 2015
M. Gorentla Venkata et al. (Eds.): OpenSHMEM 2015, LNCS 9397, pp. 3–17, 2015.
DOI: 10.1007/978-3-319-26428-8_1

not well supported by implementations, because of (or perhaps resulting in) their under-utilization in existing OpenSHMEM codes.

It is important for OpenSHMEM to provide more general interfaces for strided communication in order to support data transfer for 2-dimensional subarrays or arrays of structures with strided indexes. We propose two routines for this purpose – shmem_iputmem and shmem_igetmem. We describe in this paper how these routines may be implemented using existing OpenSHMEM contiguous and strided RMA routines. We motivate this proposal with example application codes which exhibit communication patterns that may take advantage of these proposed routines. We also provide an assessment of various implementations' support for the existing strided routines. The performance of our proposed routines, implemented in terms of the existing strided routines, is of course contingent on the performance of those existing routines. Hence, we also investigated this performance across various implementations, observing that almost all of them use a naive implementation based on contiguous RMA routines.

The contributions of this work are:

- a performance study of shmem_*TYPE*_iput and shmem_*TYPE*_iget routines in various available OpenSHMEM implementations;
- proposed extensions for efficient data transfer of aggregate data types, namely shmem_iputmem and shmem_igetmem;
- a new algorithm for implementing the proposed extensions using the existing OpenSHMEM routines: shmem_*TYPE*_iput, shmem_*TYPE*_iget, shmem_putmem and shmem_getmem;
- an evaluation of the proposed new OpenSHMEM routines and their implementations using our PGAS Microbenchmark Suite [2] and the common halo exchange algorithm.

This paper is organized as follows. In Sect. 2 we give a brief overview of various OpenSHMEM implementations and review the strided data routine in the OpenSHMEM specification. In Sect. 3, we assess the implementation of the strided routines in OpenSHMEM by performing microbenchmark tests using the PGAS Microbenchmark Suite. We follow up with the importance of these routines for application designs in Sect. 4. In Sect. 5 we propose the shmem_iputmem and shmem_igetmem routines for inclusion into OpenSHMEM, and we provide an efficient algorithm to implement them. In the experimental results presented in Sect. 6 we use a common halo exchange benchmark for testing the performance of the proposed routines. We discuss related work in Sect. 7, and we conclude in Sect. 8.

2   Background

In this section, we provide a brief overview of different OpenSHMEM implementations and describe the strided communication routines that are currently in OpenSHMEM.

2.1 Overview of OpenSHMEM Libraries

OpenSHMEM is a PGAS library interface which is a culmination of a unification effort among various vendors and users in the SHMEM programming community. It provides an API to support one-sided, point-to-point data communication. It also offers routines for collectives, atomic operations, and synchronization. There are various production-grade, closed source OpenSHMEM implementations as well as open source implementations available. Among the closed source implementations, the implementations in the Message Passing Toolkit (MPT) from SGI [3,5] and Cray [1] are popular. They are optimized to their particular environment using the communication layers XPMEM and DMAPP [19], respectively. The open source reference implementation [16], developed by University of Houston in collaboration with Oak Ridge National Laboratory (ORNL), uses GASNet [8] as its communication layer.

In this paper, we denote the reference implementation as UH-SHMEM. The vendor specific OpenSHMEM implementations from Cray and SGI are denoted as Cray-SHMEM and SGI-SHMEM, respectively. The OpenSHMEM implementation in Open MPI [4] is referred to as OMPI-SHMEM, while the MVAPICH2-X implementation from Ohio State University [6] is referred as MV2X-SHMEM. An OpenSHMEM implementation which uses the Unified Common Communication Substrate (UCCS) [18] as its communication layer is referenced as UCCS-SHMEM.

2.2 Strided Data Transfer in OpenSHMEM

OpenSHMEM provides one-sided, point-to-point RMA using various routines. Figure 1 provides an example for the two different types of remote memory access available in OpenSHMEM: contiguous and strided. The routines shmem_*TYPE*_put and shmem_*TYPE*_get are used to remotely access contiguous data, where *TYPE* refers to a basic data type defined in the base language. On the other hand, shmem_*TYPE*_iput and shmem_*TYPE*_iget are used to remotely access strided data.

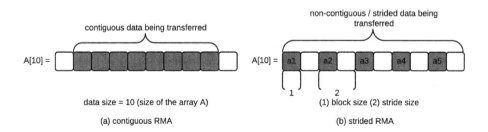

Fig. 1. Contiguous and strided remote memory accesses in OpenSHMEM

Figure 2 shows an example of the usage of OpenSHMEM RMA routines. Here, src_ptr and dest_ptr represent the source and the destination pointers, respectively, `nelems` is the number of elements to be transferred, and `pe_id` is the destination process ID. The stride for the source and destination are referred to as `src_stride` and `dest_stride`, respectively.

In Fig. 2, `shmem_putmem` is used to send data from the local `src_pointer` to the remote `dest_pointer` – `nelems` bytes are sent from local `src_pointer` to remote `dest_pointer` in PE with rank `pe_id`. Similarly, the `shmem_iput` routine is used to send data from the source to the destination with strides of `src_stride` and `dest_stride`, respectively.

```
shmem_putmem(dest_ptr, src_ptr, nelems, pe_id);
...
shmem_double_iput(dest_ptr, src_ptr, dest_stride,
              src_stride, nelems, pe_id);
```

Fig. 2. Example of the usage of the OpenSHMEM data communication routines. Note that in this example the strided routine is for array elements of type double.

Figure 1 shows also the difference between the block size and the stride in a strided transfer. While the stride can be any integer, the block size is the size of the element being transferred. The current OpenSHMEM specification, version 1.2, supports any non-character type that has a storage size equal to 32, 64, or 128 bits. This restricts the usage of these strided communication routines to arrays of basic types. This restriction is discussed in Sect. 4.

3 Assessment of Current Strided Communication Routines

In this section, we analyze the implementation of the strided routines in different OpenSHMEM implementations discussed in Sect. 2.1. There are different ways through which the strided routines may be implemented. The simplest, straightforward method is to call multiple contiguous RMA calls inside a single strided routine, which we refer to as the baseline implementation. Other methods may efficiently utilize the network's scatter and gather operations and can be considered as optimizations over the baseline implementation. In this section, we analyze the performance of these strided routines in different OpenSHMEM implementations.

We used our PGAS Microbenchmark Suite [2] for the performance assessment. We have measured and compared the bandwidth of a non-contiguous data transfer with two different implementations: using single `shmem_iput/iget` calls versus using multiple `shmem_putmem/getmem` calls. The communication is between two PEs, each of which are executing on two separate compute nodes. The purpose of this assessment is not to compare the performance of the strided routines against different OpenSHMEM implementations, but rather to understand the extent to which they are optimized in comparison to the baseline implementation.

We have used the following OpenSHMEM implementations: (1) Cray-SHMEM, (2) UH-SHMEM, (3) SGI-SHMEM, (4) MV2X-SHMEM, (5) OMPI-SHMEM and (6) UCCS-SHMEM. Table 1 shows the experimental setup. We used a Cray XC30 machine for analyzing Cray-SHMEM, an SGI Altix XE1300 system at ORNL for SGI-SHMEM, and the remaining implementations were run using Whale, an AMD Opteron machine with InfiniBand Interconnect in UH. The table also provides the configurations of these machines.

Table 1. Experimental setup and machine configuration details

Name	Nodes	Cores/Node	Processor type	Interconnect
Whale	81	8	AMD Opteron	4xInfiniBand DDR[1] 2012 switch
Cray XC30	64	16	Intel Xeon E5 Sandy Bridge	Dragonfly interconnect with Aries
SGI Altix XE1300 System	12	12	Intel Xeon X5660	Mellanox ConnectX-2 QDR HCA 1 port

[1]Voltaire Grid Director ISR 2012 switch

We summarize our experimental findings in Fig. 3. We can infer that all of the tested open-source and vendor implementations, except for Cray-SHMEM, implement strided data transfers using the naïve, baseline approach. That is, they are implemented using multiple contiguous RMA calls.

In further sections, we will discuss the importance of these strided routines in OpenSHMEM and its related usage in implementing new OpenSHMEM routines for strided communication of 2-dimensional subarrays or arrays of structure types.

4 Motivation: Importance of Strided Transfers

The current OpenSHMEM API for supporting strided transfers is greatly limited when dealing with multi-dimensional arrays or arrays of aggregate data types, such as structures. Certain communication patterns can not be efficiently supported without more flexible strided transfer routines. A distributed matrix transpose, required heavily in Fast Fourier Transforms (FFTs), is an example pattern for which the current strided routines are insufficient and where relying on contiguous communication results in inefficient memory copies. Another example is for neighbor communication for checker board domain decompositions, which for example may be employed in conjugate gradient (CG) iterative solvers. Based on the orientation of the strides in these two examples, the

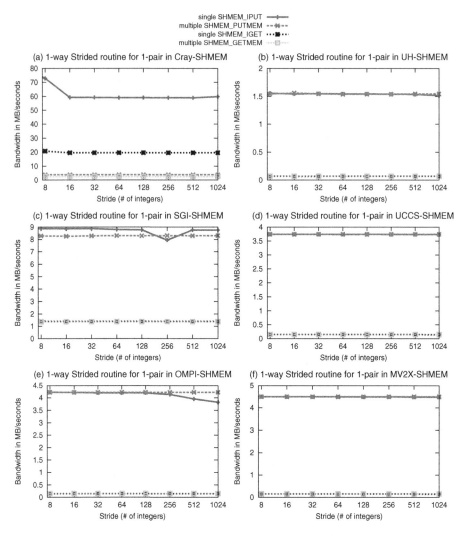

Fig. 3. Performance analysis of OpenSHMEM strided calls, comparing against baseline implementation in three different environments as shown in Table 1

array may possess a checker board orientation or matrix orientation as shown in Fig. 4(a) and (b) respectively.

Ideally, we would want to handle these communication patterns using a zero-copy implementation. The performance challenges for dealing with such communication patterns have been discussed in [11], with solutions described using MPI derived data types for implementing zero-copy algorithms. We suggest that a similar result may also be achieved through the use of more general strided routines in OpenSHMEM applications. The global transpose operation performed by FFT rearranges the given input data more than once by means of packing

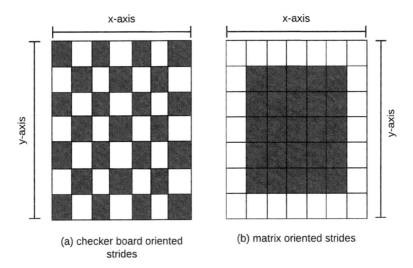

Fig. 4. Different orientations of the strides in conjugate gradient solver (a) and Fast Fourier (b)

and unpacking the given input data. This effectively means a copy operation is performed on the complete data set. Such a copy operation could be potentially avoided through the use of strided communication support, which avoids the packing and unpacking of the data. Similar performance issues for communication in CG solver employing a checker board strides orientation (Fig. 4(a)) may be handled through strided communication routines as well.

The drawback in employing the existing OpenSHMEM strided routines for the above purpose is in the type of the data being transferred. Often, implementations of FFT and conjugate gradient solvers make use of aggregate data types (e.g., structures) to represent the vectors used in the computation. However, the current OpenSHMEM strided routines do not support the use of aggregate types of arbitrary size. Hence, there is a necessity for OpenSHMEM to support more generic data types in OpenSHMEM, discussed in detail in Sect. 5.

5 OpenSHMEM Extension Proposal for Aggregate Data Types

In Sect. 4, we discussed two example applications, FFT and CG, for the strided routines. However, with the currently available strided routines in the Open-SHMEM specification (see Sect. 2.2), we can only express strided transfers for arrays of basic types, which is insufficient for these applications. This essentially means that the type of data which can be used in the strided routines is fixed to a particular type (int, float, long, double, etc.) or a particular size (32, 64 or 128 bits). However, many applications make use of arrays of aggregate data types, such as arrays or structures.

5.1 API Extension

We propose, as an extension to the OpenSHMEM API, the routines shmem_iputmem and shmem_igetmem for enabling strided communication for arrays of aggregate data types. We present the definition of these two routines in Fig. 5.

```
void shmem_iputmem(void *dest_ptr, const void *src_ptr,
            ptrdiff_t dest_stride, ptrdiff_t src_stride,
            size_t blksize, size_t nblks, int pe_id);

void shmem_igetmem(void *dest_ptr, const void *src_ptr,
            ptrdiff_t dest_stride, ptrdiff_t src_stride,
            size_t blksize, size_t nblks, int pe_id);
```

Fig. 5. OpenSHMEM extensions for strided communication of derived data and structures

Along with the source (src_ptr) and the destination (dest_ptr) pointers, source (src_stride) and destination (dest_stride) strides given in bytes, and processing element ID (pe_id), we replace nelems with two new arguments: the blksize argument gives the size of each block in bytes, and nblks gives the number of blocks from the dest and source arrays that are accessed. The specified values for dest_stride and src_stride must be greater than blksize. The block size may be the size of a structure or other aggregate data types.

5.2 Algorithm

We describe an algorithm to implement the proposed OpenSHMEM extensions. This algorithm makes use of the current existing OpenSHMEM RMA routines. Due to space restrictions, we only show the algorithm for shmem_iputmem; the case of shmem_igetmem is analogous to shmem_iputmem.

Baseline Algorithms. The baseline design and the common way to implement the shmem_iputmem routine is to call multiple shmem_putmem inside every shmem_iputmem call, as shown in Algorithm 1.

The second design is to implement the shmem_iputmem routine using multiple calls to *iput* routines. In Algorithm 2, we use multiple combinations of shmem_iput128, shmem_iput64, and shmem_iput32 calls based on the given block size in order to minimize the total number of library calls for performing the remote memory access. These combinations are the result of partitioning the original block size to the common or standard data type sizes of OpenSHMEM (32, 64, or 128 bits). In Algorithm 2, calls to *iput* routines will only be used if the block size and strides for the dest and source arrays are multiples of 4 bytes. Otherwise, it will fall back to utilizing *put* routines via Algorithm 1.

ALGORITHM 1. Baseline algorithm: use of `shmem_putmem`

---

procedure shmem_iputmem_using_putmem(void *dest_ptr, const void *src_ptr, ptrdiff_t dest_stride, ptrdiff_t src_stride, size_t blksize, size_t nblks, int pe_id);
    char *temp_target = dest_ptr;
    char *temp_source = src_ptr;
    for (int i = 1; i ≤ nblks; i++) **do**
      shmem_putmem(temp_target, temp_source, blksize, pe_id);
      temp_target += dest_stride;
      temp_source += src_stride;
end procedure

ALGORITHM 2. Baseline Algorithm: use of *iput* routines

---

procedure shmem_iputmem_using_iput(void *dest_ptr, const void *src_ptr, ptrdiff_t dest_stride, ptrdiff_t src_stride, size_t blksize, size_t nblks, int pe_id)
    char *dest = dest_ptr, *src = src_ptr;
    ptrdiff_t sst = src_stride, dst = dest_stride;
    bool stride_16 = *true*, stride_8 = *true*, stride_4 = *true*;
    if (dst *mod* 4 ≠ 0 ∨ sst *mod* 4 ≠ 0) **then**
      stride_4 = *false*; stride_8 = *false*; stride_16 = *false*;
    else if (dst *mod* 8 ≠ 0 ∨ sst *mod* 8 ≠ 0) **then**
      stride_8 = *false*; stride_16 = *false*;
    else if (dst *mod* 16 ≠ 0 ∨ sst *mod* 16 ≠ 0) **then**
      stride_16 = *false*;
    if (blksize ≥ 16 ∧ stride_16) **then**
      int size = blksize/16;
      for (int i = 1; i ≤ size; i++) **do**
        shmem_iput128(dest, src, dst/16, sst/16, nblks, pe_id);
        dest += 16; src += 16;
      blksize -= 16*size;
    if (blksize ≥ 8 ∧ stride_8) **then**
      int size = blksize/8;
      for (int i = 1; i ≤ size; i++) **do**
        shmem_iput64(dest, src, dst/8, sst/8, nblks, pe_id);
        dest += 8; src += 8;
      blksize -= 8*size;
    if (blksize ≥ 4 ∧ stride_4) **then**
      int size = blksize/4;
      for (int i = 1; i ≤ size; i++) **do**
        shmem_iput32(dest, src, dst/4, sst/4, nblks, pe_id);
        dest += 4; src += 4;
    else
      shmem_iputmem_using_putmem(dest_ptr, src_ptr, dest_stride, src_stride, blksize, nblks, pe_id);
end procedure

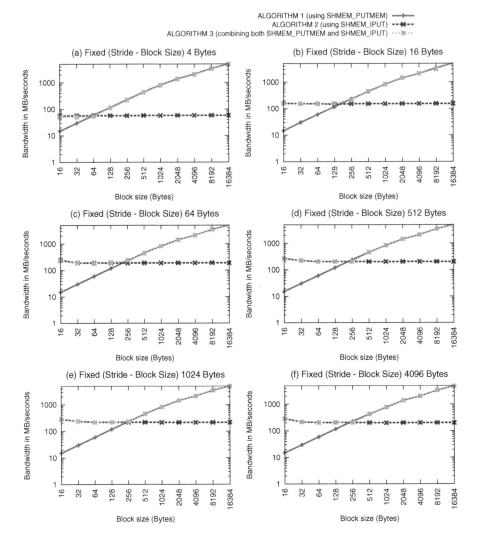

Fig. 6. Performance Analysis of Algorithms 1 and 2 to understand the usage of *iput* routines and `shmem_putmem` to implement `shmem_iputmem`. Note that the algorithm 3 line overlaps either the algorithm 1 line or the algorithm 2 line.

Measurements Using Baseline Algorithms. We have performed the following performance analysis using different stride sizes and varying block sizes to determine the most efficient way to implement our proposed extensions between Algorithms 1 and 2, or a combination of the two.

We ran these experiments on the Cray XC30 machine described in Table 1, using two PEs each on a separately allocated node. We used Cray-SHMEM version 7.2.2 for these experiments, and took the bandwidth measurements using

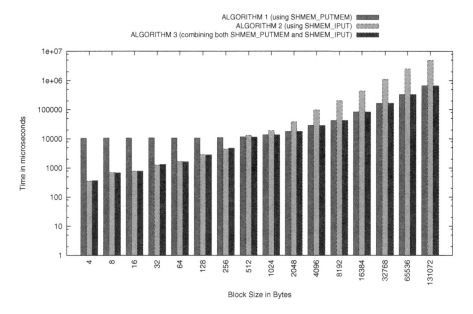

Fig. 7. Performance analysis of Algorithms 1, 2 and 3 using 2D Halo Exchange Benchmark

our PGAS Microbenchmark Suite [2], modified with additional tests for measuring the performance of `shmem_iputmem`.

We present in Fig. 6 the results when using Algorithms 1 and 2 for implementing `shmem_iputmem`. The figure shows the bandwidth as a function of block size for different strides, when the array size (i.e., $stride * nblks$) is fixed to a total of 64 MB. Again, Algorithm 1 uses only `shmem_putmem`, while Algorithm 2 uses a combination of the *iput* routines in the general case and falls back to using Algorithm 1 when the block size and strides are not multiples of 4 bytes. From the plots, we can observe the intersection point at which it becomes profitable for a given experiment to switch between an implementation based on *iput* routines and an implementation based on `shmem_putmem`. We summarize these results in Table 2.

Tuned Algorithm. Consider a parameter α, which selects either Algorithm 1 or Algorithm 2 based on a set of parameters. The previous results can be generalized in Algorithm 3, where we implement the proposed `shmem_iputmem` extension based on this α. The value of α is the result of the predicate function `predicate_lookup_table`, based on tuning parameters (here, we use the values of block size and the stride). In Algorithm 3, we select either the use of *iput* routines or `shmem_putmem` based on the value of α. A similar approach can also be employed to implement *shmem_igetmem* using *iget* routines and `shmem_getmem` routines. We implemented Algorithm 3 and ran it on the same microbenchmark, and the results have been added to Fig. 6.

ALGORITHM 3. Combining the use of *iput* routines and shmem_putmem, depending on different parameters such as block size and strides.

---

procedure shmem_iputmem(void *dest_ptr, const void *src_ptr, ptrdiff_t dest_stride, ptrdiff_t src_stride, size_t blksize, size_t nblks, int pe_id)

    bool α = predicate_lookup_table(dest_stride, src_stride, blksize);

    if *(α == 0)* **then**

        shmem_iputmem_using_iput(dest_ptr, src_ptr, dest_stride, src_stride, blksize, nblks, pe_id);

    else

        shmem_iputmem_using_putmem (dest_ptr, src_ptr, dest_stride, src_stride, blksize, nblks, pe_id);

end procedure

Table 2. Results showing which algorithm performs better based on the stride and block size, where blksize × nblks is fixed: Algorithm 1 (*putmem*) or Algorithm 2 (*iput*)

Block_Size (bytes)	(Stride - Block_Size) (bytes)					
	4	16	64	256	1024	4096
16	*iput*	*iput*	*iput*	*iput*	*iput*	*iput*
64	*iput*	*iput*	*iput*	*iput*	*iput*	*iput*
128	*putmem*	*iput*	*iput*	*iput*	*iput*	*iput*
256	*putmem*	*putmem*	*iput*	*iput*	*iput*	*iput*
512	*putmem*	*putmem*	*putmem*	*putmem*	*putmem*	*putmem*
1024	*putmem*	*putmem*	*putmem*	*putmem*	*putmem*	*putmem*
4096	*putmem*	*putmem*	*putmem*	*putmem*	*putmem*	*putmem*
16384	*putmem*	*putmem*	*putmem*	*putmem*	*putmem*	*putmem*

Note that the predicate function should be derived for different implementations and incorporated into the library implementation of OpenSHMEM. The predicate function may also be modified to take in other parameters, including the number of blocks and other system properties. The exploration of this parameter space for optimally implementating the predicate_lookup_table is left as future work.

6   Experiments

We used the same Cray XC30 machine as in the previous section and Cray-SHMEM version 7.2.2. We used a 2-dimensional halo exchange benchmark with data decomposition across one dimension for measuring the performance of the different algorithms presented in this paper.

Figure 7 shows the results of the analysis using 64 PEs distributed across 4 nodes. We compare the performance results of the halo exchange benchmark by applying the three algorithms for different block sizes, with the data size fixed to

2^{17} bytes. The x-axis shows different block sizes in bytes, and the y-axis shows the execution time in microseconds.

We can see that for small block sizes — less than 256 bytes — Algorithm 3 performs similar to Algorithm 2. For large block sizes — greater than 256 bytes — the performance becomes similar to Algorithm 1. This is because of the α value retrieved for the Cray-SHMEM implementation. The α value for block sizes below 256 bytes determines Algorithm 2 to be used and for data ranges above 256 bytes, it determines Algorithm 1 to be used. Moreover, we calculated the average execution time for each algorithm and found that when using Algorithm 3 we obtain 64.27 % improvement compared to the baseline implementation based on Algorithm 1, and we obtain 63.37 % improvement compared to an implementation based on Algorithm 2.

7   Related Work

In this paper, we have studied the usage of strided routines in OpenSHMEM and proposed extensions to support aggregate data types. The concept of strided RMA are not new to the PGAS programming model. There are other PGAS languages and libraries that make efficient use of strided data transfers. For example, Coarray Fortran (CAF) [15], a PGAS extension to Fortran, allows strided communication to be expressed as part of the standard Fortran array syntax. Portable runtime libraries designed to support PGAS languages like CAF, such as ARMCI [12,14] and GASNet [8], also provide multi-dimensional strided interfaces. Such interfaces allow transfers of n-dimensional subarrays, more general than what we propose here for OpenSHMEM, but implementations rely on a data server thread or active message handler to perform data packing and unpacking services in software.

In [10], the author proposes a similar extension shmemx_*TYPE*_aput for strided data transfers in two-dimensional arrays. However, this proposed extension will work on the basic data types defined in the standard as *TYPE* of Open-SHMEM. In our work, we extend this property and support more generic data types such as structures with the introduction of only one additional routine shmem_iputmem.

Apart from PGAS programming models, other distributed models like the Message Passing Interface (MPI) has support for strided data transfer and data transfer through MPI derived data types. There are numerous works for optimizing strided data transfers in MPI or other communication libraries provided 1-sided communication support [13,17,20]. These optimizations include exploiting scatter-gather operations made available by the network interface card, as well as utilizing NIC-based or host-based methods for packing and unpacking non-contiguous data. Note that similar implementation approaches can also be applied in the case of OpenSHMEM strides.

8   Conclusion

In this paper, we have described our study of the usage and performance of OpenSHMEM strided routines in different implementations. We motivated the need for more powerful strided routines in OpenSHMEM by discussing example communication patterns from FFT and conjugate gradient solver. We then proposed an extension for strided transfers to support communication involving arrays of aggregate types, namely shmem_iputmem and shmem_igetmem. We introduced a new algorithm for implementing the proposed OpenSHMEM extensions using the existing OpenSHMEM routines. We validated our algorithm using a halo exchange benchmark, for which we obtained close to 64 % of improvement compared to an implementation based on non-strided routines and an implementation based on the existing OpenSHMEM strided routines.

In future work, we will develop larger application codes that may take advantage of the proposed extensions for strided communication routines. We will also address the design of optimized algorithms for these routines, considering additional factors beyond block size and the source and destination strides.

Acknowledgements. This work is supported through funding from Total. This research used resources of the Oak Ridge Leadership Computing Facility (OLCF) at the Oak Ridge National Laboratory, the Texas Advanced Computing Center (TACC) at the University of Texas at Austin and Total.

References

1. Cray - Message Passing Toolkit. http://docs.cray.com/books/004-3689-001/html-004-3689-001/zfixedsllc0bet.html
2. HPCTools PGAS-Microbenchmarks. https://github.com/uhhpctools/pgas-microbench
3. Mellanox ScalableSHMEM: Support the OpenSHMEM Parallel Programming Language over InfiniBand. http://www.mellanox.com/related-docs/prod_software/PB_ScalableSHMEM.pdf
4. OpenMPI: Open Source High Performance Computing. http://www.open-mpi.org/
5. SGI - Message Passing Toolkit. http://techpubs.sgi.com/library/tpl/cgi-bin/getdoc.cgi?coll=0650&db=bks&srch=&fname=/SGI_Developer/MPT_MPI_PM/sgi_html/front.html
6. Unified MPI+PGAS Communication Runtime over OpenFabrics/Gen2 for Exascale Systems. http://mvapich.cse.ohio-state.edu/
7. Almasi, G., Padua, D.A.: Encyclopedia of Parallel Computing. Springer, cambridge (2011)
8. Bonachea, D.: GASNet Specification, V1.1. Technical report (2002)
9. Chapman, B., Curtis, T., Pophale, S., Poole, S., Kuehn, J., Koelbel, C., Smith, L.: Introducing OpenSHMEM: SHMEM for the PGAS community. In: Proceedings of the Fourth Conference on Partitioned Global Address Space Programming Model, PGAS 2010. ACM (2010)

10. Hammond, J.R.: Towards a matrix-oriented strided interface in OpenSHMEM. In: Proceedings of the 8th International Conference on Partitioned Global Address Space Programming Models, PGAS 2014 (2014)
11. Hoefler, T., Gottlieb, S.: Parallel zero-copy algorithms for fast fourier transform and conjugate gradient using MPI datatypes. In: Keller, R., Gabriel, E., Resch, M., Dongarra, J. (eds.) EuroMPI 2010. LNCS, vol. 6305, pp. 132–141. Springer, Heidelberg (2010)
12. Nieplocha, J., Carpenter, B.: ARMCI: A portable remote memory copy library for distributed array libraries and compiler run-time systems. In: Rolim, J.D.P. (ed.) IPPS-WS 1999 and SPDP-WS 1999. LNCS, vol. 1586. Springer, Heidelberg (1999)
13. Nieplocha, J., Tipparaju, V., Krishnan, M.: Optimizing strided remote memory access operations on the quadrics QsNetII network interconnect. In: Proceedings. Eighth International Conference on High-Performance Computing in Asia-Pacific Region, pp. 28–35, July 2005
14. Nieplocha, J., Tipparaju, V., Krishnan, M., Panda, D.K.: High performance remote memory access communication: the ARMCI approach. Int. J. High Perform. Comput. Appl. **20**, 233–253 (2006)
15. Numrich, R.W., Reid, J.: Co-array fortran for parallel programming. SIGPLAN Fortran Forum **17**(2), 1–13 (1998)
16. Pophale, S.S.: SRC: OpenSHMEM library development. In: Proceedings of the International Conference on Supercomputing, ICS 2011, pp. 374–374 (2011)
17. Santhanaraman, G., Wu, J., Panda, D.K.: Zero-Copy MPI derived datatype communication over InfiniBand. In: Kranzlmüller, D., Kacsuk, P., Dongarra, J. (eds.) EuroPVM/MPI 2004. LNCS, vol. 3241, pp. 47–56. Springer, Heidelberg (2004)
18. Shamis, P., Venkata, M.G., Poole, S., Welch, A., Curtis, T.: Designing a high performance openshmem implementation using universal common communication substrate as a communication middleware. In: Poole, S., Hernandez, O., Shamis, P. (eds.) OpenSHMEM 2014. LNCS, vol. 8356, pp. 1–13. Springer, Heidelberg (2014)
19. ten Bruggencate, M., Roweth, D.: DMAPP: An API for One-Sided Programming Model on Baker Systems. Technical report, Cray Users Group (CUG) (2010)
20. Wu, J., Wyckoff, P., Panda, D.: High performance implementation of MPI derived datatype communication over InfiniBand. In: 2004 Proceedings of 18th International Parallel and Distributed Processing Symposium, April 2004

Exploring OpenSHMEM Model to Program GPU-based Extreme-Scale Systems

Sreeram Potluri[1], Davide Rossetti[1], Donald Becker[1], Duncan Poole[1],
Manjunath Gorentla Venkata[2]([✉]), Oscar Hernandez[2], Pavel Shamis[2],
M. Graham Lopez[2], Mathew Baker[2], and Wendy Poole[3]

[1] NVIDIA Corporation, Santa Clara, USA
[2] Extreme Scale Systems Center (ESSC),
Oak Ridge National Laboratory (ORNL), Oak Ridge, USA
manjugv@ornl.gov
[3] Open Source Software Solutions, Knoxville, USA

Abstract. Extreme-scale systems with compute accelerators such as
Graphical Processing Unit (GPUs) have become popular for executing
scientific applications. These systems are typically programmed using
MPI and CUDA (for NVIDIA based GPUs). However, there are many
drawbacks to the MPI+CUDA approach. The orchestration required
between the compute and communication phases of the application execution, and the constraint that communication can only be initiated
from serial portions on the *Central Processing Unit* (CPU) lead to scaling bottlenecks. To address these drawbacks, we explore the viability
of using *OpenSHMEM* for programming these systems. In this paper,
first, we make a case for supporting GPU-initiated communication, and
suitability of the *OpenSHMEM* programming model. Second, we present
NVSHMEM, a prototype implementation of the proposed programming
approach, port Stencil and Transpose benchmarks which are representative of many scientific applications from MPI+CUDA model to *Open-
SHMEM*, and evaluate the design and implementation of *NVSHMEM*.
Finally, we provide a discussion on the opportunities and challenges of
OpenSHMEM to program these systems, and propose extensions to *Open-
SHMEM* to achieve the full potential of this programming approach.

1 Introduction

GPUs have become ubiquitous in High Performance Computing (HPC) clusters.
Owing to the superior performance per watt that the GPU architecture delivers,

This manuscript has been authored by UT-Battelle, LLC under Contract No.
DE-AC05-00OR22725 with the U.S. Department of Energy. The United States
Government retains and the publisher, by accepting the article for publication,
acknowledges that the United States Government retains a non-exclusive, paid-up,
irrevocable, world-wide license to publish or reproduce the published form of this
manuscript, or allow others to do so, for United States Government purposes. The
Department of Energy will provide public access to these results of federally sponsored research in accordance with the DOE Public Access Plan(http://energy.gov/
downloads/doe-public-access-plan).

M. Gorentla Venkata et al. (Eds.): OpenSHMEM 2015, LNCS 9397, pp. 18–35, 2015.
DOI: 10.1007/978-3-319-26428-8_2

they will be a key component in the road to exascale computing. A wide range of scientific applications, many of which use the Message Passing Interface (MPI), have been ported to take advantage of GPUs. They typically use the MPI + *Compute Unified Device Architecture* (CUDA) model. CUDA is used to offload compute portions of the application onto the GPU. MPI [1] two-sided communication API is used from the CPU to manage data movement. This leads to distinct phases in the application: for computation, that run on GPU, and for communication, that run on the CPU. The transition between these phases is managed by the CPU and involves waiting for MPI communication to complete before launching CUDA kernels or waiting for CUDA kernels to complete before initiating communication.

The CPU-controlled execution model on GPU clusters incurs overheads that limit the strong scalability of applications. Strong scaling where the problem size is fixed while the execution resources are increased is a critical metric of efficiency of applications and the execution environment. There is an overhead associated with launching compute kernels on the GPU. Alternating compute and communication phases result in recurring launch kernels and lead to recurring overheads. The synchronizing activity on the GPU before MPI communication leads to under-utilization of GPU resources during communication and synchronization phases. Similarly, there is under-utilization of the network when computation is in progress. Some of these issues are handled by restructuring the application code to overlap independent compute and communication phases, using CUDA streams. These optimizations make the application code complex and their benefits usually diminishes as the problem size per GPU becomes smaller [2].

One of the approaches to address these limitations is by adding the capability to initiate communication on the GPUs. Self reliance of the GPU to initiate and complete communication without synchronizing with the CPU can result in long running kernels, providing better utilization of the GPU while avoiding launch and synchronization overheads. Communication from within CUDA kernels results in a highly concurrent, finer-grained communication model in applications. Using the MPI two-sided model for GPU-initiated communication requires GPUs to perform message matching, and deal with unexpected messages. To take advantage of GPU-initiated communication while overcoming the disadvantages of two-sided communication, we explore the viability of using one-sided communication model such as *OpenSHMEM* for GPU-initiated communication.

OpenSHMEM [3] specification defines a standard *Application Programming Interface* (API) that provides portability to applications that have traditionally used various vendor-specific SHMEM libraries. While the current standard provides an API for library initialization, data object management, communication and synchronization, it is still evolving to provide API and semantics for use of *OpenSHMEM* in multi-threaded environments. The effective use of *OpenSH-MEM* on the GPU will require further extensions. For example, implementing the current *OpenSHMEM* semantics requires a Total Store Ordering(TSO) memory model on the target platform. This has to be relaxed to enable its use on GPUs which has a highly relaxed memory model. The current ordering and completion API in OpenSHMEM apply to all communication initiated by the calling PE. In a highly-threaded environment, finer grained control of communication is required for efficiency and overlap.

In this paper, we first explore the advantages of using the *OpenSHMEM* model for GPUs. Then, we provide a prototype implementation, and evaluate the opportunities and challenges of this model. At the end, we provide a discussion to address the drawbacks and propose extensions to the *OpenSHMEM* programming model that could address the drawbacks.

2   Background

2.1   Current Programming Model Approach for GPU-based Systems

Most HPC applications ported to clusters accelerated with NVIDIA GPUs currently use an MPI+CUDA hybrid programming model. The application is split into phases of communication and computation with CPU orchestrating their execution. Computation is typically offloaded onto the GPUs while MPI communication is managed from the CPU. To demonstrate the use of this programming approach, consider the stencil example listed in Fig. 1. The data grid is split into interior and boundary portions to achieve overlap between computation and communication. The execution in each iteration goes through the following steps:

```
              Traditional                          Envisioned

Loop {

    interior_compute <<<..., stream0>>>(...)

    pack_boundaries<<<..., stream1>>>(...)

    cudaStreamSynchronize (stream1)
                                          compute_exchange<<<...,stream0>>>(...)
    Exchange (MPI/OpenSHMEM)

    unpack_boundaries<<<..., stream1>>>(...)

    boundary_compute<<<..., stream1>>>(...)

    cudaDeviceSynchronize();

}
```

Fig. 1. Execution models: traditional and envisioned

1. A CUDA kernel is launched via a CUDA stream to compute interior of the data grid.
2. While this is in progress, another CUDA kernel is launched to pack the boundary cells. This is launched on a different stream. Both these CUDA streams are asynchronous from the CPU's perspective. The pack kernel is launched on

the stream with higher priority, so that it does not block behind the CUDA kernel computing the interior. This enables better overlap between computation and data exchange.

3. cudaStreamSynchronize, a blocking synchronization call on CPU, checks the completion of the packing kernel.

4. After the completion of packing, MPI (or other communication API) is used to exchange data between processes. The data exchange pattern can be classified as near-neighbor exchange. The CPU blocks until the MPI communication is complete.

5. After the data is exchanged, two CUDA kernels are used for processing the data. The first kernel unpacks the exchanged data, and the second kernel computes the boundary portion.

6. On the last step, the call to *cudaDeviceSynchronize* ensures the completion of computation on the GPU. The *cudaDeviceSynchronize* is a blocking call on the CPU and marks the end of an iteration

As this example illustrates, the existing model requires frequent synchronization between GPU and CPU. The CPU has to be running at full-speed to ensure fast synchronization and hence will stay in a high power state even though it does little useful work. The synchronization phase at end of each iteration requires the GPU to be completely drained before starting the next iteration which reduces the utilization of the GPU and also kills any opportunity of data locality and reuse. Further, when the application is scaled strongly, the interior compute time and hence the opportunity for overlap decreases. The application runtime is limited by the latency for CPU-GPU synchronization which includes: launch and synchronization of CUDA kernels and MPI communication. The envisioned approach is explained in Sect. 3.

2.2 *OpenSHMEM*

OpenSHMEM is a PGAS library interface specification. It includes routines, environment variables, and constants to implement the PGAS programming model as a library. It also defines bindings in C and Fortran languages, enabling the applications to invoke the interfaces.

OpenSHMEM presents a PGAS view of execution contexts and memory model. The execution contexts in *OpenSHMEM* is an OS process identified by integer called Processing Element (PE). An *OpenSHMEM* program has private address space and shared address space. A PE allocates and stores its private data and control structures in the private address space. The shared address space in *OpenSHMEM* is presented as symmetric objects, which are accessible by all PEs in an *OpenSHMEM* program. The symmetric objects are allocated using a collective allocation operation in *OpenSHMEM*.

OpenSHMEM provides routines for communication and synchronization with other PEs. The communication in *OpenSHMEM* is primarily one-sided. It provides many variants of Put, Get and Atomic operations to access and modify symmetric data objects that are located on remote PEs. It provides Quiet and Fence which complete communication and orders communication, respectively.

It provides interfaces for collective communication and synchronization. The group of PEs involved in a collective communication is defined by three integers called Active Set. The collectives include barrier, reductions, and data gather operations.

3 Our Approach: GPU-Initiated Communication using *OpenSHMEM*

We propose a programming approach using GPU-initiated communication which is motivated by the throughput oriented architecture of the GPU. The GPUs are designed to support tens of thousands of threads to achieve maximum parallel throughput. These threads are extremely light weight and thousands of threads are queued up for work (in groups called warps). If one warp must wait on a memory access, another warp can start executing in its place. As a separate set of registers is allocated for all active threads, there is no need for swapping of registers or state. As a consequence, this execution model has inherent latency hiding capabilities with minimal scheduling overheads. With the increasing amount of parallelism, GPU architectures can have enough state to hide latencies not only to local GPU device memory but also to remote GPU memory over a network. GPU-initiated communication can be used to take advantage of this inherent capability of the GPU hardware while relying on the CUDA programming paradigm that has been used for scaling within a GPU. Further, this improves programmability as developers will not have to rely on a hybrid model to orchestrate and overlap between different phases of the application.

Figure 1 shows the contrast of the CPU code of stencil application using the hybrid model and the model with GPU-initiated communication. The communication initiated and synced from within CUDA kernels will not only reduce the reliance on the CPU, additionally it also avoids existing synchronization overheads that limit the strong scaling. Also, to enhance the efficiency within a warp and reduce the pressure on the memory sub-system, the loads and stores can be coalesced by the hardware when alignment and access pattern requirements are met.

Using PGAS programming model such as *OpenSHMEM* suits GPU-initiated communication better. The one-sided communication model of *OpenSHMEM* requires only the caller (origin) of the interface to be active, which matches the massive parallelism and dynamic scheduling model on the GPU. Further, a combination of global address space approach and semantics of *OpenSHMEM* communication interfaces such as Put and Get is a close match to load and stores on shared-memory space of GPU.

4 *NVSHMEM*: A Prototype for GPU-Initiated Communication using *OpenSHMEM*

4.1 Overview of Implementation

NVSHMEM is a prototype implementation of *OpenSHMEM* with support for GPU-initiated communication. We do not depart significantly from the

OpenSHMEM execution model that is currently used on non-GPU clusters. Currently, each PE can be implemented using an OS process. All the resources and state associated with the use of a GPU by a host process or thread is encapsulated in a CUDA context. A context is associated with a single GPU device and only one context can be active in a OS process/thread at a given time. In our *OpenSHMEM* execution model, we extend the scope of a PE to include an OS process or thread and a CUDA context. This respects the execution boundary of the GPU and the state boundary (device address space, etc.) of the CUDA context. We consider a single symmetric heap per PE, that will be enabled by the unified memory capability of NVIDIA GPUs. We started with an intuitive separation of API that is supported on the host from that is supported on the GPU. In the current version of *NVSHMEM*, API for runtime initialization/termination, memory management and collective communication is supported from serial portions on the host. API for one-sided communication, one-sided ordering/completion, and point-to-point synchronization interfaces are supported from the inside parallel regions, on the GPU. *NVSHMEM* can be seen as a subset of the *OpenSHMEM* standard and follows the semantics defined in the standard except for a few exceptions. It assumes multi-threading support in *OpenSHMEM*, allowing all the *OpenSHMEM* calls supported on the GPU to be made concurrently by multiple threads. Current *OpenSHMEM* standard assumes a strongly consistency memory model on the architectures it is implemented on. This is relaxed in the *NVSHMEM* implementation to allow implementation on the GPU which has a highly relaxed memory model. This extension is discussed in more detail in Sect. 5.5.

NVSHMEM data movement interfaces are implemented by leveraging CUDA data movement mechanisms. CUDA has a protocol built on top of PCIe that enables direct data movement between GPUs that are connected to the same PCIe root complex. This data path completely bypasses CPU/system memory avoiding additional copies. This is referred to as the P2P protocol in CUDA and was originally limited to inter-GPU data movement within a single process. Since CUDA 4.2, it has been extended to support inter-process communication. The capability is exposed to the developer through CUDA IPC (Inter-Process Communication) API. We have used these existing technologies to build an emulation platform for experimenting with GPU initiated communication. With this environment, we can scale unto 8 GPUs connected to the same PCIe root complex. Technologies like NVLink [4] and PLX Express Fabric [5] are intended to allow larger number of GPUs to be deployed in this fashion.

Akin to shared memory on Linux clusters, CUDA IPC provides API for one process to map GPU device memory allocated by another process, into its own address space. Once the mapping has been established it can access the memory as it would access its own. The handle creation and mapping mechanism are exposed through the *cudaIpc∗* interface provided by the CUDA toolkit. In our *NVSHMEM* implementation, symmetric heap allocation and setup happens as part of the initialization function (shmem_init). Each process allocates its heap in device memory and shares the IPC handle to all other process. An all-to-all mapping of the heaps of all processes is established. Memory allocation is managed by returning symmetric chunks of memory from the heap. *NVSHMEM* also supports shmem_ptr API, which exposes remote symmetric regions for direct loads and stores in the application code. This is implemented as a simple address translation using displacement of the pointer in the local heap and calculating the corresponding pointer in the remote heap that was mapped using CUDA IPC. *NVSHMEM* also provides collective communication operations which are implemented as CUDA kernels.

As GPU-initiated communication is usually fine-grained, we use direct loads/ stores to implement Put/Get routines in *NVSHMEM* to avoid the overheads of making the CUDA API calls for small transfers. The shmem_quiet call is implemented as a __threadfence_system() call in CUDA. This waits until all prior memory requests have been performed with respect to all clients, including those over PCIe. Point-to-point synchronization calls such as shmem_wait and shmem_wait_until are implemented as active polling loops on the memory locations and have to include a call to __threadfence_system() in order to guarantee ordering of loads. Both shmem_quiet and shmem_fence have similar implementations on our multi-GPU platform.

4.2   Evaluation of the Prototype Implementation

To evaluate the design and implementation of *NVSHMEM*, we ported 2dstencil and Transpose kernels to use *OpenSHMEM* with GPU-initiated communication. These kernels are representative of commonly found computation and communication patterns in several scientific applications. Rest of the section details the implementation of kernels and its performance characteristics.

2DStencil: Fig. 2 shows the use of *NVSHMEM* in the 2dstencil code. The code snippet on the left shows the CPU code for setting up global memory and code snippet on the right shows the use of *NVSHMEM* inside the CUDA kernel. In the traditional version of the 2dstencil code, as shown in Fig. 1, computation of the interior and the boundary elements are separate to allow for overlap between a major chunk of computation and communication. The overlap is achieved using multiple streams in CUDA. The traditional version involves four kernel launches per step: for interior computation, for boundary pack-unpack and for boundary compute. There also has to be explicit CPU-based synchronization between the CUDA kernels and MPI communication. These add performance overheads and code complexity.

In the *NVSHMEM*-based implementation, the host code involves a single kernel launch that runs for the lifetime of the application. It does not require any further intervention from the CPU. The communication and synchronization are expressed as part of the kernel, using *OpenSHMEM* API. Boundary threads fetch data from the neighboring processes using shmem_float_get and kernels across neighboring processes synchronize at the end of each step using shmem_float_wait. In the current version of the code, a hierarchical synchronization is implemented with one thread per block calling shmem_int_wait while other

```
                                        __global__ void stencil_kernel (u, v, sync, ...) {

                                        i = blockIdx.x*blockDim.x + threadIdx.x;

                                        for (...) {

                                            if (i+1 > nx) {
                                                v[i+1] = nvshmem_float_g (v[1], rightpe)
                                            }

. . .                                       if (i-1 < 1) {
u = (void *) nvshmalloc (size)                  v[i-1] = nvshmem_float_g (v[nx], leftpe)
v = (void *) nvshmalloc (size)              }
sync= (void *) nvshmalloc (sizeof(int)*npeers)
. . .                                       u[i] = (v[i+1] + v[i-1] . . . //compute

. . .                                       /*peers array has left and right PE ids*/
stencil_kernel <<< >>> (u, v, sync ...)     if (i < 1 || i > n-2) {
                                                nvshmem_int_p (sync[i], 1, peers[i]);
. . .                                           nvshmem_quiet();
cudaDeviceSynchronize();                        nvshmem_wait_until (sync[i], EQ, 1);
                                            }

                                            //intra-process sync (code not shown)

                                            //compute v from u  (code not shown)
                                        }
                                        }
```

Fig. 2. Using GPU-initiated communication: example with *NVSHMEM*

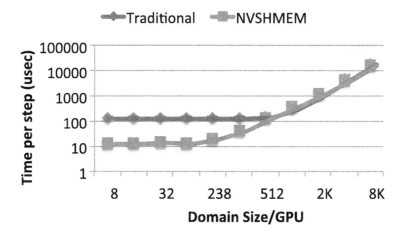

Fig. 3. Performance of 2Dstencil code using traditional model and using *NVSHMEM*

threads block on an intra-block synchronization primitive. This is to reduce the number of global memory requests that are generated. The communication pattern between these two versions of the code changes from sparse coarse-grained to dense fine-grained. Further, the overlap between compute and communication changes from an explicit programmer managed design to an implicit GPU thread-scheduler managed one.

Figure 3 shows the preliminary results, comparing the performance of the traditional version of the 2Dstencil code with the version using GPU-initiated communication. Due to the non-preemptive execution of CUDA blocks, we have to be careful to avoid deadlocks when using inter-block or inter-kernel synchronization using point-to-point synchronization primitives like shmem_int_wait. We workaround this in our experiments by limiting the number of blocks equal to the number of Streaming Multiprocessors (SMs) available. This constraint of non-preemptive execution is a limitation only the current GPU architectures. For our experiments, we use a system with K40m GPUs, and we restrict the number of blocks to 15 for all our runs. From the performance results, we can observe that the version using GPU-initiated communication shows a significant improvement in per-step time, when the problem size per GPU is small (< 512). This improvement is a consequence of avoiding the overheads of multiple kernel launches and the use of CUDA API. Moreover, when strong scaling the applications on large GPU clusters, avoiding these overheads is critical for the application performance.

Transpose: Matrix transpose forms the basis of Fast Fourier transform (FFT) transformations and is therefore widely used in signal and image processing. We have ported a multi-GPU transpose code that traditionally uses MPI+CUDA to use *NVSHMEM*.

In the MPI+CUDA version, the algorithm involves pipelining three steps: local transpose using a CUDA kernel, all-to-all data transfers between processes using MPI, and copying data to the target location using cudaMemcpy2D. Note that it is important to perform the local transpose prior to the all-to-all. Doing the transpose upfront places memory to be sent to other GPUs in contiguous memory, thus ensuring an efficient transfer. This code is complex as it involves streams, non-blocking MPI communication, and asynchronous CUDA memory copies required to achieve its pipelining.

The *NVSHMEM* version uses fine-grained communication to implement the transpose. Remote data is fetched as required by using *OpenSHMEM* API from inside the CUDA kernel. To make the implementation simple, shmem_double_get calls are used to fetch the data, whether it is local or remote. As these calls translate into direct memory loads underneath, the overheads are negligible. The host code is trivial and involves a single kernel launch.

The performance of these two versions was compared on a node with three NVIDIA Tesla K40 GPUs connected to the same socket. Figure 4 shows the bi-directional PCIe bandwidth achieved as the size of matrix increases. We can see that the version using GPU-initiated fine grained communication is able to better saturate the PCIe bandwidth for smaller problem sizes than the MPI version. This is because of the overhead in CUDA and MPI API calls and overheads of DMA copies. Saturation of the PCIe channel shows that a network with higher bandwidth will benefit the performance of MGTranspose using *NVSHMEM*. The MPI version is not able to saturate the bandwidth even for larger matrix sizes because of a limitation in the current CUDA runtime. CUDA copies involving a buffer on a remote GPU (one not actively used by the calling process) are unable to use direct P2P transfer and are instead staged through system memory. This issue does not happen with *NVSHMEM* as the transfers are implemented using memory accesses rather than as CUDA memory copies.

Further, achieving a pipeline in the MPI version introduces significant code complexity. The number of lines of code for the transpose function is 280 in this version compared to 100 in the *NVSHMEM* version, and this actually understates the complexity of the MPI implementation compared with the *NVSHMEM* version.

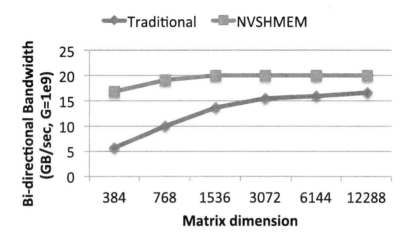

Fig. 4. Performance of Transpose code using traditional model and using *NVSHMEM*

5   Extending *OpenSHMEM* to Better Support GPU-Initiated Communication

This section highlights the extensions required to efficiently implement the *OpenSHMEM* model for GPU-based extreme scale systems with GPU-initiated communication. Firstly, the *OpenSHMEM* specification provides ordering guarantees that can only be implemented on systems with a TSO or stronger memory model. GPU on the other hand provides a highly relaxed memory model. This prevents *OpenSHMEM* to be implemented on the GPU in its current form. Secondly, the ordering and completion API apply to all the operations issued by the PE. This can be restrictive and expensive in a highly threaded environment. We see the need for finer grained isolation and control of operations within a PE. How collective operations behave within a threaded region is also not defined in the *OpenSHMEM* standard. The rest of the section explains the issues listed here in more detail and proposes extensions that can address them.

5.1   Memory Consistency Model in *OpenSHMEM*

In OpenSHMEM, the order in which updates become visible at the target PE (shmem_put) is controlled by the source PE, with ordering (shmem_fence) and completion (shmem_quiet) interfaces. No explicit *OpenSHMEM* operations are expected by the user to guarantee the correct visibility ordering on the target PE. Figure 5 shows the consistency guarantees *OpenSHMEM* provides when implementing a message passing idiom.

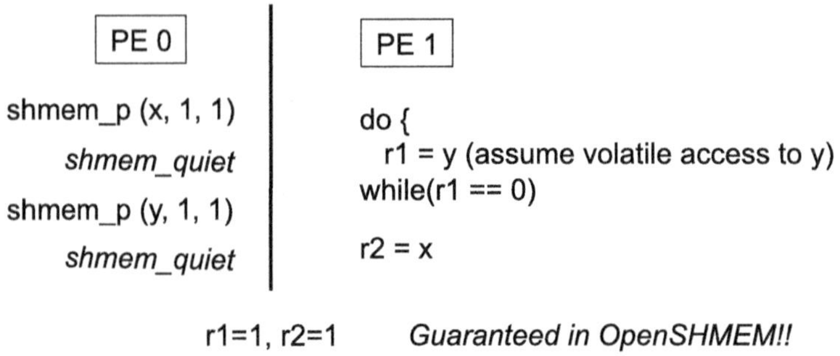

PE 0	PE 1
shmem_p (x, 1, 1)	do {
shmem_quiet	r1 = y (assume volatile access to y)
shmem_p (y, 1, 1)	while(r1 == 0)
shmem_quiet	r2 = x

r1=1, r2=1   *Guaranteed in OpenSHMEM!!*

Fig. 5. Message passing idiom implemented using *NVSHMEM*

These semantics cannot be guaranteed on systems like NVIDIA GPUs, IBM Power and ARM64, which have relaxed memory models. Additional operations are required at the target PE to guarantee visibility ordering. Implementation of the same message passing idiom using CUDA to run on a NVIDIA GPU is shown in Fig. 6. Explicit memory barrier instruction is required at the target to prevent reordering of loads that can result the update to flag being observed before the update to data. Similar instructions (lwsync or isync) are required on IBM Power architecture. *OpenSHMEM* does not provide a way to express this using portable API. This forces applications to use platform specific ordering instructions in conjunction with *OpenSHMEM* leading to non-portable code.

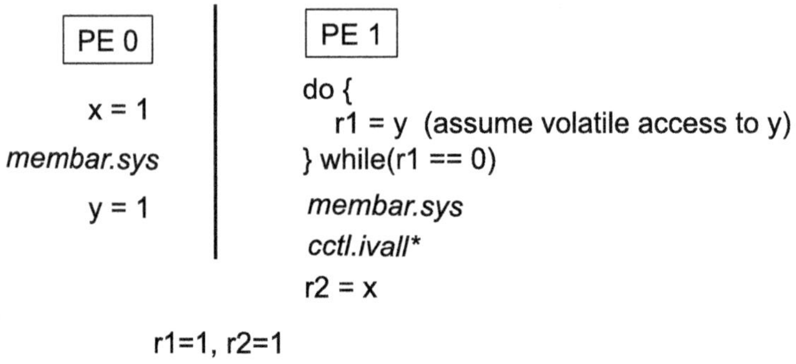

PE 0	PE 1
x = 1	do {
membar.sys	r1 = y (assume volatile access to y)
y = 1	} while(r1 == 0)
	membar.sys
	*cctl.ivall**
	r2 = x

r1=1, r2=1

Fig. 6. Message passing idiom Implemented in CUDA

One way to address this is to require the target PE to use shmem_wait (_until) to poll on a flag in order to guarantee order it sees between any prior updates and update on the flag. Figure 7 shows the message passing idiom using shmem_wait_until. This call translates to the platform specific ordering instructions on the GPU.

While this extension to semantics solves the problem in the message passing pattern, we believe there is need for a holistic solution to express ordering

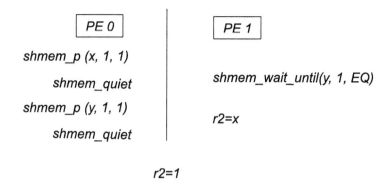

Fig. 7. Message passing idiom implemented using shmem_wait_until

in *OpenSHMEM*. For example, the ordering operation in the current standard, shmem_fence, does not identify the symmetric variable that is used for synchronization, for example y in Fig. 7. This information can allow the runtime to enforce ordering in a more efficient ways, e.g. setting IBV_SEND_FENCE flag on RDMA write to y in InfiniBand, use *STRL* to perform store release on y in ARMv8. Further, shmem_fence only guarantees ordering between updates to the same PE. The only way to guarantee consistency between updates to multiple PEs is by using shmem_quiet to complete all operations in-flight. Programming languages (C11, C++11 and Java5+) have converged on SC-DRF (Sequential Consistency - Data Race Free) as the default memory model [6]. This guarantees sequentially consistent behavior for data-race-free programs. *OpenSHMEM* standard can learn from these efforts and provide interfaces like the following which allows the flexibility to provide different ordering requirements around synchronization operations and variables.

> void shmem_int_p_fence (int* x, int value, int pe, int ordering)
> int shmem_int_g_fence (int* x, int pe, int ordering)
> void shmem_int_wait_until_fence (int* x, int cond, int value, int ordering)

Possible values for ordering can be relaxed, release and acquire. Relaxed mode does not guarantee any ordering and the interfaces can be used only for synchronization. Release guarantees that all prior Put, AMOs, and memory store operations to symmetric data objects are delivered before the Put in shmem_int_p_fence. This can be used at the sender PE when updating y in the message passing example above. Acquire prevents reordering of later Get and memory load operations with the memory read(s) in shmem_int_g_fence/shmem_int_wait_until_fence operation. This can be used at the receiver PE when reading y in the message passing example. Such an API associates the synchronization variable with the synchronization operation allowing for optimizations as mentioned above. It also makes the API extensible to provide different ordering guarantees.

5.2 Support for Memory Locality

The future extreme scale systems are expected to have heterogeneous memories with hierarchies, including DRAM, HBM (High Bandwidth Memory), and NVRAM (Non-volatile RAM). The performance characteristics of the memories such as the access latency, bandwidth, and capacities varies. Further, for an extreme scale system with GPUs, the internal memory is hierarchical with global memory that is shared across SMs and shared memory which is local to a specific block(CTA) of threads. The latencies to these memories varies significantly.

The current *OpenSHMEM* model assumes that all memory is homogeneous and is flat with no hierarchies. Following this model, for GPU based systems, we have a single symmetric heap per PE, enabled by the unified memory capability on NVIDIA GPUs. While a single heap spanning the CPU and GPU provides simplifies programming model, the locality of data in the heap impacts the performance as we deal with multiple physical memories and migration between them. Thus, implementing *OpenSHMEM* memory model for these systems can result in a negative performance impact.

To achieve performance efficiency on emerging hardware architectures, the memory allocation and access interfaces of *OpenSHMEM* should provide a way to express explicit control over the locality of the symmetric variables. The user can provide hints to the implementation about the placement of symmetric variables, and as such set expectations of it's performance. For GPU-enabled systems, this would enable the user to place the memory primarily accessed by code on GPU on device memory, and memory primarily accessed by code on CPU on DDRAM.

5.3 Support for Fine-Grained Synchronization

In the *OpenSHMEM* model, all operations are completed when a shmem_quiet is invoked. Using this interface and its semantics for GPU translates to completing all shmem_put operations issued by all threads associated with the PE. Many applications involving stencil operations, near-neighbor communication, sparse communications require more fine-grained synchronization primitives. For example, in a stencil application, computation on a boundary is split among multiple groups of threads (blocks or warps). The communication and computation in one group of threads can progress independently from that handled by another group of threads. Such patterns can benefit from finer-grained isolation, ordering and completion of communication than a PE. The completion of communication issued from the threads of CTA/warp can allow for better overlap between different CTAs.

Independent Communication Streams with Contexts: Context is a programming construct, which allows independent streams of one-sided communications to be grouped together. This concept was introduced by Dinan et al. as an approach to achieve communication-computation overlap in single-threaded *OpenSHMEM* programs, and to avoid thread-interference and resource isolation in multi-threaded *OpenSHMEM* programs [7]. We propose to use a similar construct to achieve fine-grained synchronization for GPU threads. However, we propose to add the flexibility to define a context based on a memory region. In distributed shared memory environments, we believe it can be natural for the user to isolate traffic based on the memory region being operated on rather than explicitly identifying all the operations accessing it. This can group the threads collaborating on a data region and complete their communication stream independent of other threads.

5.4 Multi-threaded *OpenSHMEM*

The current *OpenSHMEM* specification does not specify the interaction of *Open-SHMEM* and user-threads. In this absence, the thread-safe invocation of *Open-SHMEM* interfaces in the multi-threaded *OpenSHMEM* program is undefined i.e., implementing PE as a thread or invoking *OpenSHMEM* interfaces from multiple threads concurrently does not guarantee correct *OpenSHMEM* semantics. This is a significant bottleneck for using *OpenSHMEM* for many-thread systems such as GPUs, Xeon Phis, and CPUs with hundreds of hardware threads. The performance advantages of multi-thread support in the other programming model is well documented [8].

In NVSHMEM, we experiment with using one PE per GPU and invoking *OpenSHMEM* interfaces from multiple CUDA threads within the PE. Thus, we present a use case for thread-safe invocation of *OpenSHMEM*. The interfaces and semantics proposed by Cray [9] accommodates most of the needs for implementing *NVSHMEM*. However, we believe the requirement that each thread has to call shmem_thread_register before making *OpenSHMEM* calls is too restrictive in a highly parallel and dynamic thread environment like the GPU. We think the ability of threads to initiate communication should be implicit once the thread safety level of the runtime has been specified during initialization. Any information that might help optimize the runtime (number of threads, for example) can be provided as hints during the initialization. Next subsection discusses the interfaces and semantics of collectives invoked from a multi-threaded *OpenSHMEM* program.

5.5 Collectives Extensions to Operate in Thread Environment

Assuming the thread model proposed by [9] is a part of the specification, we propose two extensions to the semantics of collectives to operate in the presence of the threads.

Collectives with Thread Collaboration: In current *OpenSHMEM* standard (and even after including thread models similar to MPI), a collective is initiated through a single call from a PE. In a highly-threaded environment, this typically means, synchronizing among all the threads in a PE before allowing one thread to call into the collective, as depicted in Fig. 8. Enforcing these synchronization points can be expensive and can bring down the overall utilization of highly parallel environments such as GPU. Parallelism can be spawned transparently within the collective but this can lead to additional overheads, and deadlocks due to scheduling and interaction between runtime and the application.

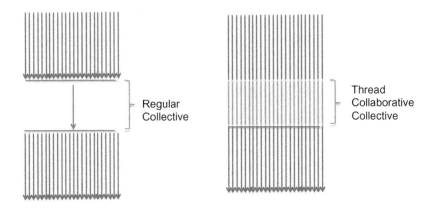

Fig. 8. Making collective a collaborative threaded operation

To address this, we propose that the *OpenSHMEM* allow multiple threads to call into a collective and thus explicitly declaring their participation. This allows the collective to be optimized using the parallelism while avoiding the synchronization point before the collective. Collectives in *OpenSHMEM* are one-sided which means the application guarantees that the target buffers on all the processes are ready to be used when the collective call is made on any process. Further in *OpenSHMEM* collectives, the transformation on each data element is independent of the transformation on other data elements at a PE. This allows parallelism to be naturally applied inside the collective without affecting the semantics or correctness. The collective implementation can suppress parallelism by partial synchronization after considering the hierarchy and topology in the hardware. On the GPU, scheduler can inherently overlap between the data movement and computation components of the collective happening at different groups of threads. This is not the same as each thread calling a collective independently as it would change the placement of data.

To demonstrate the usage, consider the example with *collect* interface. Invoking multiple independent collect operations gathers the data from all PEs for each collect operation into a contiguous location. This leaves data contributed by each PE into non-contiguous locations. This changes the nature of the collective and also prevents efficient coalescing due to non-contiguity of accesses. In a thread-collaborative collective, calls made by all the threads constitute one collective operation and result in a data arrangement where data contributed by each PE is contiguous, similar to that achieved when using a single collect operation.

Persistence in Collective Operations: To implement and optimize the collective, runtime needs information about the amount of parallelism used for a particular collective operation [10]. The synchronization of parallelism within a PE after the collective operation can be efficiently staggered and hidden if the collective is non-blocking and the application checks for its completion later in its run. These are possible with extensions in *OpenSHMEM* to define the collective ahead its use, to launch non-blocking collective and wait for its completion using request. The following API presents an example for collect operation. The parameter *ncalls* gives the number of threads/calls per PE that constitute the collective. The info argument can be used to pass information about the way collective is called among threads (for example, one call per CTA/warp).

void shmem_collect32_init (void *target, const void *source, size_t nelems, int ncalls, int PE_start, int logPE_stride, int PE_size, long *pSync, shmem_info info, shmem_request_t *request)

void shmem_start(request)
void shmem_wait(request)

6   Related Work

There have been a fair number of contributions from vendors and researchers that are geared towards enabling efficient communication from GPUs. NVIDIA's GPUDirect technologies [11,12] have helped reduce communication overheads by removing the need to copy data to CPU memory before it can be moved to other GPUs, within and across nodes. However, the CPU is still involved in initiating communication and synchronizing between computation and communication in the application. This demands a powerful CPU for best performance and incurs overheads that limit strong scaling. GPUDirect Async [13] addresses this by allowing GPU to trigger and synchronize network operations in order with compute kernels that are queued by the CPU. This will allow CPU to be put in low power states as computation and communication is progressed by the GPU. However, communication operations are scheduled only at kernel boundaries. Computation and communication phases have to be defined and queued from the CPU. This will result in multiple kernels and bulk synchronization phases whose overheads can dominate as applications are scaled strongly. In this paper, we consider communication from inside CUDA kernels as an alternative approach and show how it can enable better performance. It also improves programmability by being inline with the CUDA programming model and taking advantage of the native GPU execution model.

Several solutions have been proposed to enable efficient use of GPUs with programming models such as MPI and PGAS. Wang et al. and Potluri et al. [14,15] has proposed CUDA-aware MPI with MVAPICH2 [16] which allows use of standard MPI interfaces for moving data from GPU or host memories. They take advantage of unified virtual addressing (UVA) feature from NVIDIA. Ashwin et al. proposed use of datatype attributes to identify GPU memory in communication using standard MPI interfaces [17]. Potluri et al. proposed CUDA-aware approach for

OpenSHMEM [18]. The aforementioned works address CPU-initiated communication involving GPU device memory. Cunningham et al. have proposed the use of X10 to program GPUs and CPUs across clusters as part of their APGAS programming model [19]. Miyoshi et al. have contributed work that allows embedding MPI calls within GPU kernels in their FLAT GPU framework [20]. In our approach, we allow the GPU user to rely on the familiar CUDA programming model while using OpenSHMEM to express inter-GPU data movement inline with the CUDA model.

7   Conclusion

This paper explores the viability of using OpenSHMEM with GPU-initiated communication to program GPU-based extreme scale systems. To evaluate this approach, we design and implement, NVSHMEM, and also port compute kernels, Transpose and Stencil, from MPI+CUDA model to OpenSHMEM. Our results show that in addition to performance advantages, this approach has productivity advantages as it does not require orchestrating compute and communication phases. Based on the experience with NVSHMEM, we identify potential extensions to OpenSHMEM that can improve performance and usability of this model to program GPU-based extreme scale systems.

Acknowledgments. The work at NVIDIA is funded by U.S. Department of Energy under subcontract 7078610 with Lawrence Berkeley National Laboratory. The work at Oak Ridge National Laboratory (ORNL) is supported by the United States Department of Defense and used the resources of the Extreme Scale Systems Center located at the ORNL. In addition the authors would like to thank Stephen Poole (DoD) for his review of this work and many technical discussions that help shape the ideas presented in the paper.

References

1. The MPI Forum: MPI: A Message Passing Interface. Technical report (Version 3.0, 2012)
2. Tariq, S.: Lessons learned in improving scaling of applications on large GPU clusters. In: HPC Advisory Council Stanford Conference (2003)
3. OpenSHMEM Org.: OpenSHMEM Specification (2015). http://openshmem.org/
4. NVIDIA: Nvlink high-speed interconnect (2015). http://www.nvidia.com/object/nvlink.html
5. AVAGO: Expressfabric technology (2015). http://www.plxtech.com/applications/expressfabric
6. Sorin, D.J., Hill, M.D., Wood, D.A.: A Primer on Memory Consistency and Cache Coherence, 1st edn. Morgan & Claypool Publishers, San Rafael (2011)
7. Dinan, J., Flajslik, M.: Contexts: a mechanism for high throughput communication in openshmem. In: Proceedings of the 8th International Conference on Partitioned Global Address Space Programming Models, PGAS 2014, Eugene, OR, USA, October 6–10, 2014, pp. 10:1–10:9 (2014)

8. Gropp, W.D., Thakur, R.: Issues in developing a thread-safe MPI implementation. In: Mohr, B., Träff, J.L., Worringen, J., Dongarra, J. (eds.) PVM/MPI 2006. LNCS, vol. 4192, pp. 12–21. Springer, Heidelberg (2006)

9. ten Bruggencate, M., Roweth, D., Oyanagi, S.: Thread-safe SHMEM extensions. In: Poole, S., Hernandez, O., Shamis, P. (eds.) OpenSHMEM 2014. LNCS, vol. 8356, pp. 178–185. Springer, Heidelberg (2014)

10. Skjellum, A.: High performance MPI: extending the message passing interface for higher performance and higher predictability. In: International Conference on Parallel and Distributed Processing Techniques and Applications (PDPTA) (1998)

11. NVIDIA: Gpudirect (2015). https://developer.nvidia.com/gpudirect

12. NVIDIA: Gpudirect RDMA (2015). http://docs.nvidia.com/cuda/gpudirect-rdma

13. Rossetti, D.: Gpudirect: integrating the GPU with a network interface. In: GPU Technology Conference (2015)

14. Wang, H., Potluri, S., Luo, M., Singh, A.K., Sur, S., Panda, D.K.: Mvapich2-GPU: optimized GPU to GPU communication for infiniband clusters. Comput. Sci. **26**, 257–266 (2011)

15. Potluri, S., Hamidouche, K., Venkatesh, A., Bureddy, D., Panda, D.K.: Efficient inter-node MPI communication using gpudirect RDMA for infiniband clusters with nvidia gpus. In: Proceedings of the 2013 42Nd International Conference on Parallel Processing. ICPP 2013, pp. 80–89. IEEE Computer Society, Washington (2013)

16. MVAPICH: MPI over infiniband, 10gige/iwarp and roce (2015). http://mvapich.cse.ohio-state.edu

17. Aji, A.M., Dinan, J., Buntinas, D., Balaji, P., Feng, W.c., Bisset, K.R., Thakur, R.: MPI-ACC: An Integrated and Extensible Approach to Data Movement in Accelerator-Based Systems. In: 14th IEEE International Conference on High Performance Computing and Communications, Liverpool, UK (2012)

18. Potluri, S., Bureddy, D., Wang, H., Subramoni, H., Panda, D.K.: Extending openshmem for GPU computing. In: Proceedings of the 2013 IEEE 27th International Symposium on Parallel and Distributed Processing. IPDPS 2013, pp. 1001–1012. IEEE Computer Society, Washington (2013)

19. Cunningham, D., Bordawekar, R., Saraswat, V.: GPU programming in a high level language: compiling x10 to cuda. In: Proceedings of the 2011 ACM SIGPLAN X10 Workshop. X10 2011, pp. 8:1–8:10. ACM, New York (2011)

20. Miyoshi, T., Irie, H., Shima, K., Honda, H., Kondo, M., Yoshinaga, T.: Flat: A GPU programming framework to provide embedded MOI. In: Proceedings of the 5th Annual Workshop on General Purpose Processing with Graphics Processing Units. GPGPU-5, pp. 20–29. ACM, New York (2012)

Check-Pointing Approach for Fault Tolerance in OpenSHMEM

Pengfei Hao[1]([✉]), Swaroop Pophale[2], Pavel Shamis[3],
Tony Curtis[1], and Barbara Chapman[1]

[1] University of Houston, Houston, TX 77004, USA
{phao,bchapman}@uh.edu, tonyc@cs.uh.edu
[2] Mellanox Technologies, Sunnyvale, CA 94085, USA
swaroop@mellanox.com
[3] Oak Ridge National Laboratory, Oak Ridge, TN 37840, USA
shamisp@ornl.gov

Abstract. Fault tolerance for long running applications is critical to guard against failure of either compute resources or a network. Accomplishing this task in software is non-trivial and there is an added level of complexity for implementing a working model for a one-sided communications library like OpenSHMEM, since there is no matching communication call at the target processing element (PE). In this paper we explore a fault tolerance scheme based on check-point and restart, that caters to the one-sided nature of PGAS programming model while leveraging features very specific to OpenSHMEM. Through a working implementation with the 1-D Jacobi code, we show that the approach is scalable and provides considerable computational resource saving.

1 Introduction

As OpenSHMEM library evolves and accommodates features for petascale and exascale applications, it is imperative that more attention is given to fault tolerance and recovery. With long running applications, it is prohibitive to re-run the applications (or execute identical instance in parallel) considering the combination of time requirements along with the increasing power costs.

Latest high-performance computing (HPC) systems consist of an increasing number of computing resources, not only CPU cores but also hybrid architectures with GPUs and FPGAs. A large spectrum of HPC programs are targeted towards high volume data processing with run times extending to multiple days. Such applications require highly reliable systems with low failure rates. Achieving continuous running time without failures is nearly impossible on such large-scale systems due to the combination of failure possibilities across computing resources. Unfortunately the Mean Time To Failure (MTTF) of individual components of the HPC system is not expected to increase. We base this of the fact that the complexity, density, and sensitivity of individual components has increased over time. The hardware vendors increase the density of silicon chips

© Springer International Publishing Switzerland 2015
M. Gorentla Venkata et al. (Eds.): OpenSHMEM 2015, LNCS 9397, pp. 36–52, 2015.
DOI: 10.1007/978-3-319-26428-8_3

and the number of transistors, while constantly trying to decrease power consumption of the components. This leads to a lower MTTF of system components. According to [4], the reliability of components in HPC systems has not improved in the last ten years. Since the reliability of individual components is not expected to increase while the number of components grow, the overall MTTF of the whole system is projected to decrease.

The OpenSHMEM specification [5] currently lacks fault mitigation features, making OpenSHMEM programs vulnerable to system failures. In this paper we present a working model of fault tolerance for OpenSHMEM [7]. This model is based on User Level Fault Mitigation (ULFM) scheme where an explicit API has to be introduced by an application developer to enable checkpointing. This provides flexibility to the application developer to modulate the frequency and placement within the application where the checkpoint may be introduced.

The paper is organized as follows: Sect. 2 describes the OpenSHMEM memory model and the characteristics of the programming model that allows for selective recording of memory during checkpointing. Section 3 gives a brief background on the fault tolerance techniques used in HPC and the existing check-pointing approaches. In Sect. 4 we delve into the details of our fault tolerance model. Section 5 provides an evaluation of our scheme and we provide an overview if the related work in Sect. 6. Section 7 provides highlights of our contribution, discussion of the results we observe and the possible future direction for the work.

2   OpenSHMEM Memory Model

OpenSHMEM is a Partitioned Global Address Space (PGAS) library interface specification that provides an interpretation of the PGAS model. In OpenSHMEM an execution unit is called a Processing Element (PE). A PE has access to local memory and global memory. A symmetric partition of global memory is mapped to each PE and facilitates one-sided communication between different PEs executing the same executable. A PE can access the symmetric memory associated with a remote PE using the OpenSHMEM library interface.

As a PGAS model library, OpenSHMEM implicitly treats global variables, both initialized and uninitialized, as symmetric variables. In addition it allows a user to explicitly allocate variables from the symmetric heap (allocated by the library at initialization) by calling OpenSHMEM. Private memory can only be accessed by the PE itself (Fig. 1).

In OpenSHMEM the following kinds of data objects are symmetric:

– Fortran data objects in common blocks or with the SAVE attribute. These data objects must not be defined in a dynamic shared object (DSO).
– Global and static C and C++ variables. These data objects must not be defined in a DSO.
– Fortran arrays allocated with *shpalloc*
– C and C++ data allocated by *shmalloc*

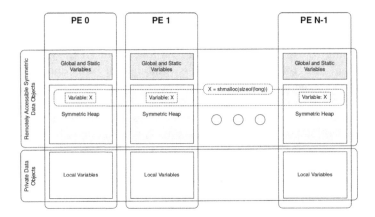

Fig. 1. OpenSHMEM memory model [5]

Since only the symmetric variables can be modified and communicated by all PEs, all applications that use the OpenSHMEM library save application critical data in symmetric variables. We use this information during our check-pointing scheme so that only a fraction of the memory consumed by the application is required to be backed up.

3   Fault Tolerance in HPC and Check-Pointing Models

In this section, we classify types of errors in the HPC environment and discuss popular fault tolerance techniques. Based on this foundation we design a Fault Tolerance model for OpenSHMEM.

3.1   Faults Definition

In order to define the fault tolerance model for OpenSHMEM it is important to classify and overview typical *High Performance Computing* (HPC) system faults. The fault tolerance community has identified three major classes of faults:

– *Permanent fault* is a result of a permanent malfunction/failure in the system. The failure is considered permanent when it causes long time unavailability of resources in the system, which requires administration intervention such as system restart or hardware replacement.
  Typically, these faults are caused by permanent hardware failures in power supply, network, CPU, or memory hardware. In certain cases, these faults might be caused by a substantial software error such as OS kernel panic and crash.
– *Transient fault* is a result of a temporary malfunction/failure in the system. Temporary failure is a short term event that results in a temporary unavailability of the system. Once system availability is back it is expected that the application availability is back with the preserved software stack.

This type of fault is typically caused by temporary malfunctions such is a bit flip in memory or temporary connection problem in the network.
- *Silent fault* (often references as "silent error") is the result of a malfunction/-failure that never got detected or got detected after extended period of time. These faults may result in invalid application behavior or incorrect computational results.
  This type of error may be caused by bit flip in the memory that is not protected with error correction code (ECC).

Silent faults we leave out of scope of this paper, since these are extremely complex to detect and are not well studied.

In this paper we focus on handling permanent and transient types of faults. Similar to most fault tolerance designs, we treat the permanent and transient faults in the same way; once the fault occurs the problematic node (or component) is marked as unavailable and notification is issued to the system manager.

3.2   Fault Handling Approaches in HPC

Fault handling approaches are well studied and researched by the HPC community. The *Message Passing Interface* (MPI) community is getting ready to introduce fault tolerance support in upcoming versions of the MPI standard. In addition, some MPI implementations already support checkpoint/restart capabilities in their libraries. Charm++, parallel programing languages also provides a built-in checkpoint/restart mechanism that supports multiple recovery algorithms. The majority of the fault tolerance approaches can be classified into the two main categories:

Masked Approach. In the masked approach the system, a communication library or hardware does not expose the errors to the application by handling it internally within a system.

The checkpoint/restart mechanism, which is also called rollback in the literature, is one of the most popular masking approaches. The checkpoint mechanism allows dumping the memory of an entire process to a storage (disk or memory). The process of taking a checkpoint may occur automatically within a certain period of time or may be explicitly requested by the application. The checkpoint of the distributed application requires substantial storage resources and time. For example, OLCF's TITAN [8] system has 710 TB of memory and the storage system reaches 240 GB/s of a peak bandwidth. Based on this information we may estimate the it takes $\frac{710\,TB}{240\,GB/s} \approx 50\,min$ to checkpoint the entire system under ideal conditions. As a result the solution is applicable for relatively small systems, but is challenging to scale with the size of future systems.

Unmasked Approach. The unmasked approach assumes that the fault is not masked and propagated to the application level. This approach substantially simplifies the software stack of a HPC system, since the major burden of the application recovery is the responsibility of the application developer. The application is responsible for handling and recovering from the fault, while the system software stack is responsible for providing the mechanisms for stabilization of the application. Once the fault is propagated, the application selects a strategy for application recovery. Since the application has the full perspective of the current state of execution, it allows the application developer to implement the best strategy for application recovery.

4   Fault Tolerance Model for OpenSHMEM

In order to develop fault tolerance design, first we identify critical design points and then based on the conclusions we define the model.

4.1   Design Points

Based on the previously discussed research work in the field we identified the following design points:

1. Coverage
   Transient faults should be handled the same way as permanent faults. If the transient fault was not handled (masked) by hardware or device driver recovery mechanisms, the failure is considered as a permanent one.
2. Minimize Overheads
   One of the primary reasons for the overheads is a lack of information about the *importance* (or usage) of various regions of the memory. As a result, the majority of the proposed solutions checkpoint the entire memory of the application.
   From this perspective, OpenSHMEM defines a convenient memory layout that separates the memory to symmetric and private regions (Fig. 1). We use this information to save only communicable symmetric data objects.
3. Choice of approach
   The unmasked approach provides a lot of flexibility for fault handling on the application level. This is one of the reasons why the MPI community is moving towards this approach. We follow the same approach and expose the basic set of operations enabling implementation of fault tolerant applications.

4.2   Checkpoint-and-Restart Model for OpenSHMEM

The checkpoint mechanism allows dumping the memory of an entire process to a storage (disk or memory). The process of taking a checkpoint may occur automatically in a certain period of time or may be explicitly requested by the application. When failure occurs, for example a fatal failure of a node, the process can be restarted from the checkpoint. The checkpoint/restart mechanisms are divided into the two types:

- Checkpoint/restart with a coordinated rollback, where all *Processing Element*(PEs) in the system are restored to the latest checkpoint
- Checkpoint/restart with a partial rollback, where only a subgroup of PEs affected by the failure is restored to the latest checkpoint.

While theoretically this approach handles all possible errors in a way that is transparent to the application and users, it has a drawback. The checkpointing of a distributed application imposes substantial overheads in terms of time and space.

One of the primary reasons for the overheads is a lack of information about the *importance* (or usage) of various regions of the memory. As a result, the majority of the proposed solutions checkpoint the entire memory of the application.

In order to mitigate the cost of the checkpoint/restart overhead researchers suggested implementation of *selective* memory checkpoint/restart, where the application explicitly specifies what memory regions are *critical* [14]. While it is possible to reduce the overhead using this approach, it offloads the burden from the programming model to the application level, where the developer has to identify the critical sections of the memory.

From this perspective OpenSHMEM (and PGAS) defines a convenient memory model that separates memory to symmetric and private regions (Fig. 1). Since, the symmetric memory is the only memory that is visible to other PEs, it is the key element that represents the state of PE in a distributed system. Failure to access this memory leads to a failure of an OpenSHMEM application which is similar to the failure of a regular process or a failure to access the physical memory. These lead to a conclusion that in order enable fault-prone execution of the process, the OpenSHMEM library has to implement a capability that enables persistent access to remote memory. Since the symmetric memory is only part of the representation of PE in the system, it is critical for the OpenSHMEM fault tolerance model to recover this particular portion of the memory. We leverage the unique characteristic of the OpenSHMEM memory model to introduce explicit checkpoint/restart functionality for symmetric memory regions only. Such a pin-pointed checkpointing technique allows reduction of the overall amount of memory backed up in the checkpoint process.

The proposed checkpoint-and-restart model consists of the following core operations:

Checkpoint: the operation checkpoints the current state of the OpenSHMEM symmetric heap and global variables. This process implicitly synchronizes; that ensures completion of all outstanding OpenSHMEM operations
Fault Detection: the operation detects a failure and notifies the OpenSHMEM application about the failure in a system.
Checkpoint Recovery: the operation rolls back the PE's symmetric memory and global variables to a previously stored checkpoint and a replacement PE takes over the role of the failed PE.

In order to implement the model and the above operations we propose the following extensions for the OpenSHMEM API:

int shmem_checkpoint_all(void) - this routine is a combination of check-pointing and fault detection. The return value indicates if a fault occurred since the previous status check. If a fault is detected, it will return a fault state immediately without checkpointing. If no fault is detected in the last computational step, it will check-point all symmetric regions and return *SHMEM_FT_SUCCESS*. The routine is a collective operation and requires a participation of all active PEs.

* *void shmem_query_fault(int **pes, int **pes_status, size_t *numpes)* - this routine is used to retrieve a list of failed PEs and reasons for their failure. It allocates memory for the *pes* and *pes_status*. A user needs to free this memory when no longer needed. *numpes* gives how many PEs failed since previous status check.

* *void shmem_restart_pes(int *pes, size_t numpes)* - this routine is a coordinated rollback operation that restores the symmetric memory region from the last checkpoint on all PEs. It will activate *sleeping* PEs to transform to a working PE. The substitute PE or PEs will leave *start_pes* when activated, skip the *shmem_ft_algo_init()* part and finally join into this function call. They will retrieve the backed up data of the dead PE, replace it and continue execution with the dead PE's PE number. The routine is a collective operation and requires a participation of all PEs.

* *int shmem_ft_algo_init(void)* - this routine returns *true* for the original PEs, while for newly spawned substitute PEs it returns *false*. The function is used to guard the initialization code in order to avoid initialization stages on substitute PEs.

Listing 1.1. ULFM frame

```
1   #include <shmem.h>
2   /* User algorithm states as global variables */
3   int step;
4   int main(int argc, const char *argv[])
5   {
6       start_pes(0);
7       if(shmem_ft_algo_init()){
8           /* User algorithm initialization goes here */
9       }
10      do{
11          if(SHMEM_FT_SUCCESS!=shmem_checkpoint_all()){
12              int *pes, *pes_status;
13              size_t numpes;
14              shmem_query_fault(&pes,&pes_status,&numpes);
15              shmem_restart_pes(pes,&numpes);
16              shmem_barrier_all();
17              free(pes);
18              free(pes_status);
19          }
20          else{
21              /* User algorithm computing loop goes here*/
22              step++;
23          }
24      }while(step<MAX_STEP);
25      /*User algorithm result report goes here*/
26      return 0;
27  }
```

In Listing 1.1 presents an pseudo code of an example that demonstrates how the above API can be used for an implementation of fault tolerant computation algorithms. On line 6 *start_pes()* is invoked in order to initialize the of OpenSHMEM environment. Lines 10 to 24 represent the loop iterating over the core computational part of the algorithm. On an iteration of the loop the application invokes *shmem_checkpoint_all()* routine that serves the two goals. First it checks if a failure has occurred since last the checkpoint, and second if no error is detected (return value SHMEM_FT_SUCCESS) it executes the checkpoint operation.

If a failure is detected (return value SHMEM_FT_FAILURE), the algorithm enters the failure branch between lines 12 and 18. *shmem_query_fault()* identifies the indexes of failed PE and a potential reason. Then *shmem_restart_pes()* is used to recover the symmetric memory segments and activate the replacement PEs. Using the call all active PEs retrieve their last checkpoint data from a backup.

It is important to point out that once replacement PEs are activated and initialized within OpenSHMEM runtime environment (*start_pes*) they reach the *shmem_ft_algo_init()* routine. For the replacement PEs the function returns *false* and therefore these PEs skip the algorithm initialization step (line 8); the replacement PEs resumes execution from the last successful checkpoint. Once all PEs are rolled back to their previous step, the algorithm invokes *shmem_barrier_all()* to synchronize between all PEs. Then the application is free to release the temporary memory allocated by *shmem_query_fault()*.

4.3   Implementation Details

In this section we describe the details of the proof-the-concept implementation of the OpenSHMEM library with checkpoint/restart capabilities. Our implementation is based on OpenSHMEM reference implementation [11] developed by University of Houston and the UCCS communication library [13]. The memory checkpoint operation is implemented using the *shmem_checkpoint_all()* routine. The routine backups symmetric memory region, its meta-data and the application *bss* and *data* memory segments that are extracted from the ELF binary format. For the rest of the paragraph all above memory segments will be referenced as a symmetric memory.

In order to store the backup each PE allocates a so-called *shadow* memory segment that is used to store the checkpoint of the symmetric, *bss,data* memory sections. In our implementation we used a simple checkpoint pattern where a PE i backs up its memory segments to PE $(i + 1)$, with the exception of the last PE N that backs up its segments to PE 0 (Fig. 2). For the memory transfer (backup) from the main memory to the shadow memory we use *shmem_mem_get* routine, which is available within the OpenSHMEM specification.

Our implementation of the checkpoint/restart is based on coordinated checkpoint methodology, therefore in an event of restart all participating PEs have to restore their symmetric memories to a previous state. This leads to a fact that, in addition to maintaining the backup information of the remote PE symmetric memory, each PE has to maintain a copy of its own symmetric memory

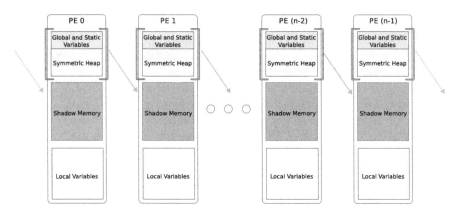

Fig. 2. Symmetric memory backup

that is used for a local rollback in event of failure of the corresponding backup
PE. As a results, the size of the shadow memory is nearly double of the size of
the symmetric memory. It is worth pointing out that this memory consumption
overhead is imposed by the nature of the coordinated checkpoint/restart mode.
For an uncoordinated restart, which is out of scope of this paper, the backup
of the local memory is not required and therefore the memory consumption is
substantially less. Our implementation of the OpenSHMEM checkpoint/restart
supports both modes of recovery, nevertheless in this work we focus on an algorithm that requires coordinated recovery.

Another challenge of the work is associated with the spawning of a new PE for
a replacement of failed one. The current OpenSHMEM runtime does not support
spawning of a new process. In order to overcome this temporary limitations
of the runtime, our implementation pre-spawns the replacement PE during the
OpenSHMEM initialization process (*shmem_start_pes()*). The pre-spawn PEs are
started in sleep mode and do not consume computational resources. Once failure
occurs, one of the pre-spawn PEs get activated and the symmetric memory of the
failed PE is transferred to the newly activated PE. The activation of the PE is a
collective operation since all PEs in the system have to be update their address
tables with the physical address (network and memory) of the replacement PE.

4.4   Assumptions

In this section we present some of core assumptions that have been made in
respect to our implementation of the checkpoint/restart capabilities:

– Dynamic linkage
  The current implementation of the checkpoint/restart mechanism assumes
  that the application is linked dynamically with the OpenSHMEM library. The
  primary reason for this assumption is the fact that the current implementation
  does not have the capability to distinguish between *bss* and *data* memory

segments of the OpenSHMEM library and the application when those are linked statically. As a result, under the static linking the recovery of the *bss* and *data* sections of the application may reset the internal global state (global and static variables) of the OpenSHMEM library. This is temporary limitation of the current implementation that can be fixed by selective recovery of the sections or a simple removal of the global and static variables from the internal usage within the OpenSHMEM library implementation.

– Address space recovery
  When a new PE is restarted and the symmetric memory is recovered from a checkpoint, the address space of the checkpointed symmetric memory may not be aligned with the base address space of the symmetric memory and the data cached in it. This is a potential side-effect of virtual memory randomization that has been recently enabled in the linux kernel. In order to overcome this challenge we remap the symmetric heap memory of the recovered process to be aligned with the rest of process. Nevertheless, the remapping process is not guaranteed and potentially may fail if the selected virtual memory region is allocated for some reason. As an alternative approach, in order to avoid the problem altogether we suggest disabling the virtual memory address randomization feature in the kernel.

– Restricted use of *shmalloc*
  In our current implementation of the checkpoint/restart capabilities the application is not allowed to call shmalloc in between of checkpoint operations. As a result, all the symmetric memory has to be allocated during the algorithm initialization stage. This restriction is imposed by the *dlmalloc* [10] memory allocation used in our implementation. *dlmalloc* uses a set of mutexes and opaque pointers to manage the *shmalloc* memory allocation requests, which makes the recovery of the meta-data very challenging. This is a temporary restriction and it can be addressed by implementation of a meta-data transferable allocator.

– Fault detection mechanism
  The current implementation of the OpenSHMEM library does not implement a fault detection mechanism. As a result, all the faults have to be simulated on the OpenSHMEM level. In order to overcome this limitation, we plan to replace our runtime with the one developed for ULFM [3] project which provides fault detection capabilities.

5   Evaluation

We tested our scheme on a distributed memory cluster with 16 nodes. Each node has four 2.2 GHz 12-core AMD Opteron 6174 processors (12 cores per socket, 48 cores total), 64 GB main memory and dual port Infiniband ConnectX HCA (20 GB per second). For all our experiments the PEs are allocated by core, so PE allocation will exhaust all available cores on a node before moving to the next node. In our figures we refer to the OpenSHMEM implementation with fault tolerance (checkpoint/restart) capabilities as *ft* and the one without such capabilities as *non-ft*. Once a failure is detected (for our experiment, we artificially introduced failures), the program loses results mid-computing. If the checkpointing backup time is T_b, recover time is T_r, single computing step time takes T_s, the total computing steps are s and f failures occur during a program execution; the time overhead of fault tolerance program T_{ft} can be calculated as:

$$T_{ft} = s * T_b + f * (T_r + T_s)$$

O_{ft} is the fraction of the total time T_{ft_total} (fault tolerance version program full running time without faults) required for fault tolerance, it can be calculated as:

$$O_{ft} = T_{ft}/T_{ft\_total}$$

Figure 3a shows checkpointing time with different heap sizes (some missing points caused by lacking system memory). The size of the global and static variables in the test program were less than 1 K so we ignore them here. From the plot we observe that the backup time grows linearly with the heap size. With more PEs backup time shows an acceptable difference, this is mainly because the total amount of communication increases while the bandwidth between PEs is fixed. Figure 3b shows a more detailed plot for the effect increasing the number of PEs has on the backup performance. As the plot shows, the increase of backup time when the number of PEs increase is very gradual, this means our fault tolerance checkpointing has good scalability characteristics.

Figure 4a shows the time required for recovery with different heap sizes (some missing points caused by a lack of system memory). Here too the size of global and static variables in test program were less than 1 K so we ignore them here. From the plot we observe that the recovery time grows with the heap size, but it is below 10 s for 64 PEs with 1024 MB of symmetric heap size, which seems negligible considering the total execution time of long running applications. Figure 4b shows the effect of increasing the number of PEs on recovery time. The recovery time is dependent on where the shadow region resides with respect to the location of the substitute PE. If the symmetric heap memory information is sent over the network, it will be affected by network traffic and related issues. This can be tackled in the future using topology information and using substitute PEs *nearest*(not on the same node) to the backup PE.

We wrote a Jacobi 1D stencil code to use OpenSHMEM and the proposed API to evaluate our fault tolerance model. Stencil codes perform a sequence of sweeps through a given array. In each time-step the stencil code updates all array elements. Our Jacobi kernel updates element cell value with the old value and its left and right neighbors, i.e., a window size three average operation. All elements need to update m times which is a user input parameter. The algorithm splits the whole array into segments and distributes them to different PEs. Each PE operates on a subset of the whole array with size N/numpes, where N is the size of the array and *numpes* is a number of PEs in the system. For every elemental computation a value from their left neighbor and right neighbor is required. To update the border elements PEs need to retrieve neighboring PEs' border value to form a complete window. The *shmem_get()* operation is used after synchronization to retrieve that value because different PEs need to synchronize processing steps to avoid using a step mismatched value.

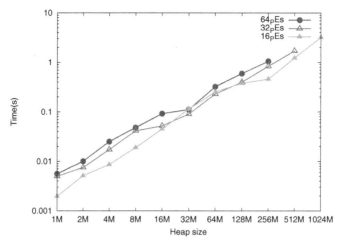

(a) Effect of symmetric heap size on checkpointing time

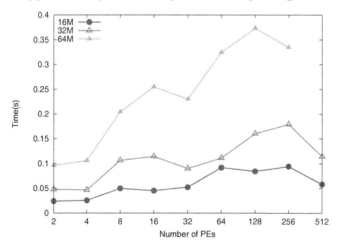

(b) Effect of number of PEs on checkpointing time

Fig. 3. Effect on checkpointing time.

At every step the border cell will consume k size buffer, hence after k rounds the border buffer is completely consumed. After that, all PEs use *shmem_barrier_all()* to synchronize, then retrieve k sized buffers from neighboring PEs to perform the next round of computation. The computing will stop after total m rounds finished. Figure 5 illustrates the buffer layout. We used a 64 MB stencil with 4096 iterations and $k = 256$ as buffer size in all tests. Each time the buffer is used up, we call *shmem_checkpoint_all()* once to back up the symmetric memory. Thus we have $4096/256 = 16$ checkpoints.

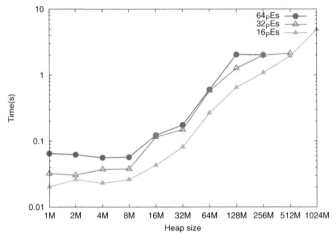

(a) Effect of symmetric heap size on recovery time

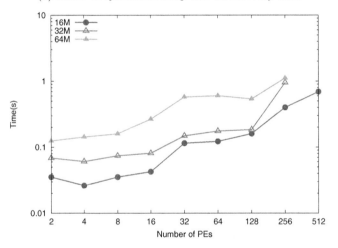

(b) Effect of number of PEs on recovery time

Fig. 4. Effect on recovery time.

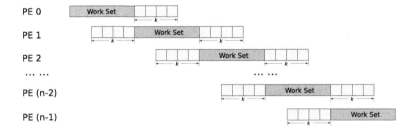

Fig. 5. Jacobi 1D stencil

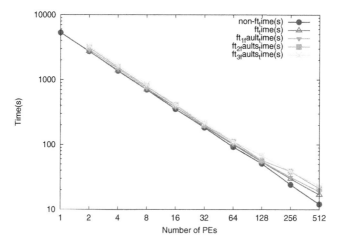

(a) Jacobi 1D runtime with *non-ft* and *ft* as a function of a number PEs with 0, 1, 2, and 3 faults

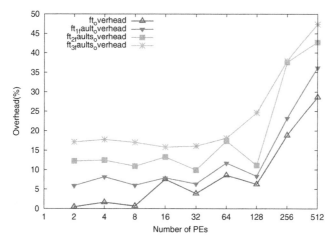

(b) Jacobi 1D fault tolerance overhead with *non-ft* and *ft* as a function of a number PEs with 0, 1, 2, and 3 faults

Fig. 6. Jacobi 1D runtime and overhead

Figure 6a is the time plot of Jacobi 1D program, with *non-ft* version, *ft* version with 0, 1, 2 and 3 faults. In log-scaled time axis these five plots are close to parallel straight lines, that implies that the fault tolerance model overhead is stable based on the problem size. Figure 6b shows the fault tolerance overhead as a percentage of the execution time of the Jacobi 1D program. We notice that depending on the number of PEs, for a fixed symmetric heap size, our fault tolerance overhead ranges from 0.4–45%, and most of the overhead is from recomputing time T_s.

6   Related Work

Research in the area of fault tolerance for the PGAS programming model is sparse. Ali, et al. [1] proposed an application-specific fault tolerance mechanism. They achieved fault-tolerance using redundant communication and shadow copies. They evaluated the approach by implementing it as a part of Global Arrays, a shared-memory programming interface for distributed systems, and using NWChem [15], a framework specifically for computational chemistry problems. Our approach is more encompassing and not limited to a specific application or kernel.

A fault tolerance mechanism based on GASPI [12] uses time-out mechanisms for all non-local procedures. Though this is more general purpose, it cannot advantageously use the unique features of OpenSHMEM. Other researchers have proposed fault-aware and fault-tolerant models for message passing models, particularly MPI. Bland et al. [2] have proposed and evaluated user level failure mitigation extensions to MPI. This provides an interface for handling faults by the user (HPC application) without aborting the entire MPI job [3]. Graham et al. [6] have proposed similar models and evaluated MPI collective algorithms in the presence of faults [9].

In this paper, we explore the best practices in the fault tolerance domain to propose a solution addressing the fault tolerance challenge for OpenSHMEM.

7   Conclusions and Future Work

Based on the investigation of different types of faults, we developed our checkpointing and restart fault tolerance model for OpenSHMEM. To the best of our knowledge, this is the first fault tolerance model implemented for OpenSHMEM. We provide a prototype API and evaluate based on the overhead observed using a Jacobi stencil code. We found that the checkpointing and restart mechanism will add about 0.4–45% overhead when compared with the non-ft version. For long running programs the overhead of checkpointing is dependent on the frequency of checkpointing.

As future work we would like to improve our current implementation, for example, we can implement a meta data transferable allocator to enable shmalloc during the computing steps. The current back up target decision uses a static ring topology which might not be the optimal for some cases, we can try to generate ad hoc backup topologies based on the processes layout on the clusters. Another aspect is the exploration for new models of computing and communication, separation of the computing resources and storage resources will allow more flexible fault recovery.

Acknowledgement. This work is supported by the United States Department of Defense and used resources of the Extreme Scale Systems Center located at the Oak Ridge National Laboratory.

References

1. Ali, N., Krishnamoorthy, S., Govind, N., Palmer, B.: A redundant communication approach to scalable fault tolerance in PGAS programming models. In: 2011 19th Euromicro International Conference on Parallel, Distributed and Network-Based Processing (PDP), pp. 24–31. IEEE (2011)
2. Bland, W., Bosilca, G., Bouteiller, A., Herault, T., Dongarra, J.: A proposal for user-level failure mitigation in the mpi-3 standard. University of Tennessee, Department of Electrical Engineering and Computer Science (2012)
3. Bland, W., Bouteiller, A., Herault, T., Hursey, J., Bosilca, G., Dongarra, J.J.: An evaluation of user-level failure mitigation support in MPI. In: Träff, J.L., Benkner, S., Dongarra, J.J. (eds.) EuroMPI 2012. LNCS, vol. 7490, pp. 193–203. Springer, Heidelberg (2012)
4. Cappello, F., Geist, A., Gropp, B., Kale, L., Kramer, B., Snir, M.: Toward exascale resilience. Int. J. High Perform. Comput. Appl. **23**(4), 374–388 (2009). http://dx.doi.org/10.1177/1094342009347767
5. Community, O.: Openshmem application programming interface (2014). http://www.openshmem.org/
6. Fagg, G.E., Dongarra, J.J.: Building and using a fault-tolerant mpi implementation. Int. J. High Perform. Comput. Appl. **18**(3), 353–361 (2004)
7. Hao, P., Shamis, P., Venkata, M.G., Pophale, S., Welch, A., Poole, S., Chapman, B.: Fault tolerance for openshmem. In: Proceedings of the 8th International Conference on Partitioned Global Address Space Programming Models, PGAS 2014, p. 23. ACM, New York (2014). http://doi.acm.org/10.1145/2676870.2676894
8. https://www.olcf.ornl.gov/titan/: Titan Super-Computer (2013)
9. Hursey, J., Graham, R.L.: Preserving collective performance across process failure for a fault tolerant mpi. In: 2011 IEEE International Symposium on Parallel and Distributed Processing Workshops and Phd Forum (IPDPSW), pp. 1208–1215. IEEE (2011)
10. Lea, D.: Doug leas malloc (dlmalloc)
11. Pophale, S.S.: Src: Openshmem library development. In: Proceedings of the International Conference on Supercomputing ICS 2011, p. 374. ACM, New York (2011). http://doi.acm.org/10.1145/1995896.1995957
12. Shahzad, F., Kreutzer, M., Zeiser, T., Machado, R., Pieper, A., Hager, G., Wellein, G.: Building a fault tolerant application using the GASPI communication layer. CoRR abs/1505.04628 (2015). http://arxiv.org/abs/1505.04628
13. Shamis, P., Venkata, M.G., Poole, S., Welch, A., Curtis, T.: Designing a high performance openSHMEM implementation using universal common communication substrate as a communication middleware. In: Poole, S., Hernandez, O., Shamis, P. (eds.) OpenSHMEM 2014. LNCS, vol. 8356, pp. 1–13. Springer, Heidelberg (2014)

14. Team, C.: Containment domains c++ api v0.1 March 2014. http://lph.ece.utexas.edu/users/CDAPI
15. Valiev, M., Bylaska, E.J., Govind, N., Kowalski, K., Straatsma, T.P., Van Dam, H.J., Wang, D., Nieplocha, J., Apra, E., Windus, T.L., et al.: NWChem: a comprehensive and scalable open-source solution for large scale molecular simulations. Comput. Phys. Commun. **181**(9), 1477–1489 (2010)

Proposing OpenSHMEM Extensions Towards a Future for Hybrid Programming and Heterogeneous Computing

David Knaak[(⊠)] and Naveen Namashivayam

Cray Inc., Seattle, USA
{knaak,nravi}@cray.com

Abstract. SHMEM is an important and popular Partitioned Global Address Space (PGAS) programming model. The OpenSHMEM API Specification Version 1.2 defines a SHMEM programming model and there are many implementations of at least most of the specification. This paper presents extensions to this API that can improve ease of programming and provide more opportunities for implementors to improve performance. Some of these features are particularly important for performance on heterogeneous system architectures with architectural features such as multi-core processors, processor accelerators, distributed memory, and heterogeneous memories. The new features described in this paper are: Alltoall Collectives, Flexible PE Subsets, Thread-Safety, Local Shared Memory Pointers, Put With Signal, and Non-blocking Put and Get. The benefits of each of these features in terms of ease of programming or program performance are also described.

1 Introduction

The original SHMEM Application Programming Interface (API) was developed by Cray Research, the predecessor of Cray Inc., and was introduced in 1993 [3]. Over time, various closed-source and open-source SHMEM implementations were developed, each with some differences. The OpenSHMEM Project, which began in 2010, is an effort to standardize the SHMEM API [3]. The OpenSHMEM API Specification Version 1.0 was derived from the Silicon Graphics (SGI) SHMEM implementation [5].

The latest OpenSHMEM API Specification, Version 1.2, was approved in March of 2015. It defines features that are adequate for developing large-scale parallel applications for high performance computing (HPC) systems. But as we move into the era of exascale computing, additional features are needed to improve performance on heterogeneous system architectures with architectural features such as multi-core processors, processor accelerators, distributed memory, and heterogeneous memories.

In recent years, Cray customers have requested extensions to Cray SHMEM [1]. Cray has worked closely with these customers to define new SHMEM APIs and has implemented the requested features. Cray has also added features based

© Springer International Publishing Switzerland 2015
M. Gorentla Venkata et al. (Eds.): OpenSHMEM 2015, LNCS 9397, pp. 53–68, 2015.
DOI: 10.1007/978-3-319-26428-8_4

on our own experience with what makes for easier programming and for better performance. For portability, both Cray and our customers would like these features, possibly in modified form, to become part of the OpenSHMEM API.

In this paper we discuss several new SHMEM features that Cray has implemented in Cray SHMEM and that we either have submitted or will submit for consideration as a part of the OpenSHMEM API. In some cases, other organizations have proposals for similar functionality. Cray is working within Open-SHMEM with the goal of reaching consensus. For each feature, we describe the motivation for it, specify its API, and present at least one use case with performance results. For brevity, the Fortran synopsis and in most cases the description of the arguments are excluded. A lot more could have been written about each feature, including a description of the research and development work done to come to the final APIs and implementation algorithms. But our primary goal is to provide enough information to demonstrate that all 6 of these features should be given careful consideration for addition to the OpenSHMEM API.

These features are not necessarily of equal importance for user productivity or for program performance and are not presented in any particular order. The features are:

- Alltoall Collectives, Sect. 3
- Flexible PE Subsets, Sect. 4
- Thread-Safety, Sect. 5
- Local Shared Memory Pointers, Sect. 6
- Put With Signal, Sect. 7
- Non-blocking Put and Non-blocking Get, Sect. 8

This paper is not intended to be a promotion of Cray but rather a promotion of OpenSHMEM. These new features are already being used to do real work for real users and we believe that many more OpenSHMEM users can benefit from having these features added to the OpenSHMEM API.

2   Experimental Setup

All of the proposed extensions are already implemented in the Cray SHMEM library, which is available in the Cray Message Passing Toolkit(MPT) [1]. We used Cray SHMEM version 7.2.2.

Tests were run on a 52 node Cray XC system with 32 core Intel Haswell processors and with the Cray Aries interconnect.

In this paper, a *node* is a group of processors, memory, and network components that acts as a network end point on the system interconnection network. The memory on a node is addressable by all processors on the node without having to go through the network. This direct addressability has lower latency and higher bandwidth than going through the network.

Since these extensions are not yet a part of the current OpenSHMEM standards, we introduce new tests in both the OSU Microbenchmark [4] and PGAS Microbenchmark [2] test suites. Additionally, other OpenSHMEM benchmarks like Matrix Multiplication and Ping-Pong were modified and used.

Each test and the corresponding performance results are discussed in detail in further Sections.

3   Alltoall Collectives

In this section we describe a new feature that supports better programmer productivity and program performance when the program has an all-to-all type of collective operation.

3.1   Motivation for Alltoall Collectives

The current set of SHMEM collective operations includes reductions, broadcast, and barrier, but does not include any all-to-all type collective operation. An all-to-all type of collective operation involves each PE exchanging data with all other PEs in the defined set of PEs. Some SHMEM programs make use of an all-to-all type communication pattern which is critical to the program. Having each program developer write his/her own all-to-all communication sequence using SHMEM primitives can be time consuming, prone to bugs, and produce sub-optimal communication performance. In addition, an algorithm that works well for a small number of data elements might not prove optimal for a larger number data elements.

Providing all-to-all collective routines simplifies programming. It also provides an opportunity for SHMEM library implementors to do optimizations, in particular system specific non-portable optimizations, that would be difficult or impractical for application developers to do.

At least two variations are important: fixed size and variable size. A fixed size all-to-all exchanges a constant number of elements with each of the other PEs in its defined group. A variable size all-to-all exchanges a possibly different number of elements with each other PE.

3.2   Alltoall Collectives API

In this subsection, we provide an overview of the proposed Alltoall API, with the C synopsis and a brief description of the functionality.

```
SYNOPSIS
    #include <shmem.h>
    void shmem_alltoall(void *dest, const void *source,
        size_t len, int PE_start, int logPE_stride,
        int PE_size, long *pSync);
    void shmem_alltoallv(void *dest, size_t *t_offsets,
        size_t *t_sizes, const void *source,
        size_t *s_offsets, size_t *s_sizes, int PE_start,
        int logPE_stride, int PE_size, long *pSync);
    void shmem_team_alltoall (void *dest, const void *source,
        size_t len, shmem_team_t myteam, long *pSync)
```

The *shmem_alltoall* routine is a collective routine; each PE in the defined set exchanges a fixed amount of data with all other PEs in the set. The data being

sent and received is stored in contiguous symmetric arrays. The jth block sent
from PE i to PE j is placed in the ith block of the destination buffer on PE j.

For *shmem_alltoallv*, each PE may send a different amount of data and provide offsets for the source and destination data.

For *shmem_team_alltoall*, the active set of PEs is specified with a   *shmem_*
team_t argument instead of the traditional active set specifiers. In Sect. 4, we
describe in detail the *shmem_team_t* arguments.

3.3   Alltoall Collectives Use Case and Performance Analysis

We introduced new tests into the PGAS Microbenchmark [2] Suite for demonstrating the performance of the *shmem_alltoall* extension. The tests were done
across 128 processes. We performed two tests and the results are shown in Fig. 1.
We implemented a basic all-to-all data transfer construct using a flat tree algorithm and we represent this as the USER DEFINED Alltoall API in Fig. 1. This
can be considered as a baseline algorithm. The author [7], describes the Flat
Tree algorithm which is used for all types of collective operations in detail. The
results of this Flat Tree algorithm is compared against the *shmem_alltoall* implementation in Cray SHMEM. We measured the latency of these two constructs
for different buffer sizes. The x-axis represents the buffer sizes in bytes, while
the y-axis represents the latency in microseconds.

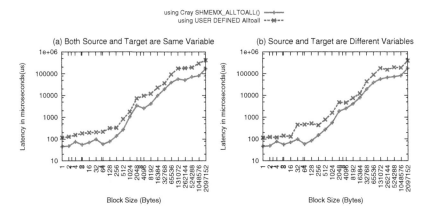

Fig. 1. Performance analysis of Alltoall API using Cray SHMEM implementation

Figure 1(a) shows the performance results when both the source and the
destination variables are same, while Fig. 1(b) shows the results when the source
and destination buffers are different variables. We can see from the results that
the *shmem_alltoall* construct improves performance and provides on an average
of 1.3X improvements in latency when compared to the user defined Alltoall
baseline algorithm.

4   Flexible PE Subsets

In this section we describe a new feature that supports ease of programming with a flexible API for specifying the active set for collective operations.

4.1   Motivation for Flexible PE Subsets

Many routines in the OpenSHMEM API operate on a subset of PEs called *the active set*. The active set is specified by three arguments to the routine: the lowest PE number of the active set of PEs, the log (base 2) of the stride between consecutive PE numbers in the active set, and the number of PEs in the active set.

For many HPC applications decomposition of work doesn't fit that required pattern. What is needed is a flexible means to specify an arbitrary sct of PEs to be included in a PE subset. The team routines provide a convenient way to manage the life cycle (creation, use, and destruction) of these subsets. Because the set of PEs is flexible, it can be easier to program than forcing a set of PEs to a fixed pattern. Performance gains are also possible with this flexibility.

MPI has always supported the concept of a flexible subset of processes which it calls a *communicator*. MPI contains a rich set of functions to support creation, use and destruction of communicators. The UPC Collectives Library 2.0 proposal from LBNL/IBM [6] has proposed a similar concept, called *teams*, to denote UPC thread subsets. Cray UPC has already implemented and delivered the UPC team functionality, based off the LBNL/IBM paper.

Cray has implemented teams in Cray SHMEM based on the UPC teams model. This provides continuity between PGAS languages and overlaps will with MPI. This fleixble PE subsets capability, called *teams*, is being proposed for OpenSHMEM.

4.2   Flexible PE Subsets API

In this subsection, we provide an overview on the proposed Flexible PE subsets API, with the C synopsis and a brief description of the functionality.

```
SYNOPSIS
    #include <shmem.h>
    void shmem_team_split(shmem_team_t parent_team,
        int color, int key, shmem_team_t *newteam);
    void shmem_team_create_strided(int PE_start,
        int PE_stride, int PE_size, shmem_team_t *newteam);
    int shmem_team_translate_pe(shmem_team_t team1,
        int team1_pe, shmem_team_t team2);
    int shmem_team_npes(shmem_team_t newteam);
    int shmem_team_mype(shmem_team_t newteam);
    void shmem_team_barrier(shmem_team_t myteam,
        long *pSync);
    void shmem_team_free(shmem_team_t *newteam);
```

The *shmem_team_split* routine is a collective routine. It partitions an existing parent team into disjoint subgroups, one for each value of color, similar to the MPI communicator concept. Each subgroup contains all PEs of the same color. Within each subgroup, each PE is assigned a rank, a value from 0 to N-1 where N is the number of PEs in the subgroup. The PEs are ranked in the order defined by the value of the argument key, with ties broken according to their rank in the parent team.

A new team is created for each subgroup and returned in the handle *newteam*. Each resulting newteam consists of a set of disjoint PEs.

A PE may supply the color value SHMEM_COLOR_UNDEFINED, in which case a value of SHMEM_TEAM_NULL is returned for newteam, as this PE will not be a member of any new team. This is a collective call over all members of the parent team, but each PE is permitted to provide different values for color and key. This routine gathers the color and key data from all PE in the parent team to determine the participants in the new team.

By default, Cray SHMEM creates two predefined teams that will be available for use once the routine *shmem_init* has been called. These teams can be referenced in the application by the constants SHMEM_TEAM_WORLD and SHMEM_TEAM_NODE. Every PE is a member of the SHMEM_TEAM_WORLD team, and its rank in SHMEM_TEAM_WORLD corresponds to the value of its global PE rank, shmem_mype. The SHMEM_TEAM_NODE team only contains the set of PEs that reside on the same node as the current PE. These predefined constants can be used as the parent team when creating new SHMEM team subsets.

Any valid SHMEM team can be used as the parent team. This function must be called by all PEs in the parent team. The value of color must be nonnegative or SHMEM_COLOR_UNDEFINED. None of the parameters need to reside in symmetric memory.

shmem_team_create_strided creates a new team based on a starting PE value, a stride, and a size.

shmem_team_translate_pe translates a given rank of one team to its corresponding rank in another team.

shmem_team_npes returns the number of PEs in the team.

shmem_team_mype returns the calling PE's rank in the team.

shmem_team_barrier is a collective synchronization routine such that no PE in the team can advance past a barrier until all PEs in the team have reached the barrier.

shmem_team_free destroys an existing team and releases all the team's resources.

4.3 Flexible PE Subsets Usage Example

Figure 2 shows an example of creating subsets of PEs using the proposed teams API. First, each PE is assigned a color based on whether its PE number is even or odd. Second, each PE is assigned a key, which is its PE number. These 2 arguments are used by *shmem_team_split* to divide the parent team, SHMEM_TEAM_WORLD, into the 2 teams. The handle for the team each PE belongs to is returned in *new_team*.

Then the rank of the PE in its team, as returned by *shmem_team_mype*, and the size of its team, as returned by *shmem_team_npes*, are printed.

shmem_team_barrier provides synchronization among the PEs in a particular team, with each team being synchronized independent of each other.

And finally *shmem_team_free* destroys the created team.

```
shmem_team_t new_team;
int color = shmem_my_pe() % 2;
int key    = shmem_my_pe();
shmem_team_split(SHMEM_TEAM_WORLD, color, key, &new_team);
if (new_team != SHMEM_TEAM_NULL) {
    int t_mype     = shmem_team_mype(new_team);
    int t_numpes   = shmem_team_npes(new_team);
    printf("I am rank %d of the %s team with %d members\n",
           t_mype, (color ? "odd " : "even"), t_numpes);
    shmem_team_barrier(new_team, bSync);
    shmem_team_free(&new_team);
}
```

Fig. 2. Usage example of the teams API for flexible PE subsets

5   Thread-Safety

In this section we describe a new feature that supports greater program performance with hybrid SHMEM and multithreading programming models.

5.1   Motivation for Thread-Safety

The OpenSHMEM API describes a programming model where all PEs have the same level of access to memory and compute resources. To take advantage of the power of various programming models, many HPC applications are now combining two or more programming models in the same program. This hybrid programming is done both for ease of programming and to take advantage of performance capabilities of different programming models. A common hybrid programming model combines MPI and OpenMP. This model uses MPI for point to point communication between the nodes and uses OpenMP inside of each node. Using this model reduces communication overhead in MPI inside each node. It also provides better scalability than pure MPI or pure OpenMP program. Another hybrid model combines Coarray Fortran and OpenMP [8].

The hybrid MPI/OpenMP programming model is possible because MPI supports thread-safety. OpenSHMEM programs could similarly benefit from a hybrid programming model with OpenMP, but that requires that OpenSHMEM support thread-safety.

The thread-safety support that is being proposed is very basic. It supports primarily simple Puts, Gets, and AMO's. Other SHMEM calls, in particular collectives, have restrictions on their use in relation to threads. The proposed support consists of minimal extensions to the OpenSHMEM API. These extensions are sufficient to enable PEs to issue small Puts, small Gets, and AMOs at higher aggregate rates than is possible in a single-threaded environment, leading to better performance for certain multi-threaded applications.

5.2   Thread-Safety API

In this subsection, we provide an overview of the proposed Thread-Safety API, with the C synopsis and a brief description of the functionality.

```
SYNOPSIS
    #include <shmem.h>
    int shmem_init_thread(int required);
    int shmem_query_thread(void);
    void shmem_thread_register(void);
    void shmem_thread_unregister(void);
    void shmem_thread_quiet(void);
    void shmem_thread_fence(void);
```

The *shmem_init_thread* routine initializes Cray SHMEM in the same way that *shmem_init* does. In addition, it performs thread-safety-specific initialization. This routine is used in place of *shmem_init* either before additional threads are created or by only one thread per process. The call supports one argument, the desired level of thread-safety. Cray SHMEM currently supports two levels.

SHMEM_THREAD_MULTIPLE specifies that processes may have multiple threads. Any thread may issue a SHMEM call at any time, subject to some restrictions.

SHMEM_THREAD_SINGLE specifies one thread per process. SHMEM_THREAD_FUNNELED and SHMEM_THREAD_SERIALIZED are not currently supported by Cray.

The *shmem_query_thread* routine returns the level of thread- safety currently being provided.

The *shmem_thread_register* routine registers threads for thread-safety purposes. If the currently provided thread-safety level is SHMEM_THREAD_MULTIPLE, any thread that will make Cray SHMEM calls must register. If the calling thread has not previously registered then the thread is registered. Otherwise this routine has no effect.

The *shmem_thread_unregister* routine unregisters previously registered threads. Any thread that has called *shmem_thread_register* must call *shmem_thread_unregister* to unregister itself properly.

The *shmem_thread_quiet* routine waits for completion of all outstanding remote writes and non-blocking Gets issued by a thread. It is the thread-specific version of the *shmem_quiet* routine. It allows an individual thread to wait for completion of Puts and non-blocking Gets it previously issued. All Put or non-blocking Get operations issued prior to the call to *shmem_thread_quiet* are guaranteed to be visible to all other processes no later than any subsequent memory load or store, remote Put or Get, AMO, or synchronization operations that follow the call to *shmem_thread_quiet*.

The *shmem_thread_fence* routine ensures ordering of delivery of puts and non-blocking gets. This is the thread-specific version of the *shmem_fence* routine. The routine ensures ordering of put (remote write) and non-blocking get operations. All such operations, which are issued by the calling thread to a particular remote processing element (PE) prior to the call to *shmem_thread_fence*, are guaranteed to be delivered before any subsequent such operations to the same PE that follow the call to *shmem_thread_fence* and are issued by the calling thread.

5.3 Thread-Safety Use Cases and Performance Analysis

A thread-safe OpenSHMEM implementation provide an opportunity to use OpenSHMEM with multithreading programming models for hybrid programming. In this performance analysis we report on the performance results of an OSU Microbenchmark and a Matrix Multiplication benchmark, both modified to use threads.

Figure 3 shows the results of a modified OSU Microbenchmark. Using the thread-safe Cray SHMEM implementation the latency was measured in one test when transferring different size messages between PEs on the same node (Intra-Node) and in another test between PEs on two different nodes (Inter-Node). Figure 3(a) shows the results for Intra-Node transfer and Fig. 3(b) shows the results for Inter-Node transfer.

We compare 2 PEs without threads to 2 PEs with each PE having 16 threads. The test, when threaded, splits the data buffer into multiple chunks. The source and destination buffers are in the symmetric heap. Each thread in the sending PE transfers a separate chunk to its corresponding thread in the receiving PE. Depending on the size of the chunk, *shmem_put128* or *shmem_put64* or *shmem_put32* is used. The results are compared against transferring the entire buffer between PEs with a single *shmem_putmem* call. On an average we observe a 84 percent improvement when using threads. But it is not surprising that using 32 cores in the threaded version will perform much better than using 2 cores in the non-threaded version.

For another test we implemented a thread-safe version of an OpenSHMEM Matrix Multiplication benchmark. The data decomposition is done across one dimension along the x-axis to obtain a contiguous set of data for transfer to other PEs. We used 8 threads per PE. The non-threaded version works on a complete data buffer. The threaded version divides the data buffer into multiple chunks and each thread works on a particular chuck.

Figure 4 shows the results. In Fig. 4, the x-axis represents both the number of threads as well as the number of PEs. For example, on x-axis scale 16 represents 16 PEs are being utilized on the non-thread matrix multiplication test and 2 PEs with each PE utilizing 8 threads on the thread-safe version test.

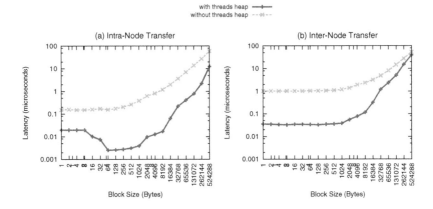

Fig. 3. Hybrid SHMEM-thread performance.

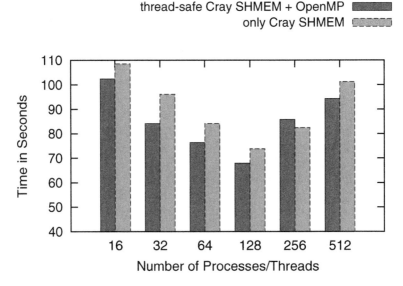

Fig. 4. Performance analysis of hybrid matrix multiplication benchmark with Cray SHMEM and OpenMP - X-axis represent both the number of processes as well as the total number of threads in all the PEs.

We observe that the performance gains on using multiple threads for this matrix multiplication benchmark is not as high as the previous microbenchmarks. We can see around 8 percent performance improvements on using the thread-safe version and this improvement is attributed to the usage of the OpenMP parallel constructs on the matrix multiplication computation and not on the usage of the threads for communication. This is because, for this analysis we have compared the number of PEs on the non-thread-safe version with the number of threads on the thread-safe version.

Usage of a thread-safe OpenSHMEM implementation can also make better use of memory. Consider the use of Intel's Xeon Phi Knights Corner processors, which has 61 cores and by hyper-threading we can extend it 244 cores. Allocating symmetric memory across all these 244 cores may not be possible, but with thread-safe Cray SHMEM we can obtain a better utilization of all the cores. Instead of having 240 PEs we can have 60 PEs and with each PE having 4 threads or 4 PEs with 60 threads on each.

6 Local Shared-Memory Pointers

In this section we describe a new feature that supports greater performance on system architectures that have non-uniform memory latency and bandwidth by allowing direct access by one PE of memory owned by another PE on the same node.

6.1 Motivation for Local Shared-Memory Pointers

When a system architecture supports direct access by one PE to memory owned by another PE without going though a network, allowing that PE to make direct accesses can be a simpler style of programming for those accesses and can be more efficient than going through an OpenSHMEM call. This sort of access is called on-node shared memory access where a node is the unit of the system architecture that allows this.

6.2 Local Shared-Memory Pointers API

In this subsection, we provide an overview on the proposed Local Shared-Memory Pointers API, with the C synopsis and a brief description of the functionality.

```
SYNOPSIS
    #include <shmem.h>
    void *shmem_local_ptr(void *dest_addr, size_t dest_len,
        int dest_pe);;
    void shmem_local_pes(int *pes, int npes);
    int shmem_local_npes(void);
```

The *shmem_local_ptr* routine takes a remote address, *dest_addr*, on the same node as the calling PE, as well as the length, *dest_len*, of the remote address space the user intends to access, and the destination PE number, *dest_pe*. It returns a local address that can be used to do local loads and stores to *dest_addr* (without the aid of SHMEM or any other communication library). The function will return NULL if *dest_pe* is not on the same node as the calling PE, or if the specified address range is not contained in the data segment or the symmetric heap.

shmem_local_ptr differs from *shmem_ptr* in that *shmem_ptr* can, for some implementations, return a pointer for a data object that is on a different node, whereas *shmem_local_ptr* will only return a pointer if the remote PE is on the same node as the calling PE.

7   Put with Signal

In this section we describe a new feature that supports a more natural programming interface to notify the destination PE that data sent to it has arrived.

7.1   Motivation for Put with Signal

SHMEM Put is a one sided operation, thus the destination PE does not have to participate directly in receiving data from a source PE. However the destination PE needs some way of knowing when the data has all arrived. In the general case the destination PE cannot simply examine the received data to determine if it has all been received. Chunks of the data might arrive out of order with respect to each other and the destination PE may not know what possibly arbitrary values the incoming data will be.

The source PE can do a *shmem_put*, then a *shmem_fence*, and then another *shmem_put* (the signal) to a different destination data object that the receiving PE can check until that signal data object has changed to some predefined value.

The proposed feature combines the two put operations into one. This simplifies, at least a little, the programmer's work. But importantly, if the underlying software and hardware can support it, the data and the signal can be sent at the same time with the requirement that the signal is not made visible to the destination PE until all the data is visible.

7.2   Put with Signal API

In this subsection, we provide an overview on the proposed Put With Signal API, with the C synopsis, and a brief description of the functionality. There are both blocking and non-blocking versions. See Sect. 8 for more on non-blocking operations.

```
SYNOPSIS
    #include <shmem.h>
    void shmem_<type>_put_signal(<type> *dest,
        const <type> *src, size_t nelems,
        uint64_t *sig_addr, uint64_t signal, int pe);
    void shmem_put<size>_signal(<type> *dest,
        const <type> *src, size_t nelems,
        uint64_t *sig_addr, uint64_t signal, int pe);
    void shmem_<type>_put_signal_nb(short *target,
```

```
      const short *source , size_t len , uint64_t *sig_addr ,
      uint64_t signal , int pe , void **transfer_handle );
void shmem_put<size>_signal_nb (void *target ,
      const void *source , size_t len , uint64_t *sig_addr ,
      uint64_t signal , int pe , void **transfer_handle );
```

The put with signal routines provide a high-performance method for copying contiguous data from a data object on the local PE to a contiguous data object on a remote PE and then setting a remote signal flag indicating the data transfer is complete.

The blocking routines return only after the data has been copied from the source data object on the local PE, but not necessarily before the data has been copied to the target data object on the remote PE. Calling shmem_quiet (or routines that call it) guarantees that all puts previously issued by this PE are complete, indicating the data has been copied to the target on the remote PE and the remote signal flag has been set.

The non-blocking routines initiate the transfer and then return, possibly before the data has been copied from the source on the local PE or before the data has been copied to the target data object on the remote PE. Calling shmem_quiet (or routines that call it) guarantees that all puts previously issued by this PE are complete, indicating the data has been copied to the target on the remote PE and the remote signal flag has been set.

7.3   Put with Signal Use Case and Performance Analysis

We used a Ping-Pong benchmark to test the performance of the *shmem_put_signal* extension. The Ping-Pong benchmark sends data from one PE to other PE and follows the data with a signal to notify the completion of the data transfer. On receiving the signal, the partner PE sends data back to the initial PE followed with a similar completion signal. This Ping-Pong operation is performed multiple times and the average time taken for a single iteration is observed. We developed two different versions of the Ping-Pong benchmark. In the first version of the benchmark we used *shmem_putmem*, then *shmem_putmem* for the signal, and *shmem_wait* by the destination PE. These are available in the current OpenSH-MEM standards. In the second version, we used the proposed *shmem_put_signal* extension, which consolidates the operation of *shmem_putmem* of the data and the *shmem_putmem* of the signal. Figure 5 shows the latency of these two different versions of the Ping-Pong benchmark across different data sizes. On an average for small data sizes, we can observe around 17 percent improvement in latency and for large data sizes we can observe around 8 percent improvements in latency.

Though we can observe some performance improvements with *shmem_put_signal*, the primary purpose for the extension is for ease of programming.

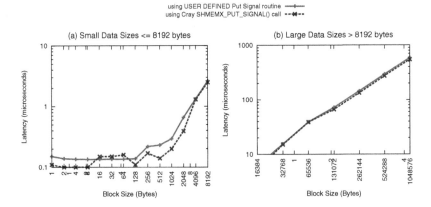

Fig. 5. Performance of *shmem_put_signal* in cray SHMEM implementation

8   Non-blocking Put and Get

In this section we describe a new feature that supports better point to point communication performance by allowing overlap of communication with computation.

8.1   Motivation for Non-blocking Put and Get

The current OpenSHMEM API specifies blocking Puts and Gets. Blocking means that while data is being moved from the source PE to the destination PE, the caller has to wait. Non-blocking versions of Put and Get would allow for the calling routine to do computation while waiting for the data transfer to complete.

Cray was not the first vendor to implement non-blocking Put and Get. We based our implementation on the HP/Quadrics API.

8.2   Non-blocking Put and Get API

In this subsection, we provide an overview of the proposed non-blocking Puts and Gets API, with the C synopsis and a brief description of the functionality.

```
SYNOPSIS
    #include <shmem.h>
    void shmem_<type>_put_nb(void *dest, const void *source,
        size_t len, int pe, void **transfer_handle);
    void shmem_put<size>_nb(void *dest, const void *source,
        size_t len, int pe, void **transfer_handle);
    void shmem_<type>_get_nb(void *dest, const void *source,
        size_t len, int pe, void **transfer_handle);
    void shmem_get<size>_nb(void *dest, const void *source,
        size_t len, int pe, void **transfer_handle);
```

In this API specification, the *transfer_handle* argument is included for a possible future extension to non-blocking explicit calls where each call returns an explicit handle that can later be used for testing completion of the communication for that call. It is not clear at this time how important that extension will be.

The non-blocking Puts and Gets have the same set of size variations as the blocking Puts and Gets.

The non-blocking Put routines provide a high-performance method for copying contiguous data from a data object on the local PE to a contiguous data object on a remote PE. These non-blocking routines initiate the transfer and then return, possibly before the data has been copied from the source on the local PE or before the data has been copied to the destination data object on the remote PE. Calling shmem_quiet (or routines that call it) guarantees that all Puts previously issued by this PE are complete, meaning that the data has been copied to the destination on the remote PE.

The non-blocking Get routines are similar to the non-blocking Put routines except that the data is transferred from a remote PE to the local PE.

9   Conclusion

Cray has implemented extensions to the OpenSHMEM API based on both customer requests and our own initiatives to improve both ease of programming and SHMEM program performance. In this paper we have demonstrated ease of programming and performance benefits. Thread-safety supports much higher computation performance when a hybrid programming model of PEs and threads is matched to a heterogeous computing architecture. Alltoall collectives support an easier way to specify all-to-all communication and performance can be tuned in implementation specific libraries to match system architectures in a way that would be impractical for program developers to do on there own. Flexible PE subsets supports user productivity with a more powerful way to specify collective operations that match the specific pattern of the program. Local shared-memory pointers support more efficient memory operations when the architecture has non-uniform memory latency and bandwidth. Non-blocking Puts and Gets support higher performance when the system architecture can offload a significant part of communication from the computation processors. Put with signal supports a more natural style of one sided point-to-point communication with potential for better performance.

For these reasons, we encourage OpenSHMEM to include these new features in future OpenSHMEM API Specifications.

Acknowledgement. The authors wish to acknowledge the Cray Inc. employees who worked on the design and implementation of these proposed extensions to OpenSH-MEM: Monika ten Bruggencate, Kim McMahon, Steve Oyanagi, and Nick Radcliffe.

References

1. Cray - Message Passing Toolkit. http://docs.cray.com/books/004-3689-001/html-004-3689-001/zfixedsllc0bet.html
2. HPCTools PGAS-Microbenchmarks. https://github.com/uhhpctools/pgas-micro bench
3. OpenSHMEM - API Standard Specification 1.2. http://bongo.cs.uh.edu/site/sites/default/site_files/openshmem-specification-1.2.pdf
4. OSU Microbenchmarks. http://mvapich.cse.ohio-state.edu/benchmarks/
5. SGI - Message Passing Toolkit. http://techpubs.sgi.com/library/tpl/cgi-bin/getdoc.cgi?coll=0650&db=bks&srch=&fname=/SGI_Developer/MPT_MPI_PM/sgi_html/front.html
6. UPC Collectives Library 2.0. http://upc.lbl.gov/publications/UPC-Collectives-PGAS11.pdf
7. Namashivayam, N., Ghosh, S., Khaldi, D., Eachempati, D., Chapman, B.: Native mode-based optimizations of remote memory accesses in openshmem for intel xeon phi. In: Proceedings of the 8th International Conference on Partitioned Global Address Space Programming Models, PGAS 2014 (2014)
8. Preissl, R., Wichmann, N., Long, B., Shalf, J., Ethier, S., Koniges. A.: Multithreaded global address space communication techniques for Gyrokinetic fusion applications on ultra-scale platforms. In: 2011 International Conference for High Performance Computing, Networking, Storage and Analysis (SC), pp. 1–11, November 2011

A Case for Non-blocking Collectives
in OpenSHMEM: Design, Implementation,
and Performance Evaluation
Using MVAPICH2-X

A.A. Awan$^{(\boxtimes)}$, K. Hamidouche, C.H. Chu, and Dhabaleswar Panda

Department of Computer Science and Engineering, The Ohio State University,
Columbus, OH, USA
{awan.10,hamidouche.2,chu.368,panda.2}@osu.edu

Abstract. An ever increased push for performance in the HPC arena
has led to a multitude of hybrid architectures in both software and hardware for HPC systems. Partitioned Global Address Space (PGAS) programming model has gained a lot of attention over the last couple of
years. The main advantage of PGAS model is the ease of programming
provided by the abstraction of a single memory across nodes of a cluster.
OpenSHMEM implementations currently implement the OpenSHMEM
1.2 specification that provides interface for one-sided, atomic, and collective operations. However, the recent trend in HPC arena in general, and
Message Passing Interface (MPI) community in specific, is to use Non-
Blocking Collective (NBC) communication to efficiently overlap computation with communication to save precious CPU cycles.

This work is inspired by encouraging performance numbers for NBC
implementations of various MPI libraries. As the OpenSHMEM community has been discussing the use of non-blocking communication, in this
paper, we propose an NBC interface for OpenSHMEM, present its design,
implementation, and performance evaluation. We discuss the NBC interface that has been modeled along the lines of MPI NBC interface and
requires minimal changes to the function signatures. We have designed
and implemented this interface using the Unified Communication Runtime in MVAPICH2-X. In addition, we propose OpenSHMEM NBC
benchmarks as an extension to the OpenSHMEM benchmarks available
in the widely used OMB suite. Our performance evaluation shows that
the proposed NBC implementation provides up to 96 percent overlap for
different collectives with little NBC overhead.

Keywords: Non-blocking collectives · PGAS model · OpenSHMEM ·
OSU micro-benchmarks · Unified communication runtime

This research is supported in part by National Science Foundation grants #OCI-
1148371, #CCF-1213084, and #CNS-1419123.

M. Gorentla Venkata et al. (Eds.): OpenSHMEM 2015, LNCS 9397, pp. 69–86, 2015.
DOI: 10.1007/978-3-319-26428-8_5

1   Introduction

Partitioned Global Address Space (PGAS) model offers the best of both worlds. It offers the convenience of programming a shared memory system as well as the performance control of a distributed programming model like message passing [33]. PGAS libraries and languages provide an alternate High Performance Computing (HPC) programming model offering light weight one-sided communication and low cost synchronization semantics. Certain applications [8,34] that have irregular communication patterns have efficiently utilized the PGAS model to their advantage. PGAS model can also benefit bandwidth limited applications [5]. There are two broad categories of the PGAS model. First is the language-based PGAS model that includes Unified Parallel C (UPC) [32], Titanium [10], Chapel [1], and Co-Array Fortran [6]. Second is the library based model provided by OpenSHMEM [3]. OpenSHMEM is an effort to bring together a variety of SHMEM and SHMEM-like implementations into an open standard.

The latest OpenSHMEM 1.2 Specification [3] provides point-to-point, one-sided, and blocking collective communication routines. However, the recent trend in HPC and specially in Message Passing Interface (MPI) paradigm, is to utilize non-blocking communication for overlapping computation and communication. Blocking communication means that the applications have to wait in the OpenSHMEM runtime (or library) till the communication gets completed. However, researchers have proposed that this blocking communication (e.g. in MPI) is a waste of CPU cycles [13]. Non-blocking communication provides an efficient alternative method of designing applications where independent computation is allowed to overlap the communication. This provides an opportunity for both one-sided and collective operations to proceed in the background while CPU is free to work on independent computation. Multiple strategies have been proposed to progress the communication in the background [9,20,30]. These studies have been proposed primarily for the message passing model but are relevant for OpenSHMEM as well.

1.1   Motivation

The primary motivation for Non-Blocking Collective (NBC) operations is to maximize the overlap while restricting the communication latency to acceptable levels. While most algorithms for blocking collectives are tuned for minimizing latency, studies suggest that the applications can get good overlap even without tuning specifically for overlap and that too with limited overhead on latency [4]. The most common scenario for an OpenSHMEM application to use the proposed NBC interface is shown in Fig. 1. We note that shmemx calls shown in Fig. 1 are experimental at this time.

Non-blocking operations for OpenSHMEM were first proposed by Poole et al. in [27]. However, the paper presented only the concept of OpenSHMEM NBC with little design and/or implementation details. In addition, the non-blocking API presented in [27] needs explicit creation of Active Sets by the user of the library. This approach makes the OpenSHMEM API more like MPI since it also requires explicit handling of communicators (MPI's Active Set equivalent)

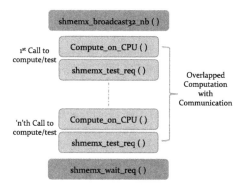

Fig. 1. Common scenario for using OpenSHMEM non-blocking collectives

by the application programmer. On the other hand, OpenSHMEM's current interface handles this requirement by the triplet *PE_start, logPE_stride, PE_end* that users can specify as part of OpenSHMEM routines. This enables the Open-SHMEM implementations to handle the task of active set management inside the runtime in a transparent fashion.

In this paper, we mainly focus on the following broad challenges and research questions:

– Can we design OpenSHMEM NBC support with minimal changes to the current blocking interface?
– Can we model the NBC interface so that it does not require the application programmer to explicitly handle creation and destruction of communicators (or Active Sets)?
– Can we implement the OpenSHMEM NBC interface in a high performance and extensible fashion?
– Can a set of micro-benchmarks be proposed that evaluate performance of any standard implementation of OpenSHMEM NBC operations?

1.2   Contributions

In order to address these challenges, we propose and design an OpenSHMEM NBC interface in this paper that is modeled along the lines of the MPI NBC interface.

Specifically, we are interested in designing the interface with minimal changes to the function signatures for NBC. Therefore, we broadly propose two options; first, we extend the blocking interface by adding only one additional argument. This argument is called **request** and is used for progressing the communication using test calls and for ending the communication using the wait call. Second, we propose to maintain the triplet based interface for OpenSHMEM NBC operations as it alleviates the user from handling the task of Active Set (or communicator) management.

For performance, we design the OpenSHMEM NBC interface on top of MVAPICH2-X [2], which is a high-performance implementation of OpenSH-MEM [19]. The performance of MVAPICH2-X can be exploited in two ways.

First, we create the communicators internally inside MVAPICH2-X. This leads to better performance as creating communicators is an expensive task. Second, we take advantage of the high-performance MPI NBC implementation of the MVAPICH2 library that provides near perfect overlap for most collectives [4,30]. Details about MPI NBC interface have been discussed in Sect. 2.

For extensibility, we use the Unified Communication Interface (UCR) [17] layer of MVAPICH2-X that unifies the runtimes for MPI and PGAS models. Our OpenSHMEM NBC implementation is extensible as it can be modified to take advantage of various optimizations offered by MVAPICH2-X library.

Since, the design and implementation of OpenSHMEM NBC interface is under discussion, we expect to see multiple implementations of this interface. Thus, we propose and design new NBC benchmarks to evaluate latency and overlap of OpenSHMEM NBC implementations in a standardized manner.

To summarize, we make the following key contributions in this paper.

- Propose high-performance and scalable designs and implementations of NBC operations in OpenSHMEM on top of the MVAPICH2-X library.
- Propose and implement new NBC benchmarks for evaluating OpenSHMEM NBC operations in a standardized manner.
- Describe important insights about latency, overlap, overhead, and effect of different number of test calls on the proposed NBC operations in OpenSH-MEM.
- Highlight the usefulness of the proposed NBC interface and benchmarks by conducting a comparative performance evaluation.

The rest of the paper is organized as follows. Relevant background information is provided in Sect. 2. Design and implementation details of OpenSHMEM NBC are discussed in Sect. 3. Proposed NBC benchmarks for evaluating overlap and latency of NBC operations in OpenSHMEM are described in Sect. 4. Comprehensive performance evaluation is presented in Sect. 5. Section 6 contains the conclusion and future work.

2   Background

In this section, we provide the necessary background information for this paper.

2.1   Non-blocking Collective Operations in MPI

The current MPI Standard, MPI-3 [26], includes interface for NBC operations. Although NBC implementations like LibNBC [11] predate the addition of NBC to the MPI standard, applications were not able to use NBC as MPI calls in their programs. However, with the addition of NBC interface in the MPI standard, various microbenchmark level [4] and application level [30] studies have been published. The benefits of overlapping computation and communication have been highlighted at different large and small scales. Open-source MPI libraries like MPICH2 [16], OpenMPI [7] and MVAPICH2 [23] offer full support for all non-blocking collectives defined by the MPI specification.

2.2 InfiniBand's Hardware Support for Collective Communication

Almost 45 percent of clusters in the Top500 [31] supercomputer list use InfiniBand [14] as an interconnect. InfiniBand provides a low-latency and high-bandwidth network interface for HPC clusters. It has excellent hardware support to accelerate communication [28]. Hardware-multicast is a novel feature of InfiniBand that provides ability to send messages to a *multicast address* and deliver them to multiple processes on different nodes. Compared to performing multiple point-to-point operations, Hardware-multicast can reduce the network load by allowing the switches to duplicate the message as well as significantly lower latency by reducing the number of operations performed at the host [24]. MVAPICH2 also supports efficient collectives based on hardware-multicast capabilities [21,25].

3 Design of Non-blocking Collectives for OpenSHMEM

In this section we explain the rationale behind the proposed OpenSHMEM NBC interface, its design and implementation, and the new benchmarks developed for its evaluation. First, we describe the proposed changes to the API for adding NBC operations in OpenSHMEM. We note that our interface differs from the API proposed in [27]. The differences are explained in Sect. 3.1. Second, we present the design and implementation details of OpenSHMEM NBC using the UCR in the MVAPICH2-X library.

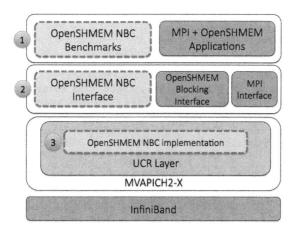

Fig. 2. Overview of design and implementation of OpenSHMEM NBC in MVAPICH2-X

3.1 The OpenSHMEM NBC Interface

Our interface is based on the non-blocking API proposed in [27] with the exception that our proposed API does not require the creation of the Active sets by the user. For better productivity, we propose to hide the complexity of creation and management of Active sets from the user. We create the communicators transparently in the underlying MVAPICH2-X library. This eliminates the need of creating Active Sets by the application programmer. It also helps to minimize the changes needed for existing OpenSHMEM applications that use blocking collectives. The only change that needs to be done at application level will be to use the additional request argument and call the shmemx_wait_req() function. The request argument will also be used to make shmemx_test_req() calls for manually progressing the communication. Further, as the creation of the active sets is an expensive operation, we have extended the MVAPICH2-X caching schemes to cache this information.

The example in Listing 1.1 highlights the difference between a blocking broadcast, a non-blocking broadcast proposed in this paper, and a non-blocking broadcast proposed in [27].

```
1  /* Blocking Broadcast - Current Implementation */
2  void
3  shmem_broadcast32 (void *target, const void *source,
4                     size_t nelems, int PE_root, int PE_start,
5                     int logPE_stride, int PE_size, long *pSync);
6
7
8  /* Non-Blocking Broadcast - Proposed in this paper */
9  void
10 shmemx_broadcast32_nb (void *target, const void *source,
11                        size_t nelems, int PE_root, int PE_start,
12                        int logPE_stride, int PE_size, long *pSync,
13                        int *request);
14
15
16 /* Non-Blocking Broadcast - Proposed by Poole et al. */
17 void
18 shmem_broadcast32_nb (void *target, const void *source,
19                       size_t nelems, struct shmem_aset aset,
20                       long *pSync, shmem_request_handle_t request);
```

Listing 1.1. Interface comparison : Blocking vs. Non-blocking broadcast

Broadly, the extended API contains two new functions for test and wait calls in addition to the non-blocking collective functions. Test calls can be used to manually progress the communication. Wait calls are called by all PEs to synchronize (or end) the communication. We note that our wait call is different than the SHMEM_WAIT defined by the OpenSHMEM specification. The shmem_wait() is a point to point synchronization routine while the wait routine defined in this paper is specific for ending a non-blocking collective operation. The proposed interface defines variants of blocking collectives in the OpenSHMEM for the proposed NBC operations. As NBC operations are yet to be standardized, the function prototypes start with a shmemx_ and end with a _nb while the x is used to indicate that the API is not yet part of the standard. The complete interface is shown in the Listing 1.2. We note that OpenSHMEM has defined reduction functions in a different fashion where each reduction function has a different datatype and operation. Due to space constraints, we have not written the full set of reduction and show just a single routine as an example in Listing 1.2. Other versions of reductions have similar function signatures except the datatypes and the operation being performed.

```
/* Test */
int
shmemx_test_req (int *request, int *flag, void *status);

/* Wait */
int
shmemx_wait_req (int *request, void *status);

/* Collect */
void
shmemx_collect32_nb (void *target, const void *source,
                     size_t nelems, int PE_start, int logPE_stride,
                     int PE_size, long *pSync, int *request);

/* Fcollect */
void
shmemx_fcollect32_nb (void *target, const void *source,
                      size_t nelems, int PE_start, int logPE_stride,
                      int PE_size, long *pSync, int *request);

/* Broadcast */
void
shmemx_broadcast32_nb (void *target, const void *source,
                       size_t nelems, int PE_root, int PE_start,
                       int logPE_stride, int PE_size, long *pSync,
                       int *request);

/* Barrier */
void
shmemx_barrier_nb (int PE_start, int logPE_stride, int PE_size,
                   long *pSync, int *request);

/* Reduction Routine for sum op. using float type */
void
shmemx_float_sum_to_all_nb (float *target, float *source,
                            int nreduce, int PE_start,
                            int logPE_stride, int PE_size, long *pWrk,
                            long *pSync, int *request);
```

Listing 1.2. Proposed extended API for Non-blocking collectives in OpenSHMEM

```
 1  #define UCR_SHMEM_REDUCE_TYPE_OP(OpCall, Name, Type, MPI_DType,
        MPI_OType)
 2
 3  void
 4  shmemx_##Name##_##OpCall##_to_all_nb (Type *target, Type *source,
 5                                        int nreduce, int PE_start,
 6                                        int logPE_stride, int PE_size,
 7                                        Type *pWrk, long *pSync, int*
                                             request);
 8
 9
10
11  UCR_SHMEM_REDUCE_TYPE_OP (sum, double, double, MPI_DOUBLE, MPI_SUM);
12  UCR_SHMEM_REDUCE_TYPE_OP (prod, short, short, MPI_SHORT, MPI_PROD);
13  UCR_SHMEM_REDUCE_TYPE_OP (max, int, int,   MPI_INT,   MPI_MAX);
```

Listing 1.3. Implementation of Non-blocking `shmemx_reduce_nb()` for OpenSHMEM in MVAPICH2-X

3.2   Design and Implementation of OpenSHMEM NBC Operations

We have used the UCR layer of the MVAPICH2-X library for implementing the non-blocking collectives. The basic design as shown in Fig. 2 highlights the multi-level design approach.

First, we design the low level functions at the UCR level inside MVAPICH2-X. In general, we handle all low level details and optimizations at this layer. We create communicator for the PEs involved in the communication. This is done only once as we utilize the internal cache for communicators inside MVAPICH2. All resources are shared between inside the unified runtime. Connections, buffers, and memory registrations are all shared for both MPI and OpenSHMEM communication operations. To illustrate clearly, we show the pseudocode for non-blocking reduction in Listing 1.3.

Second, we implement the high-level API functions in the OpenSHMEM source code that basically call UCR level routines with the correct arguments. Any application can use these functions that are listed in Listing 1.2. We note that other implementations of OpenSHMEM NBC interface will be positioned at this level. The work done in this paper is using MVAPICH2-X and its UCR layer for implementing the OpenSHMEM NBC interface in a high-performance and scalable fashion. However, other OpenSHMEM NBC implementations can choose to implement this layer in GASNet and/or any other appropriate communication runtime. We note that we are not using any vendor specific hardware or software based accelerated collectives in MVAPICH2-X. Design and implementation specific details of UCR level collectives can be studied from [18].

Third and last, in order to provide an application level example and to illustrate the benefits, we have implemented micro-benchmarks to evaluate the proposed non-blocking collectives. This layer is basically an example for the application programmer on how to use the collectives and what kind of performance to expect. The benchmarks are discussed in the next section.

4 Extending OpenSHMEM OSU Micro-benchmarks for Non-blocking Collectives

The OpenSHMEM community has been discussing about addition of non-blocking operations to the standard. We believe that NBC support will be added in the future versions of OpenSHMEM specification. in order to evaluate the performance of OpenSHMEM NBC operations in a fair manner, we propose new OpenSHMEM NBC benchmarks in this paper. These are based on current blocking OpenSHMEM benchmarks in our widely used OSU Micro-Benchmarks (OMB) suite [2]. The current version only provides support for evaluating the performance of point-to-point, one-sided, and blocking collective OpenSHMEM operations only. We have developed the proposed NBC benchmarks for Open-SHMEM by extending the blocking benchmarks in OMB.

Non-blocking OpenSHMEM NBC calls will be checked for completion by calling `shmemx_wait_req()`. We first measure the pure communication latency by calling an NBC operation like `shmemx_broadcast32_nb()` immediately followed by a `shmemx_wait_req()` call. This time is called pure communication latency. The current OpenSHMEM benchmarks in OMB display average, minimum, and maximum latency for a blocking collective. However, this does not provide any insight on the overlap, pure comm. latency, and time available for independent computation during a non-blocking operation. To address this, we have added new fields to the display. We display the overall latency (the total time taken when computation is overlapped with communication), the collective initialization time, the time for test calls, the time for computation, and the overlap percentage. We have calculated the percentage overlap based on the formula in Fig. 3. We note that the compute time in the formula includes the time of dummy computation as well as the time of `shmemx_test_req()` calls.

$$overlap \ = max(0, 100 - \left\{ \frac{overall\ time \ - \ compute\ time}{communication\ time} * 100 \right\});$$

Fig. 3. Formula to calculate overlap of communication and computation

The compute time available for the dummy compute function is pre-calculated based on the pure communication latency. This is done outside the main benchmark loop. The dummy compute function multiplies a 2D array allocated using `malloc()`. We use a cache unfriendly access and dynamic allocation to mitigate the effects of compiler optimizations. The NBC benchmark uses `shmemx_test_req()` calls as specified by the user to progress the communication. This is done to closely replicate the behavior of common applications that manually progress communication while doing the overlapped computation. This time can provide a general estimation for real applications and can be used for tuning the performance. The test calls are made at regular intervals inside the dummy compute function as shown in Fig. 1.

Different benchmarks suites have been proposed for evaluating NBC operations. However, none of these can currently be used for evaluating the Open-SHMEM NBC interface. It is possible to extend these benchmarks to evaluate NBC operations in OpenSHMEM once the interface gets published. Intel MPI Benchmarks Suite (IMB) [15] shows overall latency, pure communication latency, overlap percentage, and dummy compute time. Various other benchmarks evaluate overlap of communication and computation. NBCBench [12] that evaluates LibNBC also measures overlap of NBC operations. Both Sandia MPI Micro-Benchmark Suite (SMB) [29] and Communication Offload MPI-based Benchmark (COMB) [22] enable overlap calculation. SMB measures availability of the host during non-blocking MPI point-to-point operations by using a method called host-processor method.

5   Performance Evaluation

This section describes the experimental setup used to conduct our performance evaluation. An in-depth analysis of the results is also provided to correlate design motivations and observed behavior. All results reported here are averages of multiple (three) runs to discard the effect of system noise.

5.1   Experimental Setup

We have used the RI cluster at The Ohio State University for all the experiments. It has 160 compute nodes. Each node has 2 Intel E5630 processors clocked at 2.53 GHz. This means a total of 8 cores per node. Each node has 12 GB of RAM and is configured with RHEL 6.5 (Kernel 2.6.32–431) operating system. The nodes are equipped with Mellanox ConnectX-2 QDR InfiniBand cards (40 Gbps) and connected by one Mellanox MTS3610 196-port InfiniBand switch, which is configured as full fat-tree network.

5.2   Important Parameters for Evaluation

We have conducted the performance evaluation for multiple aspects and parameters. The parameters and terms used for evaluation are summarized in this section. Some of these have been mentioned earlier and some of them will appear in the legend of the performance graphs.

- **Pure Comm. Latency** - Latency of an NBC when we call the collective immediately followed by shmemx_wait_req() call.
- **Overall Latency** - Latency of an NBC operation when we call the collective, followed by independent computation and specified number of test calls, followed by a shmemx_wait_req() call.

- **Blocking-Avg Latency** - Average latency of a Blocking Collective operation.
- **Compute Time** - Time taken by the dummy compute (independent overlapped computation) function.
- **Test Time** - Time taken by `shmemx_test_req()` calls.
- **NBC Overhead** - This is the difference in performance of collective when its Pure Comm. latency is compared with Overall latency.

In the next few subsections, we present our performance graphs. First, we present numbers to compare the performance of blocking collectives versus non-blocking collectives in Sect. 5.3. The purpose of these numbers is to analyze the difference in behavior of blocking vs. non-blocking operations at scale. Second, we present graphs to highlight the latency and overlap for different non-blocking collectives in two modes. The first mode is pure comm. where no dummy compute and test calls are made. Second mode is where we have dummy compute as well as specified number of test calls. The legend in the graph is of type NB-MODE-NUMTESTS e.g. NB-Overall-1000 means non-blocking mode with overlapped dummy computation and 1,000 test calls interleaved with the computation. These are presented in Sect. 5.4. Third and last, we present the Overall vs Pure Comm. latency of different NBC operations. These are presented in Sect. 5.5. All the results presented use 8 processes per node in a fully subscribed manner.

5.3   Blocking Vs. Non-blocking Collectives

Figures 4, 5, 6, and 7 show the comparison of performance for blocking and corresponding non-blocking collectives. Reduce and Broadcast operations were conducted using 512 processes on 64 nodes. Fcollect operation, due its large latency, was run using 64 processes on 8 nodes only. Barrier operation has been presented for different number of processes. This configuration of processes holds for the rest of this paper as well.

We observed that for small messages, `reduce`, `broadcast`, and `fcollect` experienced very little increase in latency as compared to their blocking counterparts. However, for large messages we experienced acceptable (but somewhat significant) performance degradation in latency. This increase in latency shall not be considered in isolation as the purpose of NBC operations is to achieve both good latency and maximum overlap. We observed excellent (up to 96 percent) overlap for all NBC operations for the large message sizes. For `shmemx_barrier_nb()`, we see a small penalty for all process counts.

5.4   Latency and Overlap of NBC Operations

These graphs illustrate the overlap and latency of different NBC operations. Due to space constraints, some results have been omitted. The graphs for this section are shown in Figs. 8, 9, 10, 11, and 12. Across all these different collectives and message sizes, we observed that we achieve near perfect overlap with appropriate

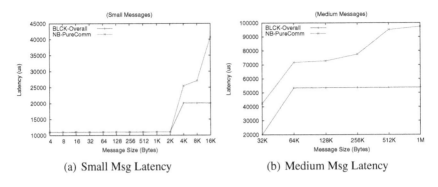

Fig. 4. Blocking vs. Non-blocking reduce (float_sum_to_all) for 512 processes

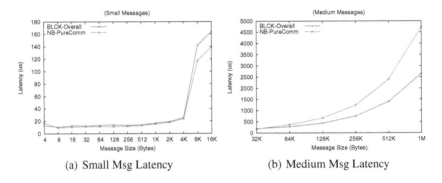

Fig. 5. Blocking vs. Non-blocking broadcast for 512 processes

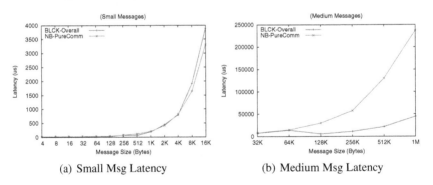

Fig. 6. Blocking vs. Non-blocking fcollect for 64 processes

number of test calls. For some collectives and message sizes, the ideal overlap is with 1,000 test calls, for others it is with 10,000 calls. Latency for small messages experiences significant penalty with 10,000 calls. We note that this is an expected outcome. On the other hand, overlap percentage is abrupt with 0 test calls for all the collectives. For large messages, 10,000 test calls provide the best overlap

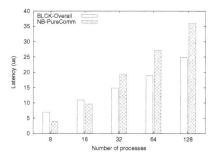

Fig. 7. Blocking vs. Non-blocking barrier

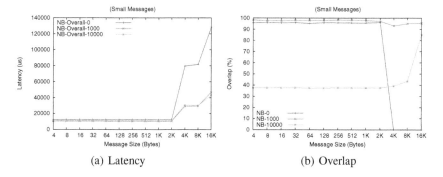

(a) Latency   (b) Overlap

Fig. 8. Performance of non-blocking broadcast : latency and overlap for small messages

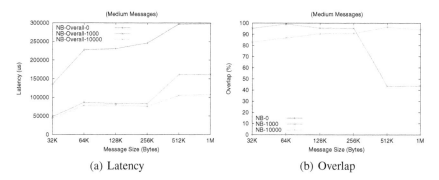

(a) Latency   (b) Overlap

Fig. 9. Performance of non-blocking broadcast : latency and overlap for medium messages

as well as latency for all collectives. For small messages, 1,000 test calls achieve the best overlap and latency for all collectives.

5.5 NBC Overhead

In order to provide insights into the overhead associated with NBC operations, we present the graphs that show performance of an NBC operation when it

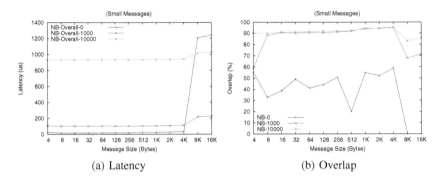

Fig. 10. Performance of non-blocking broadcast : latency and overlap for small messages

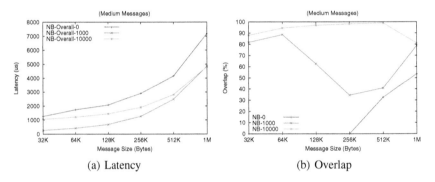

Fig. 11. Performance of non-blocking broadcast : latency and overlap for medium messages

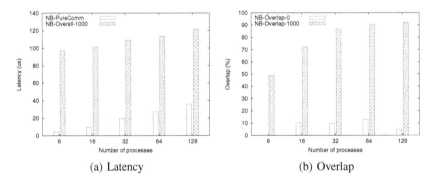

Fig. 12. Performance of non-blocking barrier : latency and overlap for different number of processes

is running in Pure Comm. mode versus when it executes in overlapped fashion with varying number of test calls. Figure 13 shows the NBC overhead for `shmemx_fcollect32_nb()`. For small messages, there is no overhead with 0 and

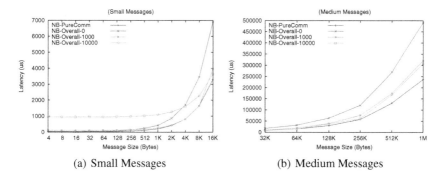

Fig. 13. Performance of non-blocking fcollect : NBC overhead

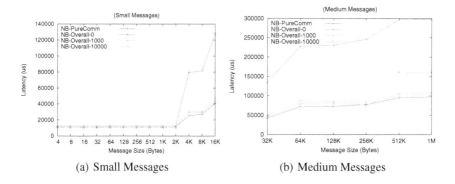

Fig. 14. Performance of non-blocking reduce : NBC overhead

1,000 test calls. Since, 10,0000 test calls will take a lot of time, we can see the performance degradation for small message sizes. For large messages, we observed that latency is very comparable to Pure Comm. with 10,000 test calls. This is expected since the latency for large messages is much higher than the time taken by 1,000 calls and these calls actually progress the communication that in turn provides lower overall latency. As Fig. 14 suggests, the trends for `shmemx_reduce_nb()` are similar to `shmemx_fcollect32_nb()`. The difference we observed here is that we achieve poor performance if we do a dummy compute and 0 test calls (see NB-Overall-0 in the graph).

6   Conclusion and Future Work

In this paper, we presented our case for adding non-blocking collective (NBC) operations to the OpenSHMEM specification. We presented the motivation for NBC and argued that MPI NBC has performed better for different applications. We then presented the proposed NBC interface for OpenSHMEM. We also presented the design and implementation details of this new interface. Our implementation takes advantage of MVAPICH2-X and its UCR layer. Further, we propose new non-blocking benchmarks as part of the OSU Micro-Benchmarks Suite. These benchmarks allow us to evaluate performance of the collectives using various parameters like varying number of test calls and a dummy compute function while the communication proceeds in the background. In addition, a detailed performance evaluation of the proposed non-blocking collectives using the proposed benchmarks was presented. The evaluation showed that most NBC operations provide near perfect overlap if tuned correctly using different number of test calls and the amount of computation.

In future, we plan to extend the OpenSHMEM NBC benchmarks for different accelerator based systems. The proposed benchmarks will be made publicly available through a future OMB release. We also plan to conduct application-level studies in future.

References

1. Chapel The Cascade High-Productivity Language. http://chapel.cray.com/
2. MVAPICH2-X: Unified MPI+PGAS Communication Runtime over OpenFabrics/ Gen2 for Exascale Systems. http://mvapich.cse.ohio-state.edu/
3. OpenSHMEM. http://www.openshmem.org/
4. Awan, A. A., Hamidouche, K., Venkatesh, A., Perkins, J., Subramoni, H., Panda. D. K.: GPU-Aware design, implementation, and evaluation of non-blocking collective benchmarks (accepted for publication). In: Proceedings of the 22nd European MPI Users' Group Meeting EuroMPI 2015. ACM, Bordeaux (2015)
5. Bell, C., Bonachea, D., Nishtala, R., Yelick, K.: Optimizing bandwidth limited problems using one-sided communication and overlap. In: Proceedings of the 20th International Conference on Parallel and Distributed Processing IPDPS 2006, pp. 84–84. IEEE Computer Society Washington, DC, USA(2006)
6. Co-Array Fortran. http://www.co-array.org
7. Open MPI : Open Source High Performance Computing. http://www.open-mpi. org
8. Cong, G., Almasi, G., Saraswat, V.: Fast PGAS implementation of distributed graph algorithms. In: Proceedings of the 2010 ACM/IEEE International Conference for High Performance Computing, Networking, Storage and Analysis, SC 2010, pp. 1–11. IEEE Computer Society, Washington, DC, USA (2010)
9. Graham, R.L., Poole, S., Shamis, P., Bloch, G., Bloch, N., Chapman, H., Kagan, M., Shahar, A., Rabinovitz, I., Shainer, G.: Overlapping computation and communication: barrier algorithms and connectx-2 core-direct capabilities. In: 2010 IEEE International Symposium on Parallel Distributed Processing, Workshops and Phd Forum IPDPSW, pp. 1–8, April 2010
10. Hilfinger, P. N., Bonachea, D., Gay, D., Graham, S., Liblit, B., Pike, G., Yelick, K.: Titanium language reference manual. Technical report, Berkeley, CA, USA (2001)
11. Hoefler, T., Lumsdaine, A.: Design, Implementation, and Usage of LibNBC. Technical report, Open Systems Lab, Indiana University, August 2006
12. Hoefler, T., Schneider, T., Lumsdaine, A.: Accurately measuring collective operations at massive scale. In: Proceedings of the 22nd IEEE International Parallel & Distributed Processing Symposium PMEO 2008 Workshop, April 2008

13. Hoefler, T., Squyres, J.M., Rehm, W., Lumsdaine, A.: A case for non-blocking collective operations. In: Min, G., Di Martino, B., Yang, L.T., Guo, M., Rünger, G. (eds.) ISPA Workshops 2006. LNCS, vol. 4331, pp. 155–164. Springer, Heidelberg (2006)
14. InfiniBand Trade Association. http://www.infinibandta.com
15. Intel MPI Benchmarks (IMB). https://software.intel.com/en-us/articles/intel-mpi-benchmarks
16. Liu, J., Jiang, W., Wyckoff, P., Panda, D. K., Ashton, D., Buntinas, D., Gropp, B., Tooney, B.: High Performance Implementation of MPICH2 over InfiniBand with RDMA Support. In: IPDPS (2004)
17. Jose, J., Kandalla, K., Luo, M., Panda, D. K.: Supporting hybrid MPI and Open-SHMEM over InfiniBand: design and performance evaluation. In: Proceedings of the 2012 41st International Conference on Parallel Processing, ICPP 2012, pp. 219–228. IEEE Computer Society (2012)
18. Jose, J., Kandalla, K., Zhang, J., Potluri, S., Panda, D. K. D. K.: Optimizing collective communication in openshmem. In: 7th International Conference on PGAS Programming Models, p. 185 (2013)
19. Jose, J., Zhang, J., Venkatesh, A., Potluri, S., Panda, D.K.D.K.: A comprehensive performance evaluation of OpenSHMEM libraries on InfiniBand clusters. In: Poole, S., Hernandez, O., Shamis, P. (eds.) OpenSHMEM 2014. LNCS, vol. 8356, pp. 14–28. Springer, Heidelberg (2014)
20. Kandalla, K.C., Subramoni, H., Tomko, K., Pekurovsky, D., Panda, D.K.: A Novel functional partitioning approach to design high-performance MPI-3 non-blocking alltoallv collective on multi-core systems. In: 42nd International Conference on Parallel Processing, ICPP 2013, pp. 611–620, Lyon, France, 1–4 October 2013
21. Kini, S.P., Liu, J., Wu, J., Wyckoff, P., Panda, D.K.: Fast and scalable barrier using RDMA and multicast mechanisms for infiniband-based clusters. In: Dongarra, J., Laforenza, D., Orlando, S. (eds.) EuroPVM/MPI 2003. LNCS, vol. 2840, pp. 369–378. Springer, Heidelberg (2003)
22. Lawry, W., Wilson, C., Maccabe, A.B., Brightwell, R.: COMB: a portable benchmark suite for assessing MPI overlap. In: IEEE Cluster, pp. 23–26 (2002)
23. Liu, J., Jiang, W., Wyckoff, P., Panda, D. K., Ashton, D., Buntinas, D., Gropp, W., Toonen, B.: Design and implementation of MPICH2 over InfiniBand with RDMA support. In: Proceedings of International Parallel and Distributed Processing Symposium, IPDPS 2004, April 2004
24. Liu, J., Mamidala, A., Panda, D. K.: Fast And scalable MPI-level broadcast using InfiniBand's hardware multicast support. In: Proceedings of International Parallel and Distributed Processing Symposium, IPDPS 2004, April 2004
25. Mamidala, A., Liu, J., Panda, D. K.: Efficient barrier and allreduce on IBA clusters using hardware multicast and adaptive algorithms. In: IEEE Cluster Computing (2004)
26. MPI-3 Standard Document. http://www.mpi-forum.org/docs/mpi-3.0/mpi30-report.pdf
27. Poole, S., Shamis, P., Welch, A., Pophale, S., Venkata, M.G., Hernandez, O., Koenig, G., Curtis, T., Hsu, C.-H.: OpenSHMEM extensions and a vision for its future direction. In: Poole, S., Hernandez, O., Shamis, P. (eds.) OpenSHMEM 2014. LNCS, vol. 8356, pp. 149–162. Springer, Heidelberg (2014)
28. Rabinovitz, I., Shamis, P., Graham, R.L., Bloch, N., Shainer, G.: Network offloaded hierarchical collectives using ConnectX-2"s CORE-*Direct* capabilities. In: Keller, R., Gabriel, E., Resch, M., Dongarra, J. (eds.) EuroMPI 2010. LNCS, vol. 6305, pp. 102–112. Springer, Heidelberg (2010)

29. Sandia MPI Micro-Benchmark Suite (SMB). http://www.cs.sandia.gov/smb/index.html
30. Subramoni, H., Awan, A.A., Hamidouche, K., Pekurovsky, D., Venkatesh, A., Chakraborty, S., Tomko, K., Panda, D.K.: Designing non-blocking personalized collectives with near perfect overlap for RDMA-enabled clusters. In: Kunkel, J.M., Ludwig, T. (eds.) ISC High Performance 2015. LNCS, vol. 9137, pp. 434–453. Springer, Heidelberg (2015)
31. TOP 500 Supercomputer Sites. http://www.top500.org
32. UPC Consortium. UPC Language Specifications, v1.2. Technical report LBNL-59208, Lawrence Berkeley National Lab (2005)
33. Yelick, K., Bonachea, D., Chen, W.-Y., Colella, P., Datta, K., Duell, J., Graham, S.L., Hargrove, P., Hilfinger, P., Husbands, P., Iancu, C., Kamil, A., Nishtala, R., Su, J., Welcome, M., Wen, T.: Productivity and performance using partitioned global address space languages. In: International Workshop on Parallel Symbolic Computation, PASCO 2007 (2007)
34. Zhang, J., Behzad, B., Snir, M.: Optimizing the barnes-hut algorithm in UPC. In: Proceedings of 2011 International Conference for High Performance Computing, Networking, Storage and Analysis, SC 2011, pp. 75:1–75:11. ACM, New York (2011)

An Evaluation of OpenSHMEM Interfaces for the Variable-Length Alltoallv() Collective Operation

M. Graham Lopez$^{(\boxtimes)}$, Pavel Shamis, and Manjunath Gorentla Venkata

Computer Science and Mathematics Division,
Oak Ridge National Laboratory, Oak Ridge, TN 37921, USA
`lopezmg@ornl.gov`

Abstract. `Alltoallv()` is a collective operation which allows all processes to exchange variable amounts of data with all other processes in the communication group. This means that `Alltoallv()` requires not only $O(N^2)$ communications, but typically also additional exchanges of the data lengths that will be transmitted in the eventual `Alltoallv()` call. This pre-exchange is used to calculate the proper offsets for the receiving buffers on the target processes. However, we propose two new candidate interfaces for `Alltoallv()` that would mitigate the need for the user to set up this extra exchange of information at the possible cost of memory efficiency. We explain the new interface variants and show how a single call can be used in place of the traditional `Alltoall()`/ `Alltoallv()` pair. We then discuss the performance tradeoffs for overall communication and memory costs, as well as both software and hardware-based optimizations and their applicability to the various proposed interfaces.

1 Introduction

`Alltoall()` is an important collective operation where each processing element (PE) in the communicating group exchanges data with every other PE, and it is used in many scientific applications as part of several basic numerical algorithms including the fast Fourier transform (FFT), matrix transpose, fast Gaussian transforms, and adaptive mesh algorithms. `Alltoallv()` provides a generalization of `Alltoall()` where each PE may transfer different amounts of data to

---

This manuscript has been authored by UT-Battelle, LLC under Contract No. DE-AC05-00OR22725 with the U.S. Department of Energy. The United States Government retains and the publisher, by accepting the article for publication, acknowledges that the United States Government retains a non-exclusive, paid-up, irrevocable, world-wide license to publish or reproduce the published form of this manuscript, or allow others to do so, for United States Government purposes. The Department of Energy will provide public access to these results of federally sponsored research in accordance with the DOE Public Access Plan (http://energy.gov/downloads/doe-public-access-plan).

© Springer International Publishing Switzerland 2015
M. Gorentla Venkata et al. (Eds.): OpenSHMEM 2015, LNCS 9397, pp. 87–101, 2015.
DOI: 10.1007/978-3-319-26428-8_6

every other PE. This type of operation is important in all of the algorithms previously listed that use `Alltoall()`, but in cases where these algorithms are used with the work distributed unevenly among the PEs. In addition, irregular `Alltoallv()` communications are needed for a variety of scan and sort algorithms; as an example `Alltoallv()` is used in the NAS Parallel Benchmark [4] integer sort (IS) benchmark.

We can most simply describe the total amount of data transfered, T_t, by `Alltoall()` as

$$T_t = c * N * (N-1) , \tag{1}$$

where each of N processes sends c bytes to $N-1$ other processes. `Alltoallv()` is a generalized form of the `Alltoall()` operation which allows a variable amount of data to be transfered. In this case, the amount of data sent from process i to process j is given by c_{ij}, and so the total data transferred is given by

$$T_t = \sum_{\substack{i,j=1 \\ j\neq i}}^{N} c_{ij} . \tag{2}$$

It is easy to see that in the special case where $c_{ij} = c$, then Eq. (2) reduces to Eq. (1). This generalization allows optimizations of algorithms like the 3D-FFT [2], CPMD [1], and others where an all-to-all exchange is required among imbalanced tasks.

Although `Alltoallv()` has been present as part of the MPI API for several years, in order to bring it to OpenSHMEM, we would like to carefully consider the function interface that will be exposed to the programmer. As we discuss in Sect. 2.1, the traditional MPI interface to `Alltoallv()` may impose unnecessary requirements on the programmer, especially when working with current Open-SHMEM memory semantics. Therefore, we present here three possible interfaces for `Alltoallv()` including the equivalent to the traditional MPI interface, and we compare and contrast them in the contexts of usability and application performance.

1.1   Related Work

Being part of the MPI standard, `Alltoall()` and `Alltoallv()` have been extensively studied and optimized in as defined that context. The linear algorithm approach to `Alltoallv()` has been optimized in the past for both internode [7] as well as shared memory [6,8] communications. Nonlinear algorithms have been proposed for `Alltoall()` such as recursive doubling [11] and Bruck's algorithm [5], but these are for messages of constant size. A logarithmic method has been implemented for `MPI_AlltoallV()` [10]. As pointed out in that work, these optimizations yield little benefit for large message sizes and so the authors focus their experiments on message sizes of 64 bytes or less. One reason for this is the memory copies necessary to merge outgoing data during the log-scaling algorithm; for large messages, these memory copies become more time consuming and can overwhelm the latency advantage of the log-scaling exchange.

In Reference [10], MPI_AlltoallV() was also optimized for intranode communication using shared memory. One result to note is that the authors observed much higher reductions in latency as the number of cores per node went up. If upcoming exascale architectures continue to move towards a higher number of smaller cores, this type of hierarchical optimization could become more important, as long as per-core memory constraints do not make it infeasible.

Cray has implemented both Alltoall() and Alltoallv() as non-standard extensions in Cray-SHMEM as part of the Cray Message Passing Toolkit [3], with an interface that very closely mimics MPI_AlltoallV(). In this work, we consider this MPI and other possible interfaces for Alltoallv() in the context of OpenSHMEM semantics and present an alternative interface that can improve its usability. We briefly discuss some of the optimzations done for MPI_AlltoallV() as they apply to the various proposals here, but a detailed study of implementations and their optimizations beyond the scope of the present work.

2   Proposed Alltoallv()Interfaces

In order to help illustrate the how Alltoallv() could be used in an application, here we present the NAS Parallel Benchmark [4] integer sort (IS) benchmark example, adapted from an OpenSHMEM port of the suite [9]. Listing 1.1 shows the key redistribution section of the benchmark as it is ported to OpenSHMEM. Since there is no Alltoall() or Alltoallv() interfaces in the current Open-SHMEM standard, we start with the code as it looks without these collective operations.

```
1   /* This is the redistribution section:  first find out how many keys
2      each processor will send to every other processor:            */
3      shmem_barrier_all();
4      for( j1=0; j1 < comm_size; j1++ ) {
5          shmem_int_put(&t_sizes[my_rank],&s_sizes[j1],1,j1);
6      }
7      shmem_barrier_all();
8
9   /* Determine the receive array displacements for the buckets */
10     t_offsets[0] = 0;
11     for( i=1; i < comm_size; i++ ) {
12         t_offsets[i] = t_offsets[i-1] + t_sizes[i-1];
13     }
14
15  /* Now send the keys to respective processors */
16     shmem_barrier_all();
17     for( j1=0; j1 < comm_size; j1++ ) {
18         shmem_int_get(&k2,&t_offsets[my_rank],1,j1);
19         shmem_int_put(&key_buff2[k2/sizeof(INT_TYPE),
20                       &key_buff1[s_offsets[j1]/sizeof(INT_TYPE),
21                       s_sizes[j1]/sizeof(INT_TYPE),j1);
22     }
23     shmem_barrier_all();
```

Listing 1.1. NPB IS benchmark: key exchange without Alltoallv()

As we move forward and present possible interfaces for Alltoallv(), we will update this snippet of code using each variant.

2.1   MPI Interface (Variant 1)

```
1   extern void
2   shmem_alltoallv(void *target, size_t *t_offsets, size_t *t_sizes,
3                   const void *source, size_t *s_offsets, size_t *s_sizes,
4                   int PE_start, int logPE_stride, int PE_size, long *psync);
```

Listing 1.2. Alltoallv() interface Variant 1 definition

This is the interface that Cray implements [3] and is very similar to that of MPI_AlltoallV(). The specification of how the data gets transferred is almost identical; the only differences between this interface and MPI_AlltoallV() show up in designating which PEs participate in the operation. The destination for the transferred data is specified by the first three arguments: target is the memory buffer that will receive the data, t_offsets[n] holds the byte offset from the beginning of target where the nth sending PE has deposited its transfer on the calling PE, and t_sizes[n] is the number of bytes that was transferred by the nth sending PE. Similarly, the source data is described by the next three parameters, with the source buffer containing the data segments to be transferred to all other PEs, s_offsets[n] containing the byte offset in the source buffer of the data to be sent to the nth receiving PE, and s_sizes[n] having the number of bytes to be transferred from the calling PE to the nth receiving PE.

```
1   /* This is the redistribution section:  first find out how many keys
2      each processor will send to every other processor:              */
3      shmem_barrier_all();
4      shmem_alltoall(&t_sizes, &s_sizes, sizeof(size_t),
5                     0, 0, shmem_n_pes(), pSync);
6      shmem_barrier_all();
7
8   /* Determine the receive array displacements for the buckets */
9      t_offsets[0] = 0;
10     for(i=1; i < comm_size; i++) {
11         t_offsets[i] = t_offsets[i-1] + t_sizes[i-1];
12     }
13
14  /* Now send the keys to respective processors */
15     shmem_barrier_all();
16     shmem_alltoallv(key_buff2, t_offsets, t_sizes,
17                     key_buff1, s_offsets, s_sizes,
18                     0, 0, shmem_n_pes(), pSync);
19     shmem_barrier_all();
```

Listing 1.3. NPB IS benchmark: key exchange using Alltoallv() Variant 1. The for loops from Listing 1.1 have been replaced by Alltoall() and Alltoallv(). The first Alltoall() performing the pre-exchange of data transfer sizes which are then used to calculate the destination offsets in the target buffer. Finally Alltoallv() is used to exchange the varying amount of key data between all of the PEs.

In order to use this interface, in many cases an extra Alltoall() is required in order to pre-exchange the amounts of data that are going to be transferred by each process using the Alltoallv() operation. Usually, this means translating s_sizes[m] to t_sizes[n] from each nth sending PE to each mth receiving PE. This information is used as input for the t_sizes parameter, and can also be used to calculate the input for t_offsets and to allocate the receiving buffer as shown in Listing 1.3.

The advantage realized from this extra pre-exchange required by the interface is the ability to more accurately allocate memory for and insert the data contiguously into the target buffers, therefore obtaining (possibly substantial) memory savings in the application, as well as accessing all of the data on each PE without gaps. However, OpenSHMEM at present only supports symmetric allocation of memory buffers on PEs which will exchange data, and so a slight extension in either the semantics for memory allocation and/or for the allowed destination buffers for remote transfers permitted by the OpenSHMEM specification would be necessary to enable applications to save as much memory as possible using this proposed Alltoallv() interface. Some of the implications for such changes in general OpenSHMEM semantics are discussed further in Sect. 4.

2.2   Max Offsets (Variant 2)

In the case where variable amounts of data are to be transferred, we could imagine simplifying the code by using Alltoall(), which would result in setting $c = c_{max} = max(c_{ij})$ in Eq. 1. There are two immediately obvious problems with using an unmodified Alltoall() in this manner. First, $O(N^2 * c_{max})$ data will be transferred, and if there is a wide variability in the c_{ij} amounts of data to be transferred and N is large, this could cause a significant performance hit by transferring extra data that is not needed by the application in the amount given by

$$T_{extra} = \sum_{\substack{i,j=1 \\ j \neq i}}^{N} (c_{max} - c_{ij}) \ . \tag{3}$$

Second, the user will have a difficult time knowing how to access only the intended amount of c_{ij} data contained within each c_{max} sized slot in the receiving target buffer.

The second proposed interface attempts to capture much of the simplicity of Alltoall() from the user's perspective, while allowing the implementation to address at least the two problems pointed out above.

```
1  extern void
2  shmem_alltoallv(void *target, size_t max_offset, void *flag,
3                  const void *source, size_t *s_offsets, size_t *s_sizes,
4                  int PE_start, int logPE_stride, int PE_size, long *psync);
```

Listing 1.4. Alltoallv() interface Variant 2 definition

This interface removes the parameters that specify the target buffer sizes and offsets arrays, t_sizes and t_offsets, respectively, and replaces them with the simpler pair of scalar parameters, max_offset and flag. As the name would imply, max_offset is the greatest possible offset required to accommodate the largest single transfer between the N^2 participating PEs, and it corresponds to

c_{max} amount of data from Eq. 3. This implies that each PE will need to allocate $N*$max_offset bytes for its receiving target buffer. The flag parameter describes a bit sequence (usually a single instance of the transfer data type) that indicates to the receiving PE the end of the meaningful data transferred into the target[n*max_offset] slot by the nth sending PE.

```
1   keys to respective processors  */
2       shmem_barrier_all();
3       shmem_alltoallv(key_buff2, max_offset, LONG_MAX,
4                       key_buff1, s_offsets, s_sizes,
5                       0, 0, shmem_n_pes(), pSync);
6       shmem_barrier_all();
```

Listing 1.5. NPB IS benchmark: key exchange using Alltoallv() Variant 2. The max_offset and LONG_MAX (serving as the flag as indicated in Listing 1.4) parameters replace the t_offsets and t_sizes parameters from Listing 1.3. The pre-exchange from Listings 1.1 and 1.3 are no longer needed.

Here, a pre-exchange of the data sizes using a separate call to Alltoall() is not required. The offset of each PE can be calculated by the implementation at communication time using the max_offset parameter, with the destination for the data from the nth PE being expected at target[n*max_offset] on the receiving PE. In addition to obviating the need for a pre-exchange Alltoall() operation, there is an additional 'get' operation saved in the implementation because all target arrays now have the same layout (divided into N segments, each max_offset bytes wide) on all PEs. This means that the sending PE may now use max_offset to calculate the destination slot in the target buffer on the receiver, instead of having to ask the receiver for the correct entry in the now absent t_offsets array that is required in the first proposed interface.

This version of Alltoallv() is very close to Alltoall() from a user perspective; identical target buffers are allocated on all processes which expect to receive the same amount of data from each transfer. However, with the addition of the sender's size and offset information provided by s_offsets and s_sizes to Alltoallv(), T_{extra} bytes of extra communication can be saved by the implementation. The user will have to manually account for the variability on the receiving side by not copying data out of the extra unused gaps in the target memory buffers. One naive solution to this is for the implementation to append a null termination character to each transfer in a manner that is familiar to users of common C-language string operations. In this interface, such a character is designated by the user by setting the flag parameter[1]. In this type of implementation, the performance advantage of the avoided 'get' operation on the t_offsets array is negated by the now extra 'put' to provide the null terminating character. However, one can imagine a couple of possible optimizations for this scenario, which we discuss further in Sect. 4.

---

[1] If the null character is unsuitable, the flag parameter can typically be chosen to be the maximum value of the corresponding datatype, e.g. LONG_MAX for long int, since there will typically be overflow issues with a data set if its domain includes this value.

2.3   Max Offsets Returning Sizes (Variant 3)

```
1   extern void
2   shmem_alltoallv(void *target, size_t max_offset, size_t *t_sizes,
3                   const void *source, size_t *s_offsets, size_t *s_sizes,
4                   int PE_start, int logPE_stride, int PE_size, long *psync);
```

Listing 1.6. Alltoallv() interface Variant 3 definition

In this final version, there is a mixture between the previous two proposed interfaces. The extra pre-exchange using a separate Alltoall() operation is still avoided, but the amount of each transfer is provided to the user as *output* from the Alltoallv() call in the t_sizes parameter. Therefore, similar to the Variant 2 interface, there will be gaps in the output buffers if less than max_offset is transferred, but unlike that case, the user can easily know how much data resides in each chunk of the output buffer without having to scan for the terminating value indicated by the flag parameter. Note that the communication advantage of eliminating the pre-exchange Alltoall() is still retained, but the saved 'get' operation in the implementaion to obtain the destination slot in the target buffer from the t_offsets array is negated, as this operation is now replaced by the single integer 'put' to the t_sizes output parameter. This is similar to the non-optimized implementation of Variant 2 which must follow the data exchange with a 'put' to insert the null terminating character, trading a 'put' for the terminating flag into the target array for an integer 'put' into the t_sizes array. Although some of the communication advantage is lost, the usage is arguably more convenient than the previous interfaces - being superior to the first by saving the pre-exchange Alltoall(), and being superior the second by avoiding the need to detect the terminating character in the output buffers.

```
7    keys to respective processors  */
8        shmem_barrier_all();
9        shmem_alltoallv_sizes(key_buff2, max_offset, t_sizes,
10                              key_buff1, s_offsets, s_sizes,
11                              0, 0, shmem_n_pes(), pSync);
12       shmem_barrier_all();
```

Listing 1.7. NPB IS benchmark: key exchange using Alltoallv() Variant 3. max_offsetis used as in Listing 1.5, but in place of the flag, the t_sizes ; it is not pre-calculated as in Listing 1.3, and the pre-exchange is avoided

As a final note about the various interfaces shown in this section, we point out that there are other options that can achieve similar results for some situations. For example, Cray has another variant of the Alltoallv() operation named shmem_alltoallv_packed which also obviates the need for the pre-exchange required by Variant 1, and is a very convenient alternative for the integer sort example as we have presented it. However, it may not be suitable for a more generalized case where information about the ordering of the received data is important, such as when trying to perform an integral transform or exchange information divided onto a mesh. The alternative interfaces for Alltoallv()

presented here provide a means to avoid the pre-exchange required by Variant 1, while remaining suitable for use in any situation where Variant 1 could have been used originally.

3   Evaluation of Proposed `Alltoallv()` Interfaces

This paper discusses the various issues regarding differences in possible interfaces for `Alltoallv()` in OpenSHMEM, and in this section we quickly compare basic, unoptimized implementations of each proposed interface. We will discuss some possible optimizations in Sect. 4 as they apply to each proposed interface, but we leave a detailed study of various enhanced implementations to a future work. Here, we simply want to determine any performance implications for choosing one of the `Alltoallv()` interface variants over the others without needing to tease out the effects of differing optimizations that might be applied to each.

Each of the `Alltoallv()` variants proposed above and labelled as "Variant [1,2,3]" in the figures in this section were implemented on equal footing using only CraySHMEM 'put' and 'get' operations. Comparing these three curves allows a performance comparison of choosing one of the proposed interfaces over any other. We also include Cray's implementation of Variant 1 in the figures, labelled "Cray," as a sanity check and to show what the performance from a quality implementation of `Alltoallv()` might look like. The experiments were performed on the "Titan" system at Oak Ridge National Laboratory using CraySHMEM 7.0.4. Each node has 16 processors with 32 GB of memory (2 GB per processor), and is connected by a Cray Gemini network arranged in a 3D torus.

Figure 1 shows the behavior of the various implementations for 8 byte message sizes among varying numbers of PEs. Most significantly, all of the proposed interfaces perform almost identically. Despite having different requirements regarding which kind of data must be exchanged *within the `Alltoallv()` call* to make the interface work (target offsets, sent sizes, terminating flag, etc.), we see that the cost of these differing requirements do cancel out as discussed in Sects. 2.2 and 2.3. We also see that there are some possible network-based optimizations that are able to increase its performance for internode communication, which can be seen when more than 16 PEs are involved in the exchange. For larger message sizes (Fig. 2) the optimizations for latency get washed out by bandwidth-based effects, but we see again that there is no inherent penalty for choosing one of the proposed interfaces over any other.

Comparing Figs. 1 and 2, we begin to get a picture of the effect of having to do the pre-exchange to populate the `t_sizes` buffer and using these to compute the entries for the `t_offsets` array that are both used as input to Variant 1 of `Alltoallv()`. The curves for the pre-exchange and the computation are distinguishable from the others by using open squares on black and grey lines, respectively. The first thing one notices from these curves is that the time cost of computing the offsets is always negligible compared to the communication times. Recalling that the pre-exchange of the sizes data is an `Alltoall()` operation with each exchange involving `sizeof(size_t)` bytes, it makes sense that

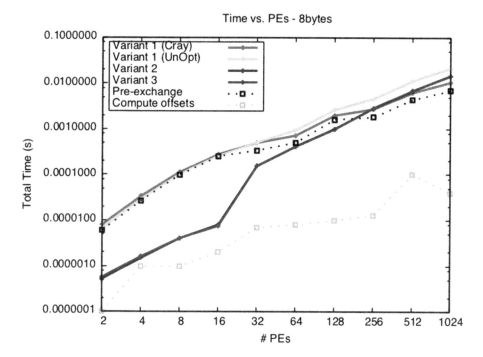

Fig. 1. Latency of small (8 byte) message size for `Alltoallv()` for varying numbers of PEs. Variant 1 is shown in two versions: "Variant 1 (Cray)" as a non-standard opaque extension in Cray-SHMEM, and "Variant 1 (UnOpt)" implemented using SHMEM 'put' and 'get' operations to comparie the interface on equal footing with the other proposed interfaces, being similarly implemented. The data for both "Variant 1" curves (solid) includes the time for the pre-exchange `Alltoall()` and offset computation operations, which are shown separately in the figure as separate curves made up of dotted lines.

for `Alltoallv()` operations involving large message sizes, the cost of doing the pre-exchange is also negligible as can be seen in Figs. 2 and 4. However, for small message sizes, the time taken by the pre-exchange `Alltoall()` and the subsequent `Alltoallv()` are comparable; in these cases, eliminating the pre-exchange could result in tangible benefits for applications with many `Alltoallv()` operations exchanging smaller payloads. Besides this performance gain, it is also a simplification for the programmer, independent of the `Alltoallv()` message size that occurs in their application.

As a final sanity check, we examine the behavior of our various interfaces as a function of varying message sizes among a modestly large number of PEs, and the results are shown in Figs. 3 and 4. We observe very consistent behavior among the three variants throughout the entire range tested from 8 bytes up to 320 kilobytes. The latency measured is almost constant for message sizes of 128 bytes and smaller, at which point all implementations begin to steadily increase in latency with the Cray optimizations becoming less significant around

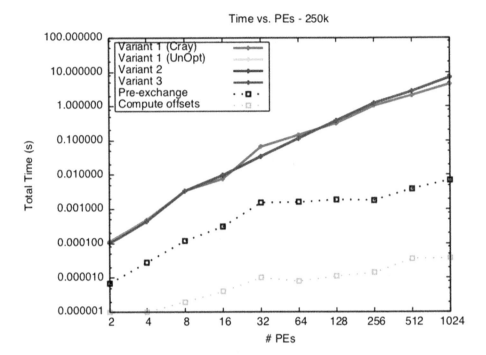

Fig. 2. Latency of large (250 kilobyte) messages for `Alltoallv()` for varying numbers of PEs. For an explanation of the various curves, see the caption for Fig. 1.

1 kilobyte but still making a difference over the three Variants that simply wrap 'put' and 'get' operations. Starting at 10 kilobytes in Fig. 4 the function has become a very well-behaved simple linear dependence. We see that it is at around 1 kilobyte where the time penalty of the `Alltoall()` pre-exchange of message sizes starts to become less of an issue for application performance.

Figure 5 shows the performance of the `Alltoallv()` interfaces when used in the NAS Parallel Benchmark Suite integer sort benchmark. Inconsistent behavior was observed in the OpenSHMEM port of the benchmark when attempting to use a large number of iterations, so that this data is subject to possibly increased noise due to the smaller iteration counts. Nevertheless, it can still be seen that the three proposed interfaces perform very similarly, while the Cray implementation shows that optimizations for `Alltoallv()` can improve application performance by almost 50 %.

4   Discussion

In this section, we briefly discuss some implementation details that should be considered when evaluating the advantages and disadvantages of the proposed interfaces to `Alltoallv()`. Although it is beyond the scope of the present work

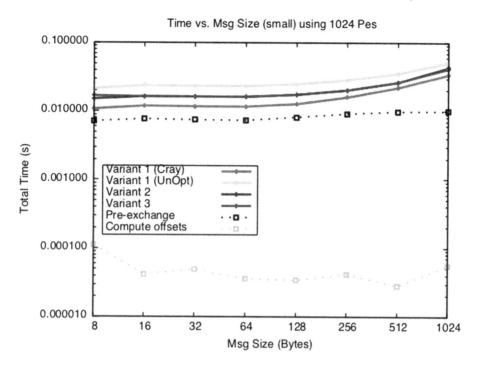

Fig. 3. Latency of small messages of varying sizes for 1024 PEs. For an explanation of the various curves, see the caption for Fig. 1.

to fully evaluate the details different implementation strategies, we nevertheless wish to highlight some of the major issues.

4.1   OpenSHMEM Semantics and Memory Usage

Besides optimizations which help decrease the overall time-to-solution, many applications which are memory-constrained benefit from considerations which allow a decrease in total memory usage. Any memory that can be saved by libraries, communication middleware, or other application overheads is then available for the application to work with larger data sets.

As pointed out in Sect. 2.2, there will necessarily be some extra memory that is allocated to hold the data received (and possibly sent) by an `Alltoallv()` operation in the case where it doesn't reduce to a uniform `Alltoall()` transfer. In fact, this unused memory will be present in all three variants, and can be calculated by Eq. 3, which could grow quickly with N relative to the available memory per PE.

This problem stems from current OpenSHMEM semantics which require that all shared objects allocated from the symmetric heap must be the same size on all PEs. There are two possible changes that would allow further memory-based optimizations for applications. First, `shmalloc()` could be extended to

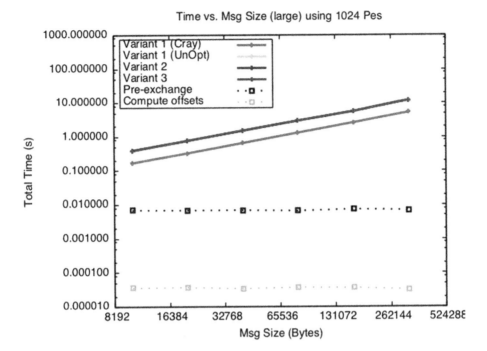

Fig. 4. Latency of large messages of varying sizes for 1024 PEs. For an explanation of the various curves, see the caption for Fig. 1.

allow for asymmetric allocations where each PE is able to specify how much remotely-accessible memory it wants to allocate for the `target` buffer. However, at least one consideration of this solution is the resulting increase in complexity for the overall OpenSHMEM implementation; most implementations depend on the fact that each shared object has the same offset from the beginning of the symmetric heap, and an increase in per-PE bookkeeping would be required if this restriction were relaxed. Another possibility is to allow remote operations direct to private memory. In fact, this semantic change need not be exposed to the user for an implementation to make use of it in a provided `Alltoallv()` where the user would simply provide the `target` argument pointing to a private memory buffer.

Note that these memory optimizations are not compatible with the benefits realized by eliminating the pre-exchange of data sizes using a separate `Alltoall()`. Unless the receiving `target` buffer were allocated during the `Alltoallv()` exchange (which might require further extensions to the interfaces proposed in this work), an `Alltoall()` pre-exchange of the send sizes will be necessary in order for the receiving PE to know how exactly much memory to allocate, whether it is allocated from the symmetric heap or private memory. However, for memory-constrained applications that have a communication pattern with potentially widely varying sizes being exchanged by `Alltoallv()`,

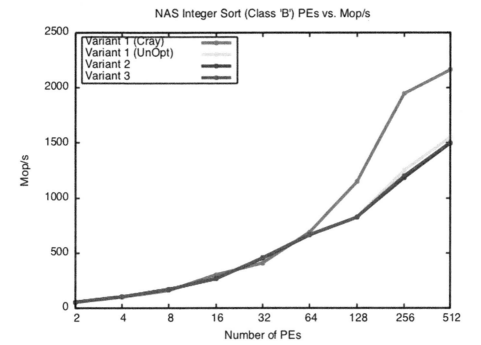

Fig. 5. Millions of operations per second for NAS Integer Sort Benchmark using the various `Alltoallv()` interfaces. The three proposed variants perform identically (within the noise) for the relatively large exchanges required by the integer sort application.

the latency of a `sizeof(size_t)` byte `Alltoall()` exchange is less likely to be a significant performance issue, and tradeoff of programmer convenience could be acceptable.

4.2 Opportunities for Optimization

Several opportunities exist for reducing the latency of the `Alltoallv()` operations described above, starting with simple things such as rotating the remote endpoints to reduce contention, and removing any extra hardware synchronizations imposed by using separate 'get' and 'put' operations in a `for` loop to implement the `Alltoallv()`. Additionally, there are more sophisticated optimizations that have been applied to `Alltoall()` and `Alltoallv()` algorithms in other progamming models and implementations such as those for MPI, as well as some possible enhancements that would be made possible by one or more of the newly proposed `Alltoallv()` interfaces.

There is an extra 'put' required by both Variant 2 and 3 to append the terminating flag or the size of the data transfer, respectively. For small message sizes especially, eliminating this extra operation would save the time required to transfer the extra bytes, as well as the corresponding overheads for performing a separate remote memory access. Appending the terminating flag and inserting into the t_sizes array can both be optimally solved with the help of underlying support from the networking hardware. If the implementation can get the information about the raw number of bytes received, this can be used on the receiving PE for both Variant 2 and 3, so that only the payload data is pushed across the network during the Alltoallv() operation. For example, the InfiniBand architecture defines *Immediate Data* transfers which in combination with the remote memory write ('put') operation generates a completion event on the target PE; the event includes an information about the number of received bytes.

Besides hardware-assisted optimizations, there are well-known algorithmic variations that can increase the performance of Alltoallv() in some cases. The most common nontrivial enhancements are log-scaling and hierarchical transfer algorithms as summarized in Sect. 1.1. The log-scaling algorithm introduced by Bruck [5] for Alltoall() requires an extra data structure when applied to Alltoallv() in order to properly handle the variable-sized data segments that are being transferred [10]. With current OpenSHMEM semantics unchanged, this could be simplified for the second and third proposed variants, especially with small message sizes, by treating the operation as a standard Alltoall() operation transferring max_offset amount of data each time. Were the semantics to be changed, or the implementation wished to save T_{extra} bytes of data during the communication for large message sizes, then the algorithm as described in Ref. [10] again becomes necessary. Hierarchical methods to take advantage of intranode shared memory capabilities face no obvious difficulties from any of the interfaces proposed here for Alltoallv(), and so known methods could be applied.

5 Summary

In this paper, we have proposed three possible interfaces for Alltoallv() which transfers variable amounts of data from every PE to every other PE in the communicating group. We implemented the three variants on equal terms using only standard OpenSHMEM 'put' and 'get' operations, and have shown some advantages over the traditional MPI interface, both from a performance standpoint for small messages as well as convenience for the programmer. We showed how these interfaces could work for an example application - integer sort as it is used in the NAS Parallel Benchmark Suite. We have discussed the implications for memory-constrained applications in the context of current OpenSHMEM memory handling semantics, and we have suggested changes that would improve memory efficiency for such applications. Finally, we discuss various optimizations for Alltoallv(), which variants would be able to take advantage of them, and what additions would be required in either the implementing hardware or software stack.

Acknowledgements. The work at Oak Ridge National Laboratory (ORNL) is supported by the United States Department of Defense and used the resources of the Extreme Scale Systems Center located at ORNL.

References

1. CPMD. http://cpmd.org/
2. Calculating the properties of materials from first principles, June 2012. http://www.castep.org/
3. Programming environments release announcement for cray XC30 systems (2013). http://docs.cray.com/books/S-9408-1306//S-9408-1306.pdf
4. Bailey, D., Barszcz, E., Barton, J., Browning, D., Carter, R., Dagum, L., Fatoohi, R., Frederickson, P., Lasinski, T., Schreiber, R., Simon, H., Venkatakrishnan, V., Weeratunga, S.: The NAS parallel benchmarks. Int. J. High Perform. Comput. Appl. **5**(3), 63–73 (1991). http://hpc.sagepub.com/content/5/3/63.abstract
5. Bruck, J., Ho, C.T., Upfal, E., Kipnis, S., Weathersby, D.: Efficient algorithms for all-to-all communications in multiport message-passing systems. IEEE Trans. Parallel Distrib. Syst. **8**(11), 1143–1156 (1997). http://dx.doi.org/10.1109/71.642949
6. Goglin, B., Moreaud, S.: Knem: A generic and scalable kernel-assisted intra-node MPI communication framework. J. Parallel Distrib. Comput. **73**(2), 176–188 (2013). http://www.sciencedirect.com/science/article/pii/S0743731512002316
7. Jackson, A., Booth, S.: Planned AlltoallV a clustered approach. Technical report, EPCC Edinburgh Parallel Computing Centre, July 2004
8. Ma, T., Bosilca, G., Bouteiller, A., Goglin, B., Squyres, J., Dongarra, J.: Kernel assisted collective intra-node mpi communication among multi-core and many-core cpus. In: 2011 International Conference on Parallel Processing (ICPP), pp. 532–541, September 2011
9. Pophale, S., Nanjegowda, R., Curtis, A.R., Chapman, B., Jin, H., Poole, S.W., Kuehn, J.A.: OpenSHMEM performance and potential: a NPB experimental study. In: PGAS, January 2012
10. Xu, C., Venkata, M., Graham, R., Wang, Y., Liu, Z., Yu, W.: Sloavx: Scalable logarithmic alltoallv algorithm for hierarchical multicore systems. In: 2013 13th IEEE/ACM International Symposium on Cluster, Cloud and Grid Computing (CCGrid), pp. 369–376, May 2013
11. Yu, W., Panda, D., Buntinas, D.: Scalable, high-performance nic-based all-to-all broadcast over myrinet/gm. In: 2004 IEEE International Conference on Cluster Computing, pp. 125–134, September 2004

Tools (Optional - Could also Go into Application Experiences)

Dynamic Analysis to Support Program Development with the Textually Aligned Property for OpenSHMEM Collectives

Andreas Knüpfer[1]([⊠]), Tobias Hilbrich[1],
Joachim Protze[2], and Joseph Schuchart[1]

[1] Technische Universität Dresden, 01062 Dresden, Germany
{andreas.knuepfer,tobias.hilbrich,joseph.schuchart}@tu-dresden.de
[2] JARA – High-Performance Computing,
RWTH Aachen University, 52056 Aachen, Germany
protze@itc.rwth-aachen.de

Abstract. The development of correct high performance computing applications is challenged by software defects that result from parallel programming. We present an automatic tool that provides novel correctness capabilities for application developers of OpenSHMEM applications. These applications follow a Single Program Multiple Data (SPMD) model of parallel programming. A strict form of SPMD programming requires that certain types of operations are textually aligned, i.e., they need to be called from the same source code line in every process. This paper proposes and demonstrates run-time checks that assert such behavior for OpenSHMEM collective communication calls. The resulting tool helps to check program consistency in an automatic and scalable fashion. We introduce the types of checks that we cover and include strict checks that help application developers to detect deviations from expected program behavior. Further, we discuss how we can utilize a parallel tool infrastructure to achieve a scalable and maintainable implementation for these checks. Finally, we discuss an extension of our checks towards further types of OpenSHMEM operations.

1 Introduction

The development of correct parallel applications is challenging. At the same time, correctness and reliability are key requirements for simulations that support decision making processes. The set of possible defects in parallel programs consists of all types of issues that can arise in sequential programming plus additional defects that arise from parallel programming. In this paper, we consider the latter and focus on defects that result from the use of collective communication operations (*collectives*). Widely used parallel programming approaches such as MPI [8] as well as Partitioned Global Address Space (PGAS) approaches [2,12] support these operations as a powerful way to exchange data between groups of

© Springer International Publishing Switzerland 2015
M. Gorentla Venkata et al. (Eds.): OpenSHMEM 2015, LNCS 9397, pp. 105–118, 2015.
DOI: 10.1007/978-3-319-26428-8_7

```
1   int main(void) {
2     ...
3     shmem_init();
4     me = shmem_my_pe();
5     npes = shmem_n_pes();
6     if (me % 2 == 0) {
7       shmem_barrier ( 0 /*PE_start*/, 0 /*stride=1*/,
8         npes /*count*/, ...);
9     } else {
10      shmem_barrier ( 1 /*PE_start*/, 0 /*stride=1*/,
11        npes-1 /*count*/, ...);
12    }
13    shmem_finalize();
14    return 0;
15  }
```

Fig. 1. Example of a program defect in an OpenSHMEM application.

parallel Processing Elements (PEs). We consider the OpenSHMEM standard as an upcoming approach to PGAS programming in this paper.

Figure 1 presents a usage error of the OpenSHMEM standard and a violation of the textual alignment property at the same time. The example executes distinct collectives in lines 7 and 10 that include distinct but overlapping groups of Processing Elements (PEs). For 4 total PEs, PEs 0 and 2 would execute a barrier that includes all PEs, while PEs 1 and 3 would execute a barrier that only includes PEs 1–3. Also, the example is not textually aligned, because the PEs execute different calls. Program defects as in this example can be detected by tools that aid application developers in the development of correct applications. We present such a tool for OpenSHMEM collectives that would detect the example usage error with a report as in Fig. 2. The prototype is an extension of the MPI correctness checking tool MUST. Our tool follows a runtime methodology, i.e., we execute the target application on an HPC system and observe its behavior on the system. This includes observing collective routines on the

MUST Output, starting date: Fri Jun 19 09:46:55 2015.

Rank(s)	Issue		
2, 1	Error		
Message	**From**	**References**	
Detected two active collectives that each include a PE that is missing in the active set of the other collective, deadlock is likely. A correct OpenSHMEM application must execute consistent collectives within groups of PEs. The first collective (A) uses the active set (start=0, logStride=0, count=4) and the second collective (B) uses the active set (start=1, logStride=0, count=3). PE 2 activated an operation for collective B, but is also part of collective A. Its active operation is detailed in the source location for this error message. PE 1 activated an operation for collective A, but is also part of collective B. Its active operation is detailed as reference 1 (rightmost column).	Representative process: rank 2: **shmem_barrier** called from: #0 main@example.c:15	Representative process: reference 1, rank 1: **shmem_barrier** called from: #0 main@example:20	

Fig. 2. Proposed runtime correctness approach (MUST) reports defects as in Fig. 1.

individual PEs. We then perform correctness analyses on this observation data to detect and report program defects.

Our contributions include the following:

- Identification of the types of checks that apply to OpenSHMEM collectives, including correctness checks and checks for textual alignment,
- A scalable design to implement these checks in a runtime correctness tool,
- And a discussion of annotation languages and extensions of our checks.

Section 2 presents related work. We then highlight that OpenSHMEM applications follow a Single Program Multiple Data (SPMD) approach in Sect. 3. Section 4 uses this notion to propose correctness checks that analyze the usage of collective operations according to the OpenSHMEM standard, as well as additional restrictions that we derive for applications that follow a stricter SPMD style. Following our runtime analysis methodology, we present a scalable concept for these checks in Sect. 5. Finally, we discuss extensions of our checks and the use of an annotation language in Sect. 6.

2 Related Work

Our approach closely relates to the OpenSHMEM Analyzer [9] that also targets the detection of OpenSHMEM programming defects. The OpenSHMEM Analyzer follows a static source code analysis methodology whereas our approach follows a runtime methodology, i.e., we execute the application under study. The former can be limited by complex input-dependent or non-deterministic control flow decisions, while the latter may not detect defects that do not manifest during an observed application run. We see a combination of the approaches as highly synergetic and promising. Information on runtime collective matching that we observe with our runtime approach could sharpen the analysis that approaches such as the OpenSHMEM Analyzer perform. Static collective matching as in the OpenSHMEM Analyzer relies on widely used source code analysis techniques [14].

Our correctness checks for collectives closely relate to runtime collective error detection approaches for MPI [3,11]. These approaches use additional communication on the application processes to detect defects in collectives. As a consequence, these approaches will deadlock if the fault causes the application to deadlock. The approach that we propose offloads information on observed collectives to additional tool owned control flows. As a result, our correctness analysis overcomes this limitation. For scalability we rely on basic analysis techniques that we apply for MPI collective operations [4] also. Thus, the scalability that we offer is not limited in comparison to these approaches.

Our extension to analyze the observed application for (strict) textual alignment relates to an existing runtime approach for the Titanium [13] language [7]. OpenSHMEM and Titanium differ in their their abstraction and in their synchronization primitives. Textual alignment is part of the Titanium language, which is not true for OpenSHMEM. Additionally, we consider alignment and correctness with a notion of scalability, while the existing approach does not consider scalability nor wider ranges of correctness analyses.

3 SPMD Executions

The SPMD (*Single Program, Multiple Data*) style is a widely used parallel programming style in High Performance Computing (HPC). It provides an easy mapping of parallel activities to HPC systems. SPMD is the dominating approach for large scale programming of leadership scale systems. The SPMD model relies on the notion that functional decomposition into many parallel functions is infeasible. For practical applications there are not enough functional tasks to employ tens or even thousands of processes. Secondly, writing as many separate pieces of source code is unmanageable.

While MPMD (Multiple Programs, Multiple Data) codes exist in HPC, they commonly use few programs of different functionality, which in turn use an SPMD style. A common example are coupled simulations that combine a few SPMD applications. Practical applications often relax the SPMD model to allow processes to take different control flow paths. Individual processes use a PE, rank, or other number to identify themselves. Processes can then branch off depending on their PE number to increase implementation flexibility, e.g., to consider domain borders where there are less communication partners.

Collective operations in a sense are the obvious communication primitives from a SPMD point of view, because all participants execute the same thing. As we illustrate in the example of Fig. 1, collectives are always issued by groups of PEs. OpenSHMEM identifies this group with a triple (`PE_start`, `logPE_Stride`, `PE_size`), also called the *active set*. The first element of the triple identifies the first PE of the group, the second element specifies a stride with $2^{\mathrm{logPE\_Stride}}$, and the third element specifies the number of PEs in the group. Collectives often concur with a strict SPMD notion. That is, all PEs of a group issue an operation that is in the same source line of the same control flow path. This is also known as *textually aligned* collectives [14].

While OpenSHMEM allows divergence from textually aligned collectives, many practical applications will adhere to it. This particularly stems from the fact that source code with textually aligned collectives is easier to understand and maintain. For such applications, any situation where collectives are not textually aligned immediately highlights a program defect. Tools that detect this situation can provide valuable feedback to application developers and can simplify the removal of defects. Especially, they can highlight unnoticed and hard to find defects. Thus, we not only propose basic correctness checks for Open-SHMEM that consider the definitions of the OpenSHMEM standard, but also checks that verify whether collectives are textually aligned.

4 Correctness Checks and Textual Alignment

OpenSHMEM matches collective primitives of PEs based on the aforementioned PE group description. As in the example of Fig. 1, ill devised PE groups can lead to deadlock. The error report in Fig. 2 highlights a check for a particular type of collective deadlock: Two overlapping PE groups exist, one of the overlapping PEs is active in the one PE group, while another overlapping PE is active in the other PE group. Such a check is helpful for a wide range of basic problems, a general deadlock detection approach requires consideration of all blocking OpenSHMEM operations however. We consider such an approach as a future extension and focus on pure collective checks. Similarly, we consider memory related checks concerning communication contents and synchronization/work arrays as a more appropriate extension for memory checkers.

Within the PE group of a collective, all active PEs must:

(A) Execute a collective of the same name,
(B) If the collective involves a *root* argument as in **broadcast**, it must be equal on all PEs,
(C) If the collective involves a reduction, the *nreduces* argument must be equal on all PEs, and
(D) If the collective is an **fcollect**, the *nelems* argument must be equal on all PEs.

Besides OpenSHMEM standard related restrictions, we consider checks for textual alignment. Since OpenSHMEM provides no language constructs to enforce textual alignment, it allows situations in which PEs issue textually aligned collectives, but from different function call stacks. As an example, a barrier could occur at the tail of a recursion, different PEs could use different depths during the recursion. Similarly, PEs can reach a collective in a function via differing call stacks. We differentiate the following levels of collective alignment:

Full Textual Alignment: The application only executes collectives that include all PEs, matching collective primitives are from the same source line with equal call stacks;
Subset Tolerant Alignment: Matching collective primitives are from the same source line with equal call stacks;
Weak Textual Alignment: The application only executes collectives that include all PEs, matching collective primitives result from the same program function; and
Weak Subset Tolerant Alignment: Matching collective primitives are from the same program function;

Figure 3 illustrates these four types of alignment. *Full textual alignment* considers the classic textual alignment. Programs may need to apply seperate behavior for distinct PEs, e.g., to utilize distinct communication payloads. Usually such distinctions reside in a single program function. As a consequence, we use *weak textual alignment* to allow for such situations, but restrict it to collectives from the same function. Consequently, we see a situation as in Fig. 3(e) more suspicious then situations as in Fig. 3(b).

In order to allow for collectives that use PE groups, we use subset tolerant alignment that requires that matching collective primitives use similar call stacks. Again, to allow for distinctions between specific PEs within a single

```
1  int main (...) {
2    ...
3    shmem_barrier_all ();
4    ...
5  }
```

(a) Full textual alignment.

```
1  int main (...) {
2    ...
3    //Odd/Even
4    if (0 == me % 2)
5      shmem_barrier_all ();
6    else
7      shmem_barrier_all ();
8    ...
9  }
```

(b) Weak (but not full) textual alignment.

```
1  int main (...) {
2    ...
3    shmem_barrier ( me % 2, 1, (
       npes + (me+1)%2) / 2, ...);
4    ...
5  }
```

(c) Subset tolerant alignment.

```
1  int main (...) {
2    ...
3    //Root has special handling
4    if (0 == me)
5      shmem_barrier ( 0, 1, (npes
         + (me+1)%2) / 2, ...);
6    else
7      shmem_barrier ( me % 2, 1,
         (npes + (me+1)%2) / 2,
         ...);
8    ...
9  }
```

(d) Weak subset tolerant alignment.

```
1  int main (...) {
2    ...
3    //Odd/Even
4    if (0 == me % 2)
5      foo ();
6    else
7      bar ();
8    ...
9  }
10
11 void foo () {
12   shmem_barrier_all();
13 }
14
15 void bar () {
16   shmem_barrier_all();
17 }
```

(e) Violation to weak textual alignment.

```
1  int main (...) {
2    ...
3    //Root has special handling
4    if (0 == me)
5      foo ();
6    else
7      bar ();
8    ...
9  }
10
11 void foo () {
12   shmem_barrier ( 0, 1, (npes +
       (me+1)%2) / 2, ...);
13 }
14
15 void bar () {
16   shmem_barrier ( me % 2, 1, (
       npes + (me+1)%2) / 2, ...);
17 }
```

(f) Violation to weak subset tolerant alignment.

Fig. 3. Examples of the proposed alignment levels and violations to them. Assume *me* and *npes* to carry the PE identifier and PE count as in the example of Fig. 1. All sketched program control flows are valid according to the OpenSHMEM standard [12].

function of the program, we add weak subset tolerant alignment. As a consequence, the example in Fig. 3(f) is more suspicious in our considerations than the situation in Fig. 3(d).

5   Scalable Runtime Checks

We follow a runtime methodology to realize checks for the proposed adherence to the OpenSHMEM standard, as well as to identify violations to the proposed types of textual alignment. That is, we execute a target application under the presence of a correctness tool and observe the behavior of the application. Such a tool requires two main components: First, a PE local instrumentation that observes all collective primitives. And second, a global analysis that exchanges information about these observations as to apply our proposed checks.

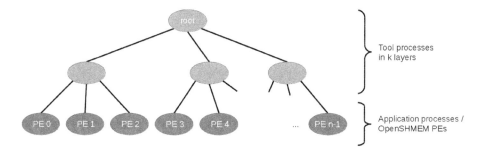

Fig. 4. Overlay tree formed from the application processes (OpenSHMEM PEs) as leaf nodes and k layers of tools processes.

Figure 4 illustrates our approach for these two components. We apply the instrumentation and observation on the PEs, which the figure illustrates with nodes labeled `PE i`. Our global analysis uses a Tree Based Overlay Network (TBON) to apply a hierarchical analysis. The widely used MRNet TBON implementation [10] demonstrated the efficiency of this concept that provides an accessible approach to distribute workloads within the tool in a scalable manner. Figure 4 illustrates the TBON with additional nodes that are owned by the tool and that drive the global analysis. In the following, we first describe the local instrumentation followed by our concept for employing the TBON to implement the proposed checks.

5.1   Instrumentation on the PEs

Collective primitives issued by the individual PEs form the input for our correctness analysis. We instrument all PEs with the profiling interface that is available for some OpenSHMEM implementations, e.g., for the OpenSHMEM reference implementation or for the Open MPI version of OpenSHMEM. These implementations use weak symbols to allow an instrumentation library to intercept the OpenSHMEM API calls. A name shifted interface then allows the instrumentation library to issue the original primitives in the actual implementation. This approach allows us to observe all collective routines. A variety of correctness checks apply to this observation data directly, e.g., analysis of whether PE descriptions in collectives use valid PEs numbers. However, such checks are not the focus of this paper. The collective analysis that we propose requires communication to combine information on matching collective operations. As to support this communication, the instrumentation library creates *event objects* that carry all information that our proposed correctness analyses require:

```
struct EventObject{
  uint8_t collId; //Identifier for the type of collective
  int PE_start;
  int logPE_stride;
  int PE_size;
  union {
    //Depending on the collective, one of the following
    int PE_root;
    int nreduces;
    size_t nelems;
    }
  std::vector<char*> callStack; // routine names with
      source file and line number
  uint64_t channelId; //Identifier for TBON aggregation
  int PEsJoined; //#PEs represented by this event
}
```

The `collId` identifies the specific collective with an identifier to differentiate a `shmem_collect32` from a `shmem_collect64` when we analyze for OpenSH-MEM restriction (A) from Sect. 4. The next three fields include the PE description. As to analyze the correctness of properties (B)–(D) from Sect. 4, we use one of `PE_root`, `nreduces`, or `nelems`, depending on the type of collective. The `callStack` field then details the call stack of the observed collective primitive[1]. Finally, the `channelId` and `PEsJoined` fields serve during our scalable analysis, which we detail subsequently.

Inside our instrumentation library we can fill all parts of the event object. We use the Dyninst [1] package to retrieve call stacks during that process. After its creation the instrumentation library passes the event object to the global analysis that we describe in the following.

5.2 Scalable Overlay Tree

As we discussed earlier, a correctness analysis checking for potential deadlocks should not use the PEs for its own analysis. We follow this notion for our proposed collective checks and analyze global correctness on tool-owned processes called *tool processes*, additional OpenSHMEM PEs in our prototype. We arrange these tool processes in a TBON (Fig. 4). We subsequently address the freedom of the fan-in ratio f, also known as branching factor. The frequency of collective operations in the target application impacts the choice for f. For MPI collective

---

[1] We replace the call stack information with a numeric identifier as to reuse information on known call stacks.

verification with a comparable technique [4] we achieve good performance with a ratio between 12 and 16.

Our instrumentation library on the leaf nodes passes all event objects to their parent nodes in the tree hierarchy. To achieve scalability, we distribute the analysis based on the following notion: The collective checks that we propose involve matching up communication primitives of PEs in associated PE groups. We must compare matching primitives of these groups to identify violations to (A)–(D) or to our textual alignment checks. This comparison is possible in a hierarchical manner that compares subsets of matching primitives with each other. If the comparison is successful we can forward a single representative from the subset. Each node in the TBON uses the event objects of its child nodes as this subset. Higher level hierarchy layers in the tree can then compare these representatives, rather than the original event objects. The root then compares representatives for all PEs in the PE group of a collective. Thus, such a hierarchical comparison does not lose precision. Most importantly, with the usage of representative events, each node in the TBON forwards at most a single event object per collective. We subsequently discuss the scalability that results from this fact.

Our event handling on the tool processes uses two data structures to process and forward the correctness analysis:

Wave: A *wave* stores event objects that belong to the same collective, i.e., the primitives that an OpenSHMEM implementation would match up.

PEGroupInfo: A `PEGroupInfo` stores incomplete waves for each PE group that a (`PE_start`,`logPE_Stride`,`PE_size`) triple of an event object describes. A `wave` stays incompleted as long as at least one event object that the tool process could receive for the PE group of a collective is missing.

We use the `channelId` and `PEsJoined` fields of an event object to decide to which incomplete *wave* in a `PEGroupInfo` it belongs. The `channelId` field identifies the node in the TBON that created the event object. A detailed study introduces these identifiers and presents their properties [6]. Every new event object with a `channelId` belongs to a wave exactly if no event object with `channelId'` exists in the wave that identifies a node in the tree that is an ancestor, descendant, or the same node as the node that `channelId` identifies.

We propose the following handling on all tool processes to realize an efficient correctness analysis of OpenSHMEM collectives. When a tool process receives an event object for a collective, it:

1. Evaluates the (`PE_start`,`logPE_Stride`,`PE_size`) triple of the event to determine the `PEGroupInfo` to which the event belongs (possibly creating a new group).
2. If this is the first event with a PE group that does not include all PEs: We store information on the event and set the flag `hadSubsetColl` to `true`.
3. The search for the `PEGroupInfo` of an event can identify situations in which PEs activate collectives that will wait cyclically for each other, as in the example of Figs. 1 and 2; We do not extend this functionality for a scalable

approach and see a more general deadlock detection approach beyond collectives as more appropriate to handle such defects.

4. We compare the `channelId` field of the new event as described above to identify the *wave* in the `PEGroupInfo` to which it belongs.
5. If no such *wave* exists: we create a new *wave* and completed the handling, i.e., the tool process does not forward the event object of the new event yet and continues with processing the next event object at Step 1.
6. If we found an existing wave: we compare the fields of the new event to the first event of the existing *wave* as follows:
   (a) To check for correctness property (A), we compare the `collId` field of the two events; If they differ we report the error and continue with Step 8;
   (b) To check for correctness properties (B)–(D) we compare the `PE_root`, `nreduces`, or `nelems` fields as applicable for the given collective; If they do not match we report the error and continue with Step 8;
   (c) If the call stacks of the two events result from the same function, but not the same source line:
       i. We report the pair of events as an instance of a weak alignment, and
       ii. We set the flag `hadWeakAlignment` to `true`.
   (d) If the call stacks of the two events result from distinct functions:
       i. We report the pair of events as a violation to weak alignment, and
       ii. We set the flag `hadWeakViolation` to `true`.
7. If the wave is complete—which we can compute from analyzing the number of PEs that a tool process can reach for the PE group and from summing up the `PEsJoined` fields of the events in the wave—we forward the first event of the wave as a representative, update its `PEsJoined` count, and set its `channelId` field to represent this tool process; We then delete the wave and continue with the next event at Step 1. Note that we do not forward an event if the wave was not completed.
8. In case of violation to (A)–(D) we forward the original events of the wave and stop the correctness analysis as follow up errors would likely be a result of the initial error.

When we observe program exit, each tool process provides a final verdict on the observed textual alignment:

1. If `hadSubsetColl == false`:
   (a) If `hadWeakAlignment == false` and `hadWeakViolation == false`: we report that the application has full textual alignment.
   (b) If `hadWeakViolation == false`: we report that the application has weak textual alignment.
2. If `hadSubsetColl == true`:
   (a) If `hadWeakAlignment == false` and `hadWeakViolation == false`: we report that the application has subset tolerant alignment.
   (b) If `hadWeakViolation == false`: we report that the application has weak subset tolerant alignment.

The root of the tree observes these verdicts and finally reports the lowest level it received a report for. A hierarchical reduction can render this process scalable.

We implemented a prototype that is based on the MPI-focused runtime correctness tool MUST [4]. This protoype uses the above handling and is based on the TBON implementation that is provided by GTI [5]. For that, we created a prototype version of GTI that is able to instrument OpenSHMEM applications and to create a TBON for these applications. However, the above concept is applicable for other TBON implementations as well.

5.3   Complexity Estimation

A common notion is that certain program defects only manifest at scale. Thus, for a runtime correctness approach it is crucial to be applicable to runs at increased scale. This notion motivates our proposed distributed and hierarchical analysis. Its influence on application runtime is driven by three main aspects: First, the frequency of collective operations in the target code. This is a given amount which cannot be controlled. Thus the following looks at the complexity induced for every single collective operation to be checked. Second, the communication overhead for the event objects that tree nodes pass between themselves. And third, there is the processing effort on every tool process.

Influence of the Communication Effort

Every node in the tree is responsible for checks for all event objects from all leaf nodes in its sub-tree with n leaf nodes corresponding to n OpenSHMEM PEs.

Our design targets situations in which collectives involve most PEs. The communication effort per tool process in such a situation is: Child nodes of the node will unify their event objects to a single event object. Thus, the node receives up to f (fan-in ratio) event objects per collective and forwards a single event object. If f is constant with increasing application scale, the communication overhead on tool nodes remains constant and balanced within the tree. A constant time communication overhead will have an acceptable influence on the application runtime, even at scale.

If collectives involve few PEs or just a single PE in the worst case, the above estimation is still correct per collective operation. Yet, many more collectives could be employed by the application at the same time. Consider a situation were all PEs issues collectives that just involve the PE itself. Then all tool processes will receive event objects about these collectives and immediately forward them. Thus, the root node will receive n events for n total PEs and becomes a scalability bottleneck. In situations where collectives are used in a degenerated manner or serve as PE-to-PE communication between few PEs, an alternative collective handling becomes necessary. This is not deemed an expected behavior of scalable OpenSHMEM applications, however.

Influence of the Processing Effort

Next to the communication cost there is also a processing cost on the tree nodes. For the leaf nodes (application PEs) we require constant time to create the event objects, assuming call stacks of bounded size. As described above, the cost of handling an event object is constant. Note that the use of the `channelId` field can introduce small additional costs. Thus, the processing effort directly correlates to the number of event objects that a tool process receives, which is bounded by f per collective operation.

Over-all Effort

If the fan-in remains constant across increasing application scale and if collectives involve most PEs, we expect constant overheads that allow a correctness tool to scale with the application. This is what we assume to be the typical scenario. Thus we optimized our approach for this case.

6   Annotation Language

The goal of our correctness analysis for textual alignment is to identify abnormal program behavior. Since we cannot guess the original intentions of the programmer, we can only report violations to textual alignment types as warnings. While these reports can identify important deviations from expected behavior, this comes with two downsides:

- If the deviation is unintentional, an error message would be advisable.
- The number of warning messages can be high for complex applications.

Thus, we propose an extension of our approach with an annotation language that allows the application programmer to specify the *intentions*. Techniques such as a C/C++ preprocessor macros, the use of compiler supported pragmas, or a tool specific API enable such an annotation. We propose a first annotation primitive `annonshmem_init` that should follow directly after `shmem_init`. This primitive informs a correctness tool that the application uses the annotation language. The tool then reports textual alignment type violations as errors instead of warnings. Additionally, the annotation language should provide annotations that can precede OpenSHMEM collectives as to notify the correctness tool of an intentional violation to one of the textual alignment types shown in Table 1. The annotations would be ignored during the normal executions of the target application without a checking tool.

With the occurrence directly before a collective, the correctness tool can include the provided information into our event object data. The scalable correctness analysis in Sect. 5 then restricts its correctness reports if the developer specified an intended violation to a textual alignment type. Furthermore, the tool can check for consistently specified annotations, as to highlight inconsistent annotations.

Table 1. Suggested annotations to be prepended to OpenSHMEM collective communication calls in the source code in order to guide the warnings or error messages produced by a tool that checks for textual alignment.

`annonshmem_subset_coll`	Intentional subset tolerant aligned collective
`annonshmem_weak_coll`	Intentional weak textually aligned collective
`annonshmem_weak_subset_coll`	Intentional weak subset tolerantaligned collective
`annonshmem_unaligned_coll`	Intentional violation to weaktextual alignment
`annonshmem_unaligned_subset_coll`	Intentional violation to weaksubset tolerant alignment

The use of the annotations allows a developer to remove unwanted reports and to highlight unexpected violations with increased visibility. Furthermore, the presence of the annotations in the source code provides helpful documentation for developers. This embedded knowledge improves maintainability of the code.

7   Conclusions and Outlook

We present a summary of runtime correctness checks for OpenSHMEM collectives and extend them with the notion of textual alignment. We provide three levels of alignment—unaligned, weak, and full—that we differentiate into regular and subset alignment. Violations to these alignment types help application developers to identify unexpected program behavior. A scalable scheme to implement these checks as part of a runtime tool highlights that these checks are applicable at scale. This is important for providing tool support when issues arise at a specific application scale. Our scheme relies on collectives that involve most PEs. In the rather uncommon case where large numbers of collectives are issued with only few PEs each, an alternative strategy may be advisable.

We are in the process of providing a prototype for these checks. The prototype uses GTI for the TBON services that we require and the MUST tool as its basis. Our goal is to provide a wide variety of helpful correctness checks in a single tool. We envision usage during unit testing and extended testing after code changes as well as when defects manifest as errors as the three main use cases of the tool.

The proposed annotation language can improve the visibility of important tool messages while at the same time increase documentation within the application's source code. Future extensions of the prototype could also offer deadlock detection and an analysis of one-sided operations.

The availability of a profiling interface as part of the OpenSHMEM reference implementation, as well as of the Open MPI implementation, simplifies tool development dramatically. In particular, it allows to hide the entire analysis complexity from the user by introducing a prefix command to be prepended before the regular command line for executing an OpenSHMEM application.

References

1. Buck, B., Hollingsworth, J.K.: An API for runtime code patching. Int. J. High Perform. Comput. Appl. **14**(4), 317–329 (2000)
2. Consortium, T.G.: GASPI: Global Address Space Programming Interface - Specification of a PGAS API for communication, version 1.01. Technical report (2013)
3. Falzone, C., Chan, A., Lusk, E.L., Gropp, W.: A portable method for finding user errors in the usage of MPI collective operations. Int. J. High Perform. Comput. Appl. **21**(2), 155–165 (2007)
4. Hilbrich, T., Hänsel, F., Schulz, M., de Supinski, B.R., Müller, M.S., Nagel, W.E., Protze, J.: Runtime MPI collective checking with tree-based overlay networks. In: Proceedings of the 20th European MPI Users' Group Meeting, EuroMPI 2013, pp. 129–134. ACM New York (2013)
5. Hilbrich, T., Müller, M.S., de Supinski, B.R., Schulz, M., Nagel, W.E.: GTI: A generic tools infrastructure for event-based tools in parallel systems. In: Proceedings of the 2012 IEEE 26th International Parallel and Distributed Processing Symposium, IPDPS 2012, pp. 1364–1375. IEEE Computer Society Washington, DC (2012)
6. Hilbrich, T., Müller, M.S., Schulz, M., de Supinski, B.R.: Order preserving event aggregation in TBONs. In: Cotronis, Y., Danalis, A., Nikolopoulos, D.S., Dongarra, J. (eds.) EuroMPI 2011. LNCS, vol. 6960, pp. 19–28. Springer, Heidelberg (2011)
7. Kamil, A., Yelick, K.: Enforcing textual alignment of collectives using dynamic checks. In: Gao, G.R., Pollock, L.L., Cavazos, J., Li, X. (eds.) LCPC 2009. LNCS, vol. 5898, pp. 368–382. Springer, Heidelberg (2010)
8. Message Passing Interface Forum. MPI: A Message-Passing Interface Standard, Version 3.1. (2015). http://www.mpi-forum.org/docs/mpi-3.1/mpi31-report.pdf. Accessed 19 June 2015
9. Pophale, S., Hernandez, O., Chapman, B.: Static Analysis for unaligned collective synchronization matching for OpenSHMEM. In: Proceedings of the 7th International Conference on PGAS Models, pp. 231–336. The University of Edinburgh, Edinburgh (2014)
10. Roth, P.C., Arnold, D.C., Miller, B.P.: MRNet: A software-based multicast/reduction network for scalable tools. In: Proceedings of the 2003 ACM/IEEE Conference on Supercomputing, SC 2003, New York. ACM (2003)
11. Träff, J.L., Worringen, J.: Verifying collective MPI calls. In: Kranzlmüller, D., Kacsuk, P., Dongarra, J. (eds.) EuroPVM/MPI 2004. LNCS, vol. 3241, pp. 18–27. Springer, Heidelberg (2004)
12. openshmem.org. OpenSHMEM Application Programming Interface v1.2, 04 (2015)
13. Yelick, K., Semenzato, L., Pike, G., Miyamoto, C., Liblit, B., Krishnamurthy, A., Hilfinger, P., Graham, S., Gay, D., Colella, P., Aiken, A.: Titanium: a high-performance Java dialect. Concur.: Pract. Exp. **10**(11–13), 825–836 (1998)
14. Zhang, Y., Duesterwald, E.: Barrier matching for programs with textually unaligned barriers. In: Proceedings of the 12th ACM SIGPLAN Symposium on Principles and Practice of Parallel Programming, PPoPP 2007, pp. 194–204. ACM, New York (2007)

Application Experiences

From MPI to OpenSHMEM: Porting LAMMPS

Chunyan Tang[1], Aurelien Bouteiller[1(✉)], Thomas Herault[1],
Manjunath Gorentla Venkata[2], and George Bosilca[1]

[1] Innovative Computing Laboratory, University of Tennessee, Knoxville, USA
{bouteill,bosilca,herault}@icl.utk.edu, ctang7@vols.utk.edu
[2] Oak Ridge National Laboratory, Oak Ridge, USA
manjugv@ornl.gov

Abstract. This work details the opportunities and challenges of porting a Petascale, MPI-based application —LAMMPS— to OpenSHMEM. We investigate the major programming challenges stemming from the differences in communication semantics, address space organization, and synchronization operations between the two programming models. This work provides several approaches to solve those challenges for representative communication patterns in LAMMPS, e.g., by considering group synchronization, peer's buffer status tracking, and unpacked direct transfer of scattered data. The performance of LAMMPS is evaluated on the Titan HPC system at ORNL. The OpenSHMEM implementations are compared with MPI versions in terms of both strong and weak scaling. The results outline that OpenSHMEM provides a rich semantic to implement scalable scientific applications. In addition, the experiments demonstrate that OpenSHMEM can compete with, and often improve on, the optimized MPI implementation.

1 Introduction

OpenSHMEM [12] is an emerging partitioned global address space (PGAS) library interface specification that provides interfaces for one-sided and collective communication, synchronization, and atomic operations. The one-sided communication operations do not require the active participation of the target process when receiving or exposing data, freeing the target process to work on other tasks while the data transfer is ongoing. It also supports some collective communication patterns such as synchronizations, broadcast, collection, and reduction

This manuscript has been authored by UT-Battelle, LLC under Contract No. DE-AC05-00OR22725 with the U.S. Department of Energy. The United States Government retains and the publisher, by accepting the article for publication, acknowledges that the United States Government retains a non-exclusive, paid-up, irrevocable, world-wide license to publish or reproduce the published form of this manuscript, or allow others to do so, for United States Government purposes. The Department of Energy will provide public access to these results of federally sponsored research in accordance with the DOE Public Access Plan (http://energy.gov/downloads/doe-public-access-plan).

© Springer International Publishing Switzerland 2015
M. Gorentla Venkata et al. (Eds.): OpenSHMEM 2015, LNCS 9397, pp. 121–137, 2015.
DOI: 10.1007/978-3-319-26428-8_8

operations. In addition it provides interfaces for a variety of atomic operations including both 32-bit and 64-bit operations. Overall, it provides a rich set of interfaces for implementing parallel scientific applications. OpenSHMEM implementations are expected to perform well modern high performance computing (HPC) systems. This expectation stems from the design philosophy of Open-SHMEM on providing a lightweight and high performing minimalistic set of operations, a close match between the OpenSHMEM semantic and hardware-supported native operations provided by high performance interconnects and memory subsystems. This tight integration between the hardware and the programming paradigm is expected to result in close to optimal latency and bandwidth in synthetic benchmarks.

In spite of a rich set of features and a long legacy of native support from vendors, like SGI, Cray [3], and Quadrics (no longer available), OpenSHMEM has seen a slow and limited adoption. The current situation is analogous to a freshly plowed field ready for seeding, in this case, with an initial effort to design software engineering practices that enable efficient porting of scientific simulations to this programming model. This paper explores porting LAMMPS [11], a production-quality Message Passing Interface (MPI) based scientific application, to OpenSHMEM. Due to big differences in semantic and syntax between MPI [9] and OpenSHMEM, there is no straightforward one-to-one mapping of functionality. In particular, OpenSHMEM features one-sided communication and partitioned global address space, unlike most legacy MPI applications which employ two-sided MPI communication and a private address space for each MPI process. Furthermore, MPI provides explicit controls over communication patterns (e.g., communicator division and communication based on process grouping and topology) to improve programming productivity, while OpenSHMEM does not yet have support for these fine grained controls. Hence, transforming an MPI-based program into an OpenSHMEM-based one remains a difficult, and largely unexplored exercise.

2   Related Work

Despite salient differences in key concepts, MPI-3 [4] provides advanced one-sided operations, and investigations are ongoing to understand how to port from MPI-1 to MPI-3 RMA; initial results have demonstrated significant speedup [8]. OpenSHMEM, as an open standard for all SHMEM library implementations [2], was first standardized in 2012. Despite its expected benefits, the scientific computing community is still in the initial phase of exploring the OpenSHMEM concepts, hence a limited number of works using OpenSHMEM are available. Pophale et al. [13] compared the performance and scalability of unoptimized OpenSHMEM NAS benchmarks with their MPI-1 and MPI-2 counterparts. They showed that even without optimization, the OpenSHMEM-based version of the benchmarks compares favorably with MPI-1 and MPI-2. Li et al. [7] re-designed an MPI-1 based mini-application with OpenSHMEM. They demonstrated a 17 % reduction in total execution time, compared to the MPI-based design. Similar results have been demonstrated for the Graph500 benchmark [6], while in [5], the authors have refactored an Hadoop parallel sort into an hybrid MPI+OpenSHMEM application, demonstrating a 7x improvement over the Hadoop implementation.

The work presented in this paper also focuses on leveraging OpenSHMEM in an application. However, instead of working on a mini-app or benchmark, we tackle a realistic, large-scale HPC application. We aim at understanding the opportunities and challenges of using the OpenSHMEM programming paradigm to translate and design highly scalable scientific simulations. Our work reveals strengths and limitations in OpenSHMEM, demonstrates better performance than legacy MPI in a large-scale performance evaluation, and discusses the merits of some optimization strategies.

3 Background

This section presents the target application, LAMMPS. It also presents a summary explaining the major differences between OpenSHMEM and MPI.

3.1 LAMMPS

Large-scale Atomic/Molecular Massively Parallel Simulator (LAMMPS) is a classical molecular dynamics (MD) code developed by Sandia National Laboratories[1]. In essence, LAMMPS integrates Newton's equations of motion with a variety of initial and/or boundary conditions. The Newton's equations calculate the motion of collections of atoms, molecules, or macroscopic particles that interact via short- or long-range forces [11].

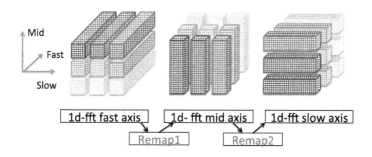

Fig. 1. Parallel 3D-FFT in 2D decomposition.

To compute the long-range Coulomb interactions, LAMMPS employs the three dimensional fast Fourier transform (3D-FFT) package, a transpose based parallel FFT developed by Steve Plimpton [10]. Transpose-based FFT performs

---

[1] http://lammps.sandia.gov/.

one dimension of 1D-FFT at a time, and transposes the data grid when needed. The 2D decomposition of parallel 3D-FFT is shown in Fig. 1. The three dimensions of the real space are labeled as Slow, Mid, and Fast axes, respectively. A data grid of size $l \times m \times n$ is divided between $1 \times p \times q$ processes. Hence the split size of the sub-domain is $nfast = l$, $nmid = m/p$, and $nslow = n/q$. Each process contains a sub-domain (pencil) of the data. First, each process performs the 1D-FFT along the Fast axis, where the data on this direction are local. The processes then transpose the Mid and Fast axes in order to perform the local 1D-FFT along the Mid axis. Finally, processes transpose the Mid and Slow axes and then perform a 1D-FFT along the Slow axis.

As an initial step to the analysis, we collected statistical information about MPI usage in LAMMPS with the MPI profiling tool (mpiP [14]). We used the *rhodopsin* test case (as provided by the LAMMPS test suite). The input file for this benchmark provides a basic problem size of 32 K atoms. The problem size for profiling is scaled to $8 \times 8 \times 8 \times 32$K atoms. In this strong scaling benchmark, the portion of time spent in MPI function over the total application time is 5.5 % for 256 processes, 12.6 % for 512 processes, 18.1 % for 1024 processes, 25.4 % for 2048 processes and 38.5 % for 4096 processes, respectively. Clearly, communication is a dominating factor in the overall performance, therefore reducing the communication time has the potential to improve LAMMPS performance significantly at scale.

In this test case, LAMMPS has 167 sites with calls to MPI functions. Doing a complete port of MPI-based LAMMPS to OpenSHMEM is a large undertaking which is unlikely to be completed in short order. Instead we chose to focus our efforts on the most data exchange intensive site, the `remap_3d` function, which is responsible for the transpose operations in the 3D-FFT. The `remap_3d` function employs a set of MPI point-to-point operations (`MPI_Send`, `MPI_Irecv`, `MPI_Waitany`) which concentrate the largest share of the overall transmitted MPI byte volume (32.45 % for 4096 processes). Consequently, any communication performance improvement in this function is expected to yield a sizable overall acceleration.

The resulting application is a hybrid MPI-OpenSHMEM application, where the legacy MPI application is accelerated with OpenSHMEM communication routines in performance critical sections.

3.2   OpenSHMEM Vs. MPI

To transform the above MPI-based implementation into one based on OpenSH-MEM, we must account for four salient differences between the two programing models.

Address Space Differences: MPI considers a distributed address space, where each process has a private memory space, in which addresses are purely local. In contrast, OpenSHMEM features a partitioned global address space, in which each processing element (PE) has a private memory space, but that memory space is mapped to symmetric addresses, that is, if a program declares a global array `A`, the local address of the element `A[i]` is the relevant parameter in a communication call to target `A[i]` at every PE. The main advantage of the latter model is that it enables the origin process in the operation to compute all the remote addresses for the operation, which it can then issue directly without first converting the addresses to the target's address space. This is a major feature that eases the development of applications using the one-sided communication paradigm.

Communication Semantics Differences: OpenSHMEM is based on one-sided communication. This is in contrast to the two-sided communication employed in MPI LAMMPS. Although MPI has provided one-sided communication since MPI-2 (i.e., `MPI_Get` and `MPI_Put`), two-sided communication programs dominate the common practice of using MPI. In two-sided operations, every Send operation matches a Receive operation. Each process provides a buffer, in the local address space, in which the input or output are to be accessed. In contrast, in the one-sided model, communications are issued at the origin, without any matching call at the target. Therefore, the operation progresses without an explicit action at the target, which is then considered to be *passive*, and, the origin PE must be able to perform all the necessary steps to issue and complete the communication without explicit actions from the target. In particular, the target doesn't call an operation to provide the address of the target buffer, so the origin must be able to locate this memory location (which is usually simple, thanks to the symmetric address space).

Synchronization Differences: Although MPI provides an explicit synchronization operation (*i.e.*, `MPI_Barrier`), most MPI two-sided communication operations carry an implicit synchronization semantic. As long as a process does not pass a particular memory location as a buffer in one of the MPI communication functions, the process knows it enjoys an exclusive use of that memory location, and it cannot be read from, nor written to, by any other process, until it is explicitly exposed by an MPI operation. Similarly, when the Send or Recv operations complete, the process knows that any exposure of that memory has ceased, and once again that memory can be considered exclusive. However, this is not true in the one-sided communication model, where a process can be the target of an operation at any time and the symmetric memory is exposed by default, at all times. As a consequence, when a process performs a `shmem_put`[2], it cannot rely on a corresponding `MPI_Irecv` to implicitly synchronize on the availability of the target buffer, and that synchronization must now be explicit. OpenSH-MEM indeed provides a more flexible set of explicit synchronization operations, like `shmem_fence`, which guarantees ordering between two operations issued at that origin; `shmem_quiet`, which guarantees completion of all operations issued at that origin (including remote completion); and `shmem_barrier_*`, a set of group synchronizations that also complete all operations that have been posted

---

[2] For brevity, in this paper we use the simplified nomenclature `shmem_put`, `shmem_get`, which are not actual OpenSHMEM functions, but refer to the actual typed operations (like `shmem_double_put`, `shmem_long_get`, etc.).

prior to the barrier. Although the explicit management of synchronization can be complex, compared to the implicit synchronizations provided by the two-sided model, the cost of synchronizing can be amortized over a large number of operations, and thereby has the potential to improve the performance of applications that exchange a large number of small messages.

Collective Operations Differences: MPI proposes a fully featured interface to manage fine grain grouping of processes that participate in communication operations. The communicator concept permits establishing arbitrary groups of processes which can then issue communication operations (collective or otherwise) that span that subgroup only. In contrast, OpenSHMEM attempts to avoid having to perform message matching to reduce the latency, and consequently does not have such fine-grained control over the group of processes participating in a collective operation. OpenSHMEM features two kinds of collective operations, those that involve all PEs (like `shmem_barrier_all`), and those that involve a structured group of PEs, in which processes involved in the communication are those whose identifier is separated by a constant stride, which must be a power of 2. This lower flexibility in establishing groups of processes on which collective operations can operate can cause additional complications. Of particular relevance is the case where a collective synchronization is needed. Because the OpenSHMEM group synchronization operations are operating on groups that do not necessarily match the original grouping from the MPI application (like the *plans* in the `remap_3d` function), one is forced to either (1) use point-to-point synchronizations to construct one's own barrier that maps the PE group at hand, which could prove more expensive than an optimized barrier operation; or (2) use a global synchronization operation that spans all PEs, thereby synchronizing more processes than are necessary, with the potential outcome of harming performance with unnecessary wait time at theses processes.

4   Methodology

In this section we expose the challenges we have faced when porting the `remap_3d` LAMMPS function from MPI to OpenSHMEM. We then discuss a number of optimization strategies for the explicit management of process synchronization.

4.1   MPI Features in the `remap_3d` Function

The `remap_3d` function we focus on in this work employs non-blocking communication primitives to exchange data between MPI processes of a particular subgroup. Peers and message sizes are calculated and obtained from the remap *plan* data structure. Each *plan* corresponds to a subset of processes (in each direction) and is mapped to an MPI communicator. Three nested `for` loops enclose the `MPI_Irecv`, `MPI_Send`, and `MPI_Waitany` calls and form a many-to-many, irregular communication pattern. Of particular interest is the usage of the `MPI_Send` function in the original code, which sequentializes the multiple *sends* from a process, thereby creating a logical ordering and implicit synchronizations between groups of processes.

During the 3D-FFT transpose, the data to be transferred for each PE comes from the *in* buffer, however from non-contiguous memory locations. The MPI implementation packs the scattered data to a contiguous buffer before performing the send operation. Similarly, the receive process stores the incoming data in a temporary contiguous *scratch* buffer as well. Only after the MPI_Irecv is issued can the data reach the target *scratch* buffer. The received data is then unpacked to the corresponding locations in the *out* buffer.

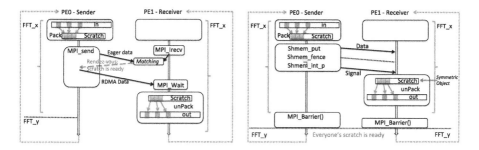

Fig. 2. Communication pattern between two processes, with MPI (left), and OpenSH-MEM (right). For simplification, in the figure, a process is shown as having an exclusive role; in reality every process is both a sender and a receiver with multiple peers during each FFT iteration.

4.2   Initial Porting Effort

In this section we discuss the porting effort to create a basic OpenSHMEM code which is functionally equivalent to the original MPI remap_3d function. Different performance optimizations will be presented in later sections.

From two-sided to one-sided: The two-sided MPI_Send and MPI_Irecv pair can be transformed into a one-sided operation by either issuing a shmem_put at the sender, or a shmem_get at the receiver. In this test case, shmem_put is selected because it improves the opportunity for communication and computation overlap. With the shmem_get semantic, the operation completes when the output buffer has been updated (that is, the communication has completed). Essentially, shmem_get is a blocking operation, and there are no non-blocking variants in the current OpenSHMEM specification. Therefore, in a single threaded program, shmem_get leaves little opportunity for initiating concurrent computations. The shmem_put semantic is more relaxed: the shmem_put operation blocks until the input buffer can be reused at the origin. It does not block until the remote completion is achieved at the target, which means that the operation may complete while communication is still ongoing (especially on short messages). More importantly, the approach closely matches the original MPI code logic, in which computation is executed at the receiver after posting non-blocking MPI_Irecv

```
1   ...
2   shmem_int_max_to_all(&scratch_size, &scratch_size, 1, 0, 0, nprocs,
3                       pWrk1, pSync1);
4   plan->scratch = (FFT_DATA *) shmem_malloc(scratch_size*sizeof(FFT_DATA));
5   ...
```

Listing 1.1. Allocating the *scratch* buffers in the Partitioned Global memory space, as needed for making them targets in **shmem_put**.

```
1   ...
2   plan->remote_offset = (int *) shmem_malloc(nprocs*sizeof(int));
3   for( i = 0; i < plan->nrecv; i++)
4     shmem_int_p(&plan->remote_offset[me], plan->recv_bufloc[i],
5                plan->recv_proc[i]);
6   shmem_fence();
7   ...
```

Listing 1.2. Exchanging the offsets in the target scratch buffers; a parameter to **shmem_put** that was not required with **MPI_Send**.

operations so as to overlap the communication progress, meanwhile blocking sends are used, which have the same local completion semantic as **shmem_put** operations.

Allocating the Symmetric Scratch Buffers: In **shmem_put**, the target data buffer (the *scratch* buffer in our case) must be globally addressable. Hence, the memory space referenced by **plan->scratch** is allocated in the partitioned global address space of OpenSHMEM (line 4 in Listing 1.1). The user is responsible for ensuring that the **shmem_malloc** function is called with identical parameters at all PEs (a requirement to ensure that the allocated buffer is indeed symmetrical). As a consequence, although processes may receive a different amount of data during the irregular communication pattern, the *scratch* buffer must still be of an identical size at all PEs, which must be sufficient to accommodate the maximum size across all PEs. This concept simplifies the management of the global memory space at the expense of potentially increasing the memory consumption at some PEs. Another benign consequence is the need to determine, upon the creation of the *plan* structure, the largest memory space among all PEs (line 2 in Listing 1.1).

Irregular Communication Patterns and Target Offsets: Except for the above communication semantics difference, most of the communication parameters at the sender remain the same (*e.g.*, send buffer address and size, target peer processes). A notable exception is that, unlike in the two-sided model in which the receiver is in charge of providing the target buffer address during the **MPI_Irecv**, in the OpenSHMEM version it must be known at the origin before issuing the **shmem_put**. Although the *scratch* buffers are in the symmetric address space, and it is therefore simple to compute the start address of this buffer, the particular offset at which a process writes into the *scratch* buffer is dependent upon the cumulative size of messages sent by processes whose PE identifier is lower. As the communication pattern is irregular, that offset is not symmetric between the different PEs and cannot be inferred at the origin independently. Ultimately, this complication stems from the different synchronization models between one-sided and two-sided operations: as the sender doesn't synchronize to establish a rendezvous with the receiver before performing the remote update, in the one-sided model, the target address must be pre-exchanged explicitly. Fortunately, we noted that, in the `remap_3d` function, the offset in the target buffer is invariant for a particular *plan*, hence we only need to transmit the offset in the target buffer to the sender once, when the `remap_3d` *plan* is initially created. An extra buffer named `plan->remote_offset` is allocated in the *plan*, and used to persistently store the offsets in the peers target buffer locations, as shown in Listing 1.2. When the same *plan* is executed multiple times, `shmem_put` operations can thereby be issued directly without further exchanges to obtain the target offset.

Signaling `shmem_put` *Operations Completion:* The original MPI program can rely on the implicit synchronization carried by the explicit exposure of the memory buffers between the `MPI_Irecv`, `MPI_Send`, and `MPI_Waitany` operations in order to track completion of communication operations. In the OpenSHMEM-based implementation, the target of a `shmem_put` is passive, and cannot determine if all the data has been delivered from the operation semantic only. To track the completion of the `shmem_put` operations, we add an extra array `plan->remote_status` which contains the per origin readiness of the target buffer. The statuses are initialized as `WAIT` before any communication happens. After the `shmem_put`, the sender uses a `shmem_int_p` to update the status at the target to `READY`. A `shmem_fence` is used between `shmem_put` and `shmem_int_p` to ensure the order of remote operations. The target PEs snoop the status memory locations to determine the completion of the `shmem_put` operations from peers.

Signaling Target Buffer Availability: It is worth noting that the same remap *plan* is used multiple time during the 3d-FFT process. Hence the scratch buffer could be overwritten by the next `shmem_put`, if the sender computes faster and enters the next iteration before the data is unpacked at the receiver. It is henceforth necessary to protect the scratch buffer from early overwrite. In the initial version, we implemented this receive buffer readiness synchronization in OpenSHMEM with an `MPI_Barrier` (this version of the code thereafter referred to as *Hybrid-Barrier*). We use an `MPI_Barrier` rather than any of the `shmem_barrier_*` functions because we need to perform a synchronization in a subgroup whose shape is not amenable to OpenSHMEM group operations, while `MPI_Barrier` is able to force a synchronization on an arbitrary group. Figure 2 reflects the schematic structure of applying `shmem_put` for point-to-point communication in `remap_3d`.

An arguably more natural way of preventing that overwrite would be to synchronize with `shmem_int_p` when the receiver scratch buffer can be reused, and have the sender issue a `shmem_wait` to wait until that target buffer becomes available. However, each process updates the scratch buffers at multiple targets, and this strategy would result in ordering these updates according to the code flow order, rather than performing the `shmem_put` operations opportunistically on the first available target. Hence, it would negate one of the advantages over the traditional `MPI_Send` based code, without making the overlap of computation and communication more likely when uneven load balance can make some targets significantly slower than others. We will discuss alternative approaches that avoid this caveat in the optimization Sect. 4.3.

4.3   Optimizations

Non-blocking `shmem_put` *to Avoid Packing Data:* As mentioned above, the MPI implementation of LAMMPS packs the non-contiguous data into a contiguous buffer before sending. A root reason comes from the higher cost of sending multiple short MPI messages compared to a single long one. The one-sided model, and the decoupling of the transfer and synchronization offer an opportunity for reaching better performance with OpenSHMEM when multiple small messages have to be sent, henceforth opening the possibility to directly transfer small, scattered data chunks without first copying into an intermediate pack buffer. As an example, `shmem_put` demonstrates a great performance advantage for sending multiple small messages when it is implemented over the `dmapp_put_nbi` function, a non-blocking implicit *put* in the Cray DMAPP API [1].

Still based on the *HybridBarrier*, a new version (called *NoPack*) removes the data packing. Each PE transfers the scattered data of size *nfast* to its peers directly, without resorting to an intermediate pack buffer. To transfer a full sub-domain of size *nslow* × *nmid* × *nfast*, a number of *nslow* × *nmid* `shmem_put` operations are required.

Eliminating Synchronization Barriers: In the *HybridBarrier* version, MPI point-to-point communications are replaced with OpenSHMEM one-sided communication semantics. To enforce synchronization between a sender and a receiver, a polling mechanism is employed. However, even with such a mechanism, an additional synchronization, in the initial OpenSHMEM version implemented with an `MPI_Barrier`, is still needed to prevent the next iteration from issuing `shmem_put` and modifying the dataset on which the current iteration is computing. This barrier could cause some performance loss, especially at large scale or when the load is not perfectly balanced.

In the *ChkBuff* version, the barrier is replaced by a fine grain management of the availability of the *scratch* buffer. A pair of communication statuses, `WAIT` and `READY`, are introduced to mark the status of the receiver's *scratch* buffer. A new array `plan->local_remote_status` stores, at the sender, the statuses of target receive buffers at all remote PEs. Before issuing a remote write on a particular PE's *scratch* buffer, the origin checks the availability status of the buffer in its local array. If the status is still set to `WAIT`, the `shmem_put` is delayed to a later date when, hopefully, the target PE will have unpacked the *scratch* buffer, thereby making it safe for reuse. When the target finishes unpacking the *scratch* buffer, it remotely toggles the status at the sender to `READY` (with a `shmem_int_p` operation), to inform the sender that it may start issuing `shmem_put` operations safely.

These synchronizations mimic the establishment of rendezvous between two-sided matching send-recv pairs. However, the MPI two-sided rendezvous can start at the earliest when both the sender and the receiver have posted the operations. In contrast, in the one-sided version, the receiver can toggle the availability status much earlier at the sender, as soon as the *unpack* operation is completed, which makes for a very high probability that the status is already set to `READY` when the sender checks for the availability of the target buffer. Unfortunately, we found that on many OpenSHMEM implementations, the delivery of `shmem_int_p` may be lazy, and delayed, negating the aforementioned advantage. The simple addition of a `shmem_quiet` call after all `shmem_int_p` have been issued is sufficient to force the immediate delivery of these state changes, and henceforth improves the probability that the state is already set to `READY` when a sender checks the status.

Opportunistic Unpacking: In the *ChkBuff* implementation, a PE unpacks its incoming data only after it completed the puts for all the outgoing data. The slightly modified *AdvChkBuff* version embraces a more dynamic, opportunistic ordering of the *unpack* operations. After issuing the `shmem_put` targeting the ready peers, the sender skips the peers which are still marked as in state `WAIT`, and instead switches to the task of unpacking the available incoming data. Before the next iteration, the sender then checks if it still has un-issued `shmem_put` operations from the current *plan* and satisfies them at this point. A major advantage of this method is that it overlaps the rendezvous synchronization wait time at the sender with data unpacking.

A design feature in the LAMMPS communication pattern, however, adds some complexity to the *AdvChkBuff* strategy. In the same `remap_3d`, the *in* and *out* buffers could point to the same memory blocks, in certain cases. This is not an issue when a PE sends out (or packs) all the outgoing data from the *in* buffer before it starts unpacking the received data from the *scratch* buffer. However, in the *AdvChkBuff* strategy, the unpack operation can happen before `shmem_put`. A memory block from the *in* buffer, where the data is waiting to be transferred to a slow PE, could thereby be mistakenly overwritten by the unpacking of the *scratch* buffer, touching that same block through the aliased pointer in the *out* buffer. This unexpected memory sharing between the two data buffers obviously threatens program correctness. To resolve this cumbersome sharing, in the conditional case where that behavior manifests, a temporary duplicate of the *out* buffer is allocated, and the unpack happens in that copy instead. The next iteration of the 3D-FFT will then consider that buffer as the input memory space, and the original buffer is discarded when the iteration completes (hence the `shmem_put` operations have all completed as well).

5   Evaluation

5.1   Experimental Setup

During the evaluation, we perform both strong and weak scaling experiments. In both cases we consider the *rhodopsin protein simulation* input problem. For the strong scaling case, the input problem size remains constant at $8 \times 8 \times 8 \times 32\,\mathrm{K}$ atoms. For the weak scaling tests, the input problem size is set proportionally to the number of PEs, so that each processor handles a load of $32\,\mathrm{K}$ atoms.

The evaluations are performed on Titan, a Cray XK7 supercomputer located at ORNL (with Cray-MPICH 6.3.0 and Cray-shmem 6.3.0 software stacks). On this machine, even when two different allocations request the same number of nodes, they may be deployed on different physical machines, connected by a different physical network topology. This has been known to cause undesired performance variability that prevents directly comparing the performance obtained from different allocations. We eliminate this effect by comparing MPI versus OpenSHMEM on the same allocation, and by taking averages over 10 samples of each experiment. We present the total time of the LAMMPS application with error bars to illustrate any increase (or lack thereof) in the performance variability, and we then present the speedup of the considered OpenSHMEM enhanced variants over the MPI implementation.

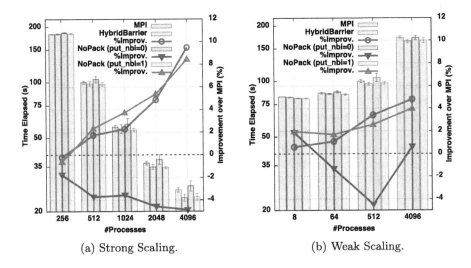

(a) Strong Scaling.   (b) Weak Scaling.

Fig. 3. Total LAMMPS execution time comparison between the following versions: original MPI, *HybridBarrier*, and *NoPack* (with and w/o non-blocking `shmem_put`).

5.2   Comparison Between the *HybridBarrier* and MPI Versions

Figure 3 presents the strong scaling and weak scaling of LAMMPS for the original version where the `remap_3d` function is purely implemented with MPI, and the two hybrid versions (*HybridBarrier* and *NoPack*) where the `remap_3d` function features `shmem_put` communication and OpenSHMEM based communication completion signaling; yet the protection against premature inter-iteration data overwrite relies on an `MPI_Barrier` synchronization. The first observation is that the standard deviation of results is very similar between all versions. The conversion to OpenSHMEM has not increased the performance variability. In terms of speedup, the *HybridBarrier* version enjoys better performance than the MPI version in all cases. The strong scaling experiments demonstrate an improvement from 2 % at 512 PEs, to over 9 % at 4096 PEs, which indicates that the OpenSHMEM APIs indeed accelerate the whole communication speed by amortizing the cost of multiple communication in each synchronization. This is mainly due to the per-communication cost of synchronization; in the original loop over MPI_Send, each individual communication synchronizes with the matching receive, in order; in contrast, and despite the coarse granularity of the MPI_Barrier synchronization, which may impose unnecessary wait times between imperfectly load balanced iterations, the cost of synchronizing in bulk numerous shmem_put operations to multiple targets is amortized over more communications and permits a relaxed ordering between the *puts*. Even in the weak scaling case, in which the communication speed improvement is mechanically proportionally diminished, the *HybridBarrier* version still outperforms the MPI version by 4 % at 4096 PEs, and as the system scale grows, the performance benefit of OpenSHMEM increases, which indicates that the OpenSHMEM programming approach has the potential to exhibit better scalability. One has to remember that these improvements are pertaining to the modification of a single function in LAMMPS, which represents approximately 30 % of the total communication time, meanwhile the communication time is only a fraction of the total time. Such levels of communication performance improvements are indeed significant, and would be even more pronounced should all MPI operations, which are still accounting for the most communication time in the hybrid version of LAMMPS, were ported to OpenSHMEM.

5.3   Consequences of Avoiding Packing

Figure 3 also compares the *NoPack* version to the MPI version. When the default environment respects the full, blocking specification for shmem_put operations (DMAPP_PUT_NBI=0), the performance of the *NoPack* version is reduced compared to both the MPI and *HybridBarrier* versions, which both pack the data. With this strict semantic, the injection rate for small messages is limited by the wait time to guarantee that the source buffer can be reused immediately. On the Cray system, the parameter (DMAPP_PUT_NBI=1) permits relaxing the shmem_put operation semantic: the shmem_put operations are allowed to complete immediately, but the source buffer can be modified only after a subsequent synchronization operation (like a shmem_quiet) has been issued. With this option, neither the MPI nor the *NoPack* versions performance are modified (an expected result, that parameter has no effect on MPI, and the *HybridBarrier* version exchanges large messages, and is therefore essentially bandwidth limited). However, the *NoPack* version's performance improves tremendously, as the injection rate for small messages is greatly increased. This observation provides strong evidence that the addition of a non-blocking shmem_put could result in significant benefits for some application patterns with a large number of small size message exchanges.

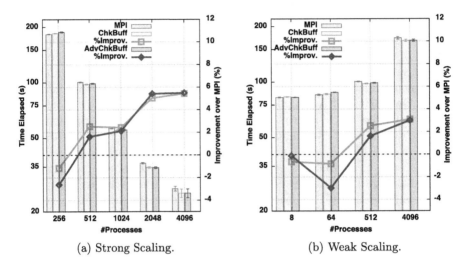

(a) Strong Scaling.   (b) Weak Scaling.

Fig. 4. Total LAMMPS execution time comparison between the following versions: original MPI, *ChkBuff*, and *AdvChkBuff*.

However, as is illustrated in the `remap_3d` function, the packing strategy proves to be an effective workaround: even with non-blocking puts, the *NoPack* version closely matches the performance of the *HybridBarrier* version.

5.4   Performance When Eliminating Group Barriers

The goal of the *ChkBuff* and *AdvChkBuff* versions is to eliminate the group synchronization, employed in the *HybridBarrier* version, that avoid the premature overwrite of the *scratch* buffer by a process that has advanced to the next iteration. Their performance is compared to the MPI version in Fig. 4. The strong scaling of these versions (Fig. 4a) generally perform better than the MPI version, with a 2 % improvement from 512 PEs, and upto 5 % for 4096 PEs. In the weak scaling case, the benefit manifests only for larger PEs counts, with a 3 % improvement.

However, when comparing to the *HybridBarrier* version, presented in the previous Fig. 3, no further performance improvement is achieved. Although the barrier has been removed, it is likely that the introduction of synchronization between pairs of peers still transitively synchronize these same processes. In addition, the busy waiting loop on the peer's buffer status scans the memory and increases the memory bus pressure. It finally appears that, in the OpenSHMEM model, trying to optimize the scope of synchronizations can result in decreasing performance, by synchronizing at too fine a granularity, which actually mimics the traditional implicit synchronization pattern found in MPI two-sided applications.

5.5   Discussion

This porting effort has led to a few observations on the entire process. Today, MPI is considered as the de-facto programming paradigm for parallel applications, and PGAS type languages are still only challengers. Shifting from one programming model to another is not an easy task: it takes time and effort to educate the developers about the new concepts, and then correctly translate the application from one programming paradigm to another.

The Good: Although MPI is a more stable, well-defined API, PGAS based approaches have clear advantages for some types of usage patterns. Until Open-SHMEM reaches the same degree of flexibility and adaptability, being able to compose the two programming paradigms in the context of the same application is a clear necessity. Our experience confirmed that it is indeed possible to mix the programming models, and to upgrade an application in incremental steps, focusing on performance critical routines independently in order to take advantage of the strong features of each model, and improve the performance and scalability of a highly-optimized MPI application.

An area where the PGAS model exhibit a clear advantage over MPI is the handling of unexpected messages. when MPI applications get out of sync due to imbalance in the workload or system noise, most messages become unexpected, forcing the MPI library to buffer some data internally to delay the delivery until the posting of the corresponding receive call. This temporary buffering has an impact on the memory accesses as it implies additional memory copies and thus extra overhead on the memory bus. As the memory is always exposed in OpenSHMEM, even when the target is passive, this pathological usage pattern cannot be triggered. In exchange, some of the implicit synchronization semantic carried by the send-recv model is lost, and explicit synchronization becomes necessary.

The Bad: One of the most unsettling missing features from the OpenSHMEM standard is the capability to work with irregular process groups. The current group collective operations are limited to well defined process topologies, mostly multi-dimensional cubes. As a consequence, they lack the flexibility of their MPI counterparts which operate on communicators and can express collective behaviors across arbitrary groups of processes. This leads to less natural synchronization points, especially in non-symmetric cases.

Another missing feature is a standardized support of the non-blocking *put* capabilities of the network. Forcing the shmem_put operation to ignore its strict specification and relaxing the total completion of the operation to the next synchronization does improve tremendously the injection rate for small messages. However, today, one has no portable way to achieve this result in the OpenSH-MEM specification, and relying on packing still remains the best bet to achieve the maximum bandwidth when the input data are scattered.

The Ugly: One of the selling points of OpenSHMEM is the exposure at the user level of *bare metal* network primitives, with a promise for a more direct access to the hardware and higher performance compared with more abstract programming paradigms, such as MPI. However, the restricted API of OpenSHMEM, and especially the lack of high level primitives such as collective communication with neighborhood communication patterns, forces the application developers to design and implement their own synchronization operations, making the applications sensitive to hardware and network topological feature variations. Furthermore, the explicit management of synchronization from the user code (instead of the implicit synchronization carried by the two-sided operations) can result in notable performance differences, depending on the strategy one employs to restore the required synchronization for a correct execution. We found that some theoretically promising optimizations can actually yield a negative effect on overall performance, and that the reasons for these detrimental consequences are often subtle and hard to predict. Overall, the balance between portability and performance is weaker than in MPI.

6   Conclusions and Future Work

In this work, we explore the process of converting the communication-intensive part of an MPI-based application, LAMMPS, to OpenSHMEM. We reveal some major programming challenges introduced by the semantics and syntax differences between the two programing models. We demonstrate how to transform a common communication pattern based on MPI point-to-point communication into the corresponding OpenSHMEM version. We evaluate our work on the Titan supercomputer looking at both strong scaling and weak scaling tests up to 4096 processes. While our work was successful in demonstrating a clear advantage in terms of performance for the OpenSHMEM hybridized version, choosing between different approaches and optimizing is not straightforward. Looking at more details and differences between different versions employing OpenSHMEM reveal counter-intuitive and significant performance differences between the possible explicit synchronization strategies that are not always matching expectations. It becomes apparent that a mechanical conversion from MPI to OpenSHMEM is not the most suitable approach. Instead, extracting the most performance from a programming paradigm requires adapting the underlying algorithm to the concepts exposed by the paradigm, rather than a simple one-to-one translation.

Our future work will address this last point, making deeper changes in the algorithm to avoid the additional synchronizations between processes. This includes investigating the opportunities to reduce the number and scope of synchronizations in the OpenSHMEM-based LAMMPS. We can also combine the presented optimizations, for example investigate if it is possible to remove the packing in the *AdvChkBuff* version. Last, with only a subset of the communication routines upgraded to OpenSHMEM, we have observed a significant reduction in runtime for the entire application. We will therefore identify other communication-intensive functions in LAMMPS and start the process of replacing them with their OpenSHMEM counterparts.

Acknowledgements. This material is based upon work supported by the U.S. Department of Energy, under contract #DE-AC05-00OR22725, through UT Battelle subcontract #4000123323. The work at Oak Ridge National Laboratory (ORNL) is supported by the United States Department of Defense and used the resources of the Extreme Scale Systems Center located at the ORNL.

References

1. Using the GNI and DMAPP APIs. Technical Report S-2446-3103, Cray Inc. (2011). http://docs.cray.com/books/S-2446-3103/S-2446-3103.pdf
2. OpenSHMEM application programming interface (version 1.2). Technical report, Open Source Software Solutions, Inc. (OSSS) (2015). http://www.openshmem.org
3. Barriuso, R., Knies, A.: SHMEM's user's guide for C. Technical report, Cray Research Inc. (1994)
4. Gerstenberger, R., Besta, M., Hoefler, T.: Enabling highly-scalable remote memory access programming with MPI-3 one sided. Sci. Program. **22**(2), 75–91 (2014). doi:10.3233/SPR-140383
5. Jose, J., Potluri, S., Subramoni, H., Lu, X., Hamidouche, K., Schulz, K., Sundar, H., Panda, D.K.: Designing scalable out-of-core sorting with hybrid MPI+PGAS programming models. In: Proceedings of the 8th International Conference on Partitioned Global Address Space Programming Models, PGAS 2014, pp. 7:1–7:9. ACM, New York (2014). doi:10.1145/2676870.2676880
6. Jose, J., Potluri, S., Tomko, K., Panda, D.K.: Designing scalable graph500 benchmark with hybrid MPI+OpenSHMEM programming models. In: Kunkel, J.M., Ludwig, T., Meuer, H.W. (eds.) ISC 2013. LNCS, vol. 7905, pp. 109–124. Springer, Heidelberg (2013)
7. Li, M., Lin, J., Lu, X., Hamidouche, K., Tomko, K., Panda, D.K.: Scalable MiniMD design with hybrid MPI and OpenSHMEM. In: Proceedings of the 8th International Conference on Partitioned Global Address Space Programming Models, PGAS 2014, pp. 24:1–24:4. ACM, New York (2014). doi:10.1145/2676870.2676893
8. Li, M., Lu, X., Potluri, S., Hamidouche, K., Jose, J., Tomko, K., Panda, D.: Scalable graph500 design with MPI-3 RMA. In: 2014 IEEE International Conference on Cluster Computing (CLUSTER), pp. 230–238, September 2014. doi:10.1109/CLUSTER.2014.6968755
9. MPI Forum. MPI: A Message-Passing Interface Standard (Version 2.2). High Performance Computing Center Stuttgart (HLRS), September 2009
10. Plimpton, S.: Parallel FFT package. Technical report, Sandia National Labs. http://www.sandia.gov/~sjplimp/docs/fft/README.html
11. Plimpton, S.: Fast parallel algorithms for short-range molecular dynamics. J. Comput. Phys. **117**(1), 1–19 (1995). doi:10.1006/jcph.1995.1039
12. Poole, S.W., Hernandez, O.R., Kuehn, J.A., Shipman, G.M., Curtis, A., Feind, K.: OpenSHMEM - toward a unified RMA model. In: Padua, D.A. (ed.) Encyclopedia of Parallel Computing, pp. 1379–1391. Springer, Heidelberg (2011). doi:10.1007/978-0-387-09766-4_490
13. Pophale, S., Nanjegowda, R., Curtis, T., Chapman, B., Jin, H., Poole, S., Kuehn, J.: OpenSHMEM Performance and Potential: An NPB Experimental Study. In: Proceedings of the 6th Conference on Partitioned Global Address Space Programming Model, PGAS 2012. ACM, New York (2012)
14. Vetter, J.S., McCracken, M.O.: Statistical scalability analysis of communication operations in distributed applications. SIGPLAN Not. **36**(7), 123–132 (2001). doi:10.1145/568014.379590

Scalable Out-of-core OpenSHMEM Library for HPC

Antonio Gómez-Iglesias[1]([✉]), Jérôme Vienne[1], Khaled Hamidouche[2],
Christopher S. Simmons[3], William L. Barth[1], and Dhabaleswar Panda[2]

[1] Texas Advanced Computing Center, The University of Texas at Austin,
Austin, TX, USA
agomez@tacc.utexas.edu
http://www.tacc.utexas.edu

[2] Department of Computer Science and Engineering, The Ohio State University,
Columbus, OH, USA

[3] Institute for Computational Engineering and Sciences (ICES),
The University of Texas at Austin, Austin, TX, USA

Abstract. Many HPC applications have memory requirements that
exceed the typical memory available on the compute nodes. While many
HPC installations have resources with very large memory installed, a
more portable solution for those applications is to implement an out-of-
core method. This out-of-core mechanism offloads part of the data typically onto disk when this data is not required. However, this presents a
problem in parallel codes since the scalability of this approach is clearly
limited by the disk latency and bandwidth. Moreover, in parallel file systems this design can lead to high loads of the file system and even failures. We present a library that provides the out-of-core functionality by
making use of the main memory of devoted compute nodes. This library
provides good performance and scalability and reduces the impact in the
parallel file system by only using the local disk of each node. We have
implemented an OpenSHMEM version of this library and compared the
performance of this implementation with MPI. OpenSHMEM, together
with other Partitioned Global Address Space approaches, represent one
of the approaches for improving the performance of parallel applications
towards the exascale. In this paper we show how OpenSHMEM represents an excellent approach for this type of application.

1 Introduction

Out-of-core methods represent a very interesting alternative for codes with large
memory requirements. In cases where the main memory is not enough to keep
all of the data required by the computation, additional resources can be used
to temporarily store some part of it. Typically data is temporarily stored onto
disk to be retrieved when needed. The problem of this approach is the very low
performance of this model, since access to local disk is slow, and its low scalability for large scale problems. However, out-of-core is critical in many large scale
applications designed to run in distributed clusters. Modern clusters present an

© Springer International Publishing Switzerland 2015
M. Gorentla Venkata et al. (Eds.): OpenSHMEM 2015, LNCS 9397, pp. 138–153, 2015.
DOI: 10.1007/978-3-319-26428-8_9

increasing number of nodes while the memory per node is not significantly changing. Several reasons lead to this: cost of memory, energy consumption, efficiency,
and so on. Therefore, applications that could take advantage of the increased
number of cores, find a bottleneck in the memory installed on each node.

As stated above, one typical approach is to offload the data that does not
fit into memory onto disk. This is the typical scenario that has been used
by several applications in different scientific fields, like graphics [4,7] or linear algebra [11]. There are also efforts to improve the performance of these
applications by improving the prefetching in the code [2]. However, this solution
presents a problem with its scalability; when the number of processes doing I/O
increases, the performance of the file system might degrade. In global file systems, this can even lead to timeouts in the file system since this system is not
capable of keeping up with the number of I/O requests. This cannot only affect
the performance, but it can also have a negative impact on other users of the file
system. Some efforts can be found focused on using local disk based solutions for
parallel problems [1]. However, when focusing in performance, I/O is a very slow
operation when compared to accessing main memory. On large clusters, where
the number of available nodes is high, using the main memory of some nodes
instead of the local or parallel file system represents a more optimal approach,
with high performance and low dependency on the file system.

Our approach was to design a library that could allow any application to
have access to this out-of-core functionality. This tool would take advantage
of the design of existing clusters, where each node has access to its own main
memory as well as local disk. By using local resources to each node, the idea was
to reduce or even remove the impact on the distributed file system. The library
would use the main memory of nodes devoted just to data management as a
high-performance distributed memory cache. When a core needed more memory
that what it is installed in that particular node, it would offload part of its data
to a remote node. This remote node stored the data in main memory or used
the local disk in the case that no more memory was available on that node.

Originally designed to work with the CFOUR (Coupled-Cluster techniques
for Computational Chemistry) code [10], the main motivations of this out-of-core
library can be resumed as: (i) reduce the I/O load of the file system; (ii) improve
application performance by replacing disk-based I/O with main memory usage
and data transfers across high-speed interconnects; (iii) create a solution that can
adapt to several computing infrastructures; (iv) provide an Application Program
Interface (API) that allows the model to be easily adopted. A previous version
of this library using MPI has been already implemented [9]. However, earlier
research work [6] shows that MPI might not be the best programming model for
applications with irregular communication patterns. Partitioned Global Address
Space (PGAS) models are gaining attraction as the best fit for such patterns.

OpenSHMEM is a standardized API for parallel programming using PGAS
[3]. It represents an attempt to standardized what vendors have been offering to
used shared memory (SHMEM) in distributed environments. The implementations of each vendor have diverged because of the lack of a standard specification.

It is also a library that enables Remote Memory Access (RMA) between multiple processes. SHMEM includes one-sided point-to-point as well as collective communication. Since PGAS models have been defined as a key element in the path to exascale [5], we are interested on studying the performance that can be achieved by this model when compared with MPI, the de facto standard approach in HPC. PGAS models aim at improving programmability by providing a shared memory abstraction while exposing the locality control required for performance.

We want to study if OpenSHMEM represents a good alternative to MPI to implement an out-of-core library. Our interest is to compare how an OpenSHMEM version of our out-of-core library performs against the existing MPI implementation. For this, we carry out an evaluation and comparison of our OpenSHMEM design with the original MPI implementation. In this paper we also present different designs that might be considered for this programming model and study how those designs behave in terms of performance. We have developed a benchmark that uses our out-of-core library. This benchmark is useful to measure the performance of our implementation. Real world applications using this library will benefit from library that provides the best possible performance for different message sizes and core counts. An out-of-core library that uses main memory instead of the filesystem removes many of the problems that applications using traditional implementations of this method pose in large clusters, so this an important type of library to consider with a potential large impact in those applications.

The rest of this paper is as follows: Sect. 2 describes the design of the out-of-core library, while Sect. 3 details some of the specifics of the OpenSHMEM implementation. Section 4 presents a detailed analysis of the results comparing MPI and OpenSHMEM and, finally, Sect. 5 summarizes the work presented.

2   Design

The design of the MPI version of the library has not been modified for this new implementation. The library consists of mainly three stages: (i) initialization; (ii) communication; (iii) termination. During the initialization stage the library initializes a set of performance counters that will be used to provide statistics about the performance achieved and will read a configuration file that indicates some general configuration parameters. These parameters include the maximum amount of main memory that can be used by each process in the memory pool and the maximum size of the file in local disk that each process has access to. This configuration file is only read by one process that will broadcast this information to all the elements involved in the communication process. The performance counters will be collected during the termination process using collective communication. These are the only collectives used in the library.

Most of the exchange of data takes place on the second stage of the execution. This communication, shown in Fig. 1, is a point-to-point communication where the master process (the process which needs to store and retrieve data

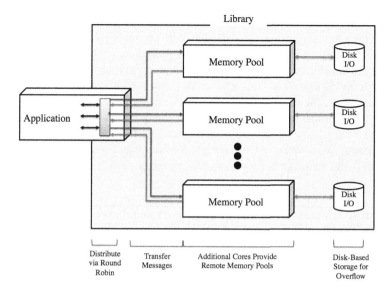

Fig. 1. Overview of the out-of-core library.

from the memory pool) exchanges information with one and only one process in the memory pool. The processes in the memory pool are solely dedicated to performing data related operations (storing and retrieving).

The data is sent to a specific member of the memory pool. The library uses a round-robin allocation mechanism to decide which remote process will receive the data while maintaining a good balance among the available resources. When it needs the data back, it already knows which process has it. Other approaches for deciding the process that will store the data could be considered. For example, giving different priorities to the processes based on the network topology. This would reduce the impact of data transfer in the execution time. However, some level of round-robin or variability would be required in that model: consecutive read/write operations to the same process would lead to delays since the process needs to find the specific data for read operations or store the data in memory for write operations. Reading/writing the data has an associated execution time. In the case of reading, there is not much that can be done to improve the situation. However, in the case of storing, the master can just sent the data and continue to the next process. If the process is the same, it has to wait until the previous transfer has finished. When using a round-robin mechanism, the time between consecutive operations is usually large enough for the previous operation to have finished in the remote process.

The processes in the memory pool group remain in an active polling state waiting for instructions for the next action that they must perform. Algorithm 1 shows the method run by these processes. In Line 1 the processes allocate enough memory to store the maximum data that they can have. This maximum value had been previously broadcast during the initialization stage. In Line 3 the process remains in an active polling state waiting for a message from the master process. This message is a set of fields that indicate the process what to do (store information, retrieve information or finalize). Based on this message, the process will store information in its own main memory or local disk (Line 5). This process starts by receiving the data from the master method, which includes a key that identifies that specific message. This data is then stored in main memory using a container that allows constant time access in local disk. The retrieve mechanism in Line 8 retrieves one of the messages that had been previously stored. The master process sends a request to retrieve the message identified by a key. If the key is found, the message is sent from the memory pool.

Algorithm 1. Main method of memory pool members

```
 1  Initialize_Local_Storage();
 2  while True do
 3  │   action ← Read_Action();
 4  │   switch action do
 5  │   │   case Store
 6  │   │   │   data, key ← Read_Data();
 7  │   │   │   Store_Data (data, key);
 8  │   │   case Retrieve
 9  │   │   │   key ← Read_Key();
10  │   │   │   data ← Retrieve_Data(key);
11  │   │   │   Return_Data(data);
12  │   │   case Finalize
13  │   │   │   return;
```

As it can be seen in Algorithm 1, the elements in the memory pool and the master process need to be synchronized in order to receive and store the correct actions and data. The action that the master process is sending to a remote process is particular to that specific process in that specific point of the program. The master process cannot continue until the element in the memory pool has acknowledged the action or the data have been received so that these messages are not overwritten. The synchronization mechanism in MPI is easily implemented through MPI_Send and MPI_Recv. However in the OpenSHMEM implementation we want to avoid excessive message passing by taking advantage of some of the instructions provided by the API.

3   Implementation

The library is implemented in C++. Its structure allows other developers to easily extend its functionality. Since the goal of this paper is to study the performance of the library specifically from the communication point of view, we have

developed a benchmark that mimics the characteristics of an external application reading and writing fixed records in random order as part of an out-of-core
solve procedure. We have grouped all the store operations at the beginning of
the benchmark and all the retrieve actions after them. This benchmark does not
perform any computation; instead, the application only generates a number of
sequences of values that need to be stored in the memory pool. When those values are later on retrieved from the memory pool, the integrity of the sequences
is checked to test that the process worked without any lost of information.

The processes use the heap memory to store an array. This array will contain
the data being exchanged at any particular time. The slaves keep all the data
they store in a map. When they receive new data that needs to be put in their
memory, they read the shared array and the key sent by the master and put
those two elements into the map. The master process does not have to wait for
the operation of inserting the data in the map to finish. When the data needs to
be restored, the master sends the key that identifies the data, the remote process
retrieves the data associated with that key, and moves the information to the
shared array.

The library is designed so that the processes in the memory pool only perform
the operation of storing/retrieving data. Certain scientific applications with very
large memory requirements can only run in this mode. Although this might
seem to represent a waste of resources, it represents the approach with the best
performance, since the alternative would be to use large files in the filesystem
that would: (i) slow down the computation; (ii) significantly increase the I/O
load in the system.

3.1   Using Locks as Synchronization Mechanism

The algorithm presented in Sect. 2 has a fairly straightforward implementation
using locks. The master process sets or unsets a lock every time it has to access
data in the member of the memory pool. Those processes in the memory pool
check for specific values in some shared variables that indicate the operation that
they have to perform. They also set or unset locks in the master to establish the
communication mechanism.

We used *shmem_set_lock* and *shmem_clear_lock* to implement the locking
mechanism. The performance achieved with this implementation when compared
to MPI was far from optimal as it can be seen in Table 1. In this table we show
the additional percentage of time required by the OpenSHMEM implementation
to run the same benchmark than the MPI implementation. It can be seen how,
especially for small messages, OpenSHMEM was up to 43.22 % slower than MPI.
This difference became smaller when the message size was 32 KB, but it again
increased for larger messages.

The small difference when the message size is 32 KB is due to the default eager
threshold (16 KB for inter-node communication and 8 KB for the intra-node
case). Increasing the threshold value improved the results achieved in the MPI
version. This large difference between the OpenSHMEM and the MPI implementations indicated that either OpenSHMEM was not able to provide good results

Table 1. 128 cores

Message size (KB)	Speed difference
8	39.47 %
16	43.22 %
32	1.19 %
64	15.67 %
128	13.86 %

for this particular problem or that our implementation was far from optimal. Considering that the main difference between the two implementations was the usage of locks in OpenSHMEM, we tried to avoid using them.

3.2 Removing Locks by Implementing an Active Polling Mechanism

A second implementation consisted of removing the locking mechanism and implementing an active polling on the processes involved in the communication. Instead of using *shmem_set_lock* and *shmem_clear_lock*, we used *shmem_wait* to implement our synchronization model. Processes in the memory pool wait until a given order is received using this mechanism. Once the order is received, a process will check for a second value indicating that the data has been received when the operation is storing data, or it will simply put its data into the requesting process memory. The synchronization process is exactly the same one used with locks. This approach significantly improved the results (as shown in Sect. 4).

4 Performance Evaluation

For these results we used the benchmark previously introduced in Sect. 3. We focus on the exchange of data as well as synchronization between the master process and the memory pool. Also, in order to reduce the impact of other factors in the results, none of the cases here presented makes use of the local file system storage that each member of the memory pool has access to. Using the local file system would introduce delays especially during the retrieve stage. On storage, the master process sends the data to the memory pool and continues with the next message without waiting for the process in the memory pool to finalize writing to the local disk.

All the tests have been performed on Stampede[1]. Stampede contains 6400 dual socket eight-core Sandy-Bridge E5-2680 server nodes with 32 GB of memory. The nodes are interconnected by InfiniBand HCAs in FDR mode [12] and the operating system used is CentOS 6.4 with kernel 2.6.32-358.el6. We have used MVAPICH2-X 2.1rc1 [6] as MPI library. The C++ compiler using for these tests is Intel Compiler 14.0.1.

---

[1] https://www.tacc.utexas.edu/stampede/.

For the sake of completeness, we include the latency values achieved with MPI and OpenSHMEM between 2 nodes on Stampede for the OSU Micro-Benchmarks 4.4.1[2]. Figure 2a shows the latency for *put* operations. It can be seen how the MPI implementation using one-sided communication offers the best result in terms of latency. It can also be seen that for OpenSHMEM there is a significant difference for small message sizes when using heap or global, but that difference disappears for larger messages and the total latency is similar to the value achieved with MPI_Send and MPI_Recv. Figure 2b shows the latency for *get* operations. In this operation, MPI still offers the best results but only for large messages. For small messages, OpenSHMEM has a shorter latency when transferring data that is in the stack. Also, for large messages, there is not a significant difference between using data in the heap or the stack memory when using OpenSHMEM. Our OpenSHMEM implementation makes use of both global and heap memory. The MPI version of the library makes use of MPI_Send and MPI_Recv.

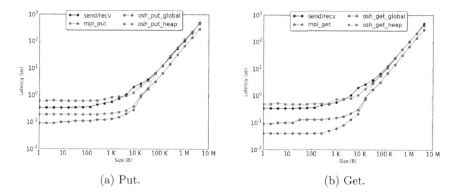

(a) Put.   (b) Get.

Fig. 2. Latency of put/get operations. For completeness we also include the latency of send/recv MPI operations.

4.1 Default MPI Configuration

Figure 3 shows the bandwidth achieved when 64 processes are used when 30000 messages of the sizes specified in the x axis are first sent from the master process to the memory pool (Store) and then those messages are received (Retrieve). We are using all of the cores on each node of Stampede for this test, so considering that each node has 16 cores and 32 GB or RAM, we have a limitation of 128 GB of total memory. A large drop in the MPI store performance can be seen in the figure. That is the effect of the default eager threshold in MVAPICH2-X. Figure 4 shows the execution time for the same test. For this particular case,

---

[2] http://mvapich.cse.ohio-state.edu/benchmarks/.

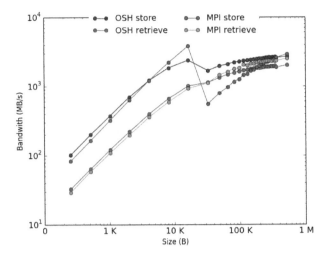

Fig. 3. Bandwidth using 64 processes.

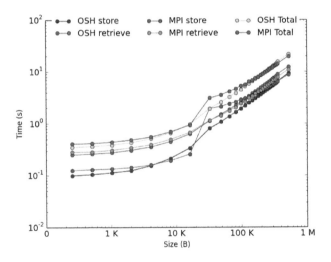

Fig. 4. Timing using 64 processes.

only for medium-sized messages OpenSHMEM outperforms MPI, starting at the default eager threshold value.

We also tried 128 cores (8 nodes, 256 GB of memory). These results are shown in Fig. 5 for the bandwidth and Fig. 6 for the time. Although the results are very similar to those achieved with 64 processes, it is also clear that the bandwidth for larger core counts is lower and the timing is higher. This is due to the optimizations implemented using shared memory by MPI and the impact of intra-node communication.

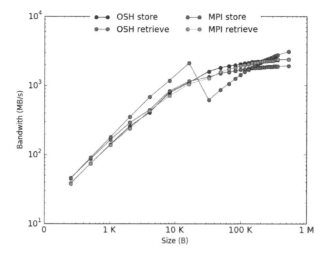

Fig. 5. Bandwidth using 128 processes.

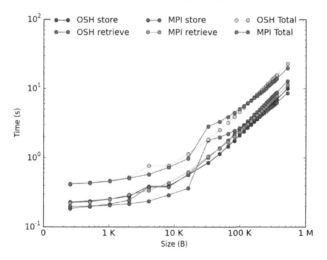

Fig. 6. Timing using 128 processes.

Instead of running more tests with this default configuration, we decided to study the effect of increasing the eager threshold, which should allow the MPI implementation to take advantage of the lower synchronization level. The goal was to find if the differences between the implementations were only due to the rendezvous protocol.

4.2   Using MPI Eager Protocol

For our next tests we increased the value for the eager threshold limit [8] so that we only used this protocol in the inter-node communication. The default

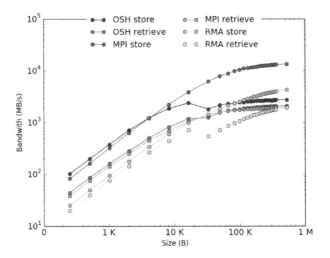

Fig. 7. Bandwidth using 64 processes. Increased eager threshold.

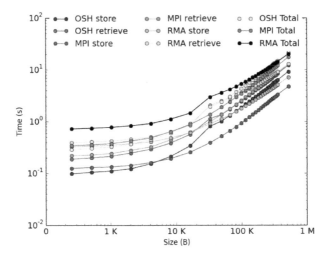

Fig. 8. Timing using 64 processes. Increased eager threshold.

value threshold limit was at the point where the MPI version of the library becomes slower than OpenSHMEM in the previous results. We wanted to study whether this was the cause of that behavior. Increasing this value should make the MPI implementation to take advantage a lower level of synchronism. Since RMA (Remote Memory Access) seemed to have the lowest latency (as it can be seen in Fig. 2a and b, we also implemented a version of the GRVY library using only MPI_Put. Figures 7 and 9 show the resulting bandwidth when using 64 and 128 processes respectively. It can be seen how the large drop in the MPI version disappeared. With this communication protocol, MPI outperforms

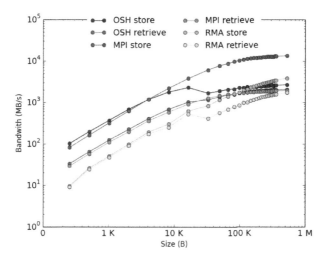

Fig. 9. Bandwidth using 128 processes. Increased eager threshold.

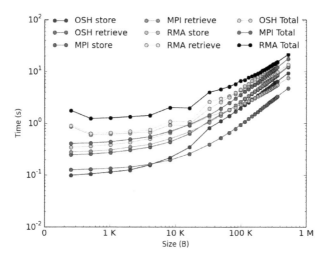

Fig. 10. Timing using 128 processes. Increased eager threshold.

OpenSHMEM for medium size messages (among the messages chosen for these tests). Also for larger sizes it can be seen how the difference between both implementations have increased mainly due to the improvement in the store component of the benchmark in the MPI implementation. Further investigation is required to understand the decrease in the performance of the OpenSHMEM store operations after a given threshold. The testing that we performed with different configuration parameters of MVAPICH2-X did not provide different results and it our research indicates that it is related to memory management in both the master process and the memory pool members. However, this does not

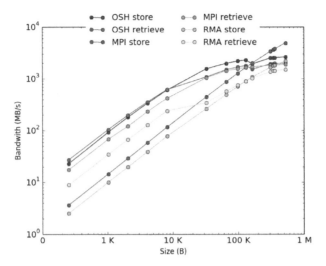

Fig. 11. Bandwidth using 2048 processes. Increased eager threshold.

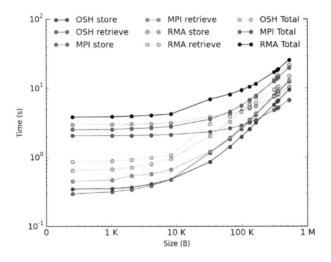

Fig. 12. Timing using 2048 processes. Increased eager threshold.

explain why the results achieved when the default eager threshold was used do not show the same behavior (compare Figs. 5 and 9). The timings for the same number of cores can be seen in Figs. 8 and 10.

For this configuration we tried with a larger number of processes in the memory pool. In this case, we ran with 2048 cores (4 TB of total main memory and 10 TB or local disk) and 4096 cores (8 TB of distributed main memory). For calculations with very large data requirements, it might be necessary to run at this scale in order to avoid using disk for storage. The results can be seen in Figs. 11 and 12 for 2048 cores and Figs. 13 and 14 for 4096 cores. It is important

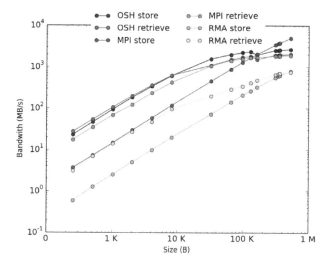

Fig. 13. Bandwidth using 4096 processes. Increased eager threshold.

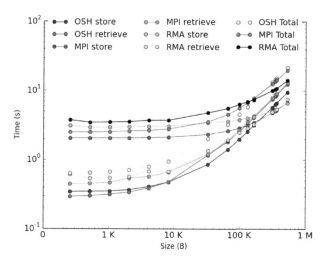

Fig. 14. Timing using 4096 processes. Increased eager threshold.

to mention that we do not include the initialization time in these results and that these figures only consider the time required by the exchange of data between processes. At this scale, it is clear when it becomes optimal to OpenSHMEM instead of MPI. Only for large messages MPI provided better results than Open-SHMEM, and the difference for those sizes was not very significant. However, for small and medium-sized messages OpenSHMEM offered far better results. Also, it can be seen how the RMA implementation always provides the worst results when using 2048 cores, but for larger number of cores it outperforms both

OpenSHMEM and MPI for large messages, even though its performance is very low for smaller messages when compared to OpenSHMEM.

The results suggest that MPI provides better results at small scale. This can be due to a more regular communication pattern. Even at that scale, the difference between MPI and OpenSHMEM is not very large. For increased number of cores, OpenSHMEM becomes an excellent approach, with large differences in performance between OpenSHMEM and MPI. The lighter-weight one-sided communication used by OpenSHMEM allow to achieve these results. The overhead of synchronization of the MPI point-to-point communication represents a bottleneck for that implementation. Also, the optimizations introduced in MVAPICH2-X for PGAS models help allow our OpenSHMEM implementation to outperform the RMA implementation.

5   Conclusion

In this paper we have shown an OpenSHMEM implementation of an out-of-core library that uses the main memory of distributed nodes to efficiently implement this functionality. Our OpenSHMEM implementation is able to outperform MPI or get very similar results to the MPI version. Our results show when it is more interesting from a performance point of view to use OpenSHMEM or MPI when using our out-of-core library. We have also demonstrated how OpenSHMEM represents a great alternative for this library especially when using larger number of cores, which is critical for applications that use out-of-core methods with very large memory requirements, especially when using small and medium-sized messages.

Two different approaches for our OpenSHMEM development have been presented. We have shown how it is critical to choose the best design to attain good results. An active polling mechanism has achieved good results for the communication requirements of our out-of-core library. However, an implementation using locks offered a poor performance when compared to MPI. We have also compared our OpenSHMEM version with RMA, another light-weighted communication model, showing that OpenSHMEM is the best option to consider when using this out-of-core library.

The results indicate that, at large scale, OpenSHMEM is the best option for small and medium-sized messages, while MPI or RMA might be better for large messages. For small numbers of cores, MPI provides better or very similar performance than the OpenSHMEM implementation. Since our interest is to develop a library that can be used by any application that needs to implement an out-of-core mechanism, it is up to the users of the library to decide when to use each implementation of the library.

The OpenSHMEM implementation shows a good scalability in the tests that we have performed. It represents an excellent approach for parallel and distributed implementations of applications. A further exploration of other possible techniques that might help improving the performance of OpenSHMEM is expected as future work. We also plan on considering other PGAS models to study their performance.

Acknowledgment. Research reported in this publication was supported by National Science Foundation under award number 1213084, *Unified Runtime for Supporting Hybrid Programming Models on Heterogeneous Architectures.*

References

1. Bordawekar, R., Choudhary, A., Kennedy, K., Koelbel, C., Paleczny, M.: A model and compilation strategy for out-of-core data parallel programs. In: Proceedings of the Fifth ACM SIGPLAN Symposium on Principles and Practice of Parallel Programming, pp. 1–10. PPOPP 1995, ACM, New York, NY, USA (1995)
2. Brown, A.D., Mowry, T.C., Krieger, O.: Compiler-based I/O prefetching for out-of-core applications. ACM Trans. Comput. Syst. **19**(2), 111–170 (2001)
3. Chapman, B., Curtis, T., Pophale, S., Poole, S., Kuehn, J., Koelbel, C., Smith, L.: Introducing OpenSHMEM: SHMEM for the PGAS community. In: Proceedings of the Fourth Conference on Partitioned Global Address Space Programming Model, pp. 2:1–2:3. PGAS 2010, ACM, New York, NY, USA (2010)
4. Cox, M., Ellsworth, D.: Application-controlled demand paging for out-of-core visualization. In: Proceedings of the 8th Conference on Visualization 1997, pp. 235-ff. VIS 1997, IEEE Computer Society Press, Los Alamitos, CA, USA (1997)
5. Gropp, W.: MPI at exascale: challenges for data structures and algorithms. In: Ropo, M., Westerholm, J., Dongarra, J. (eds.) PVM/MPI. LNCS, vol. 5759, pp. 3–3. Springer, Heidelberg (2009)
6. Jose, J., Zhang, J., Venkatesh, A., Potluri, S., Panda, D.K.D.K.: A comprehensive performance evaluation of openSHMEM libraries on infiniband clusters. In: Poole, S., Hernandez, O., Shamis, P. (eds.) OpenSHMEM 2014. LNCS, vol. 8356, pp. 14–28. Springer, Heidelberg (2014)
7. Lindstrom, P.: Out-of-core simplification of large polygonal models. In: Proceedings of the 27th Annual Conference on Computer Graphics and Interactive Techniques, pp. 259–262. SIGGRAPH 2000, ACM Press/Addison-Wesley Publishing Co., New York, NY, USA (2000)
8. Liu, J., Panda, D.: Implementing efficient and scalable flow control schemes in MPI over InfiniBand. In: 2004 Proceedings of the 18th International Parallel and Distributed Processing Symposium, pp. 183–193, April 2004
9. Simmons, C.S., Schulz, K.W.: A distributed memory out-of-core method on HPC clusters and its application to quantum chemistry applications. In: Proceedings of the 1st Conference of the Extreme Science and Engineering Discovery Environment: Bridging from the eXtreme to the Campus and Beyond, pp. 1:1–1:7. XSEDE 2012, ACM, New York, NY, USA (2012)
10. Simmons, C.S.: Development of a computational framework for quantitative vibronic coupling and its application to the NO_3 radical. Ph.D. thesis, University of Texas at Austin, Austin, May 2012
11. Toledo, S.: A survey of out-of-core algorithms in numerical linear algebra. External Mem. Algorithms Vis. **50**, 161–179 (1999)
12. Vienne, J., Chen, J., Wasi-ur-Rahman, M., Islam, N.S., Subramoni, H., Panda, D.K.: Performance analysis and evaluation of infiniband FDR and 40GigE RoCE on HPC and cloud computing systems. In: IEEE 20th Annual Symposium on High-Performance Interconnects, HOTI 2012, Santa Clara, CA, USA, August 22–24, 2012, pp. 48–55. IEEE Computer Society (2012)

Graph 500 in OpenSHMEM

Eduardo F. D'Azevedo[1](✉) and Neena Imam[2]

[1] Computer Science and Mathematics Division,
Oak Ridge National Laboratory, Oak Ridge, TN 37831, USA
dazevedoef@ornl.gov
[2] Computing and Computational Sciences Directorate,
Oak Ridge National Laboratory, Oak Ridge, TN 37831, USA
imamn@ornl.gov

Abstract. This document describes the effort to implement the Graph 500 benchmark using OpenSHMEM based on the MPI-2 one-side version. The Graph 500 benchmark performs a breadth-first search in parallel on a large randomly generated undirected graph and can be implemented using basic MPI-1 and MPI-2 one-sided communication. Graph 500 requires atomic bit-wise operations on unsigned long integers but neither atomic bit-wise operations nor OpenSHMEM for unsigned long are available in OpenSHEM. Such needed bit-wise atomic operations and support for unsigned long are implemented using atomic condition swap (CSWAP) on signed long integers. Preliminary results on comparing the OpenSHMEM and MPI-2 one-sided implementations on a Silicon Graphics Incorporated (SGI) cluster and the Cray XK7 are presented.

Keywords: Graph 500 · Graph benchmark · OpenSHMEM

This report was prepared as an account of work sponsored by an agency of the United States Government. Neither the United States nor any agency thereof, nor any of their employees, makes any warranty, express or implied, or assumes any legal liability or responsibility for the accuracy, completeness, or usefulness of any information, apparatus, product, or process disclosed, or represents that its use would not infringe privately owned rights. Reference herein to any specific commercial product, process, or service by trade name, trademark, manufacturer, or otherwise, does not necessarily constitute or imply its endorsement, recommendation, or favoring by the United States Government or any agency thereof. The views and opinions of authors expressed herein do not necessarily state or reflect those of the United States Government or any agency thereof. This manuscript has been authored by UT-Battelle, LLC under Contract No. DE-AC05-00OR22725 with the U.S. Department of Energy. The United States Government retains and the publisher, by accepting the article for publication, acknowledges that the United States Government retains a non-exclusive, paid-up, irrevocable, world-wide license to publish or reproduce the published form of this manuscript, or allow others to do so, for United States Government purposes. The Department of Energy will provide public access to these results of federally sponsored research in accordance with the DOE Public Access Plan (http://energy.gov/downloads/doe-public-access-plan).

© Springer International Publishing Switzerland 2015
M. Gorentla Venkata et al. (Eds.): OpenSHMEM 2015, LNCS 9397, pp. 154–163, 2015.
DOI: 10.1007/978-3-319-26428-8_10

Graph 500 in OpenSHMEM   155

1   Introduction

The MPI [5] communication library is the *de facto* standard used by many applications in the area of high performance computation. The traditional and commonly used programming approach of using matched send and receive calls for data transfer and synchronization is called *two-sided communication*. However, for certain unstructured computations, such as graph algorithms for large-scale data analysis, a *one-sided communication* is a more natural programming paradigm. In one-sided communication, a processor can directly access the data in the exposed remote memory of another processor using Put and Get operations. One-sided communication is implemented in libraries such as SHMEM [13], ARMCI [8] and in MPI-2 [7]. One-sided communication is also supported in Partitioned Global Address Space (PGAS) languages such as Co-array Fortran [9], Unified Parallel C (UPC) [4], and Chapel [2].

This document describes the effort to implement the Graph 500 (http:// www.graph500.org) benchmark using OpenSHMEM based on the MPI-2 one-sided version of the benchmark. The Graph 500 benchmark performs a breadth-first search (BFS) in parallel on a large randomly generated undirected graph and has a reference implementation based on using OpenMP on a shared memory machine. For execution on a distributed memory cluster, the benchmark uses basic MPI-1 or MPI-2 one-sided communication. An OpenSHMEM implementation complements the Graph 500 benchmark and allows an interesting comparison of one-sided communication libraries using MPI-2 one-sided and OpenSHMEM implementations.

One major challenge in the implementation is the Graph 500 benchmark is the benchmark requires atomic bit-wise operations (such as bit-wise AND/OR and MIN/MAX) on unsigned long integers. However, neither such atomic operations, nor support for unsigned long integers are available in OpenSHMEM 1.0. In this effort, the needed atomic operations are emulated using atomic condition swap (CSWAP) on signed long integers. Other challenges are in reimplementing a subset of MPI-2 one-sided operations such as MPI_Accumulate and MPI_AlltoAllv in OpenSHMEM.

In Sect. 2, the operations performed in Graph 500 benchmark is described. In Sect. 3 the conversion of the MPI-2 one-sided implementation to OpenSHMEM is presented. Preliminary experimental results comparing the MPI-2 one-side implementation and OpenSHMEM version are presented in Sect. 4, followed by concluding remarks in the final section.

2   Graph 500

The Graph 500 benchmark (http://www.graph500.org) is inspired by the HPL (High Performance Linpack) Top 500 benchmark (http://www.top500.org) used for ranking the top 500 supercomputers. The HPL benchmark mostly measures the floating point capability in solving a large dense matrix problem via LU factorization. This benchmark has very high spatial and temporal locality. In contrast, the Graph 500 benchmark was designed for emulating large-scale data intensive applications (such as computing breadth-first search (BFS) on large undirected graphs) that are not dominated by floating point calculations and has low spatial and temporal locality. This benchmark has fine-grained communication and seemingly random access patterns. The Graph 500 benchmark has reference implementations in GNU Octave (www.octave.org), parallel C version with OpenMP, basic MPI-1 and MPI-2 one-sided communication.

The benchmark proceeds in several phases. The first phase is the parallel generation of graph edges using the Kronecker graph generator, which is similar to the Recursive MATrix (R-MAT) graph generator [1]. The benchmark then records the time for the conversion from the distributed edge list for an undirected graph to a compact representation as compressed storage format. The size of the graph is described by the two parameters `scale_factor` and `edge_factor`. The number of graph vertices is give by 2^{scale_factor} and $2 \times$ `edge_factor` is the average vertex degree. For example, `scale_factor` $= 20$ produces an undirected graph with $2^{20} = 1,048,576$ vertices. The total memory requires is $2^{scale\_factor} \times$ `edge_factor` $\times 2 \times 8$ bytes. For ranking purpose, the benchmark defines several scale settings: toy (2^{26} vertices, 17 GBytes of RAM), mini (2^{29}, 137 GBytes), small (2^{32}, 1.1 TBytes), medium (2^{36}, 17.6 TBytes), large (2^{39}, 140 TBytes), and huge (2^{42}, 1.1 PBytes).

The next stage records the time for the generation of the breadth-first search (BFS) tree on 64 randomly selected vertices. The benchmark collects statistics on the run-time for construction of BFS search tree. A validation phase checks the correctness of the resulting BFS search tree that it has no cycles, each edge connects vertices that differ by 1 level, and all vertices in the connected component are visited. This verification of BFS search tree can be time consuming and is also used to estimate the performance of the computer system by measuring the number of traversed edges per second (TEPS).

3   Conversion to OpenSHMEM

The pure OpenSHMEM [3, 10–12] implementation of Graph 500 was performed using the MPI-2 one-sided code base. Although the Graph 500 benchmark has the option of writing out the generated graph into file using MPI parallel file I/O operations, this capability was not implemented in the OpenSHMEM version since there is no equivalent capability in OpenSHMEM.

One major challenge in the conversion to OpenSHMEM is the Graph 500 benchmark has the option to encode edge information in a packed format in unsigned long integer. It also uses unsigned long integers as bit arrays to keep track of which vertices have been visited in the breadth-first search. For example, atomic minimum on signed long and atomic bit-wise OR operations on unsigned long are performed using `MPI_Accumulate`. The atomic minimum and operations on unsigned long are not natively supported in OpenSHMEM 1.0 specification (http://www.openshmem.org). One contribution of this effort is the development a library that implements such remote operations on unsigned long integer type. In particular, atomic operations, such as minimum and bit-wise OR, are implemented using atomic conditional swap (CSWAP) for signed long integer.

Graph 500 in OpenSHMEM   157

The following documents some of the details in converting from MPI-2 one-side implementation to OpenSHMEM.

The array passed to `MPI_Win_create` is the MPI window for remote one-sided access. This array is allocated using `shmalloc`. The global maximum array size across all processing elements (PE) is first determined to ensure all calls to `shmalloc` are identical. The `MPI_Win_free` is a collective operation and this is emulated using `shmem_barrier_all`. Note that the call `MPI_Win_fence` is not equivalent to `shmem_fence` nor `shmem_quiet` since the `MPI_Win_fence` is a collective operation. This is emulated using `shmem_barrier_all`.

There is a direct correspondence between `MPI_Put` with `shmem_putmem` and `MPI_Get` with `shmem_getmem`. Atomic minimum on signed long integer can be implemented using conditional swap (CSWAP) on signed long (see Fig. 1). The call to atomic `shmem_long_fadd` is first used to retrieve the current value. A small optimization checks first whether the remote target value is already smaller than the procedure argument value before entering the loop to use atomic conditional swap `shmem_long_cswap`. Similarly, atomic bit-wise OR on unsigned long can be implemented using conditional swap (CSWAP) on signed long (see Fig. 2). Note that to maintain full portability, a call to `memcpy` is used (instead of simple direct assignment) to ensure that no changes in bit pattern can occur due to integer overflow or integer conversion for assignment between unsigned long and long integers.

A call to `MPI_Allreduce` with bit-wise OR on a single unsigned long variable is currently emulated in a straight-forward $O(\text{npes})$ manner since this is not expected to be a time consuming operation. A call to `MPI_Allreduce` with maximum value reduction on a single unsigned long variable can also be implemented directly in OpenSHMEM using the long double type in `shmem_longdouble_max_to_all` if long double type has sufficient precision in the mantissa. This is condition is checked as (`sizeof(long double) > sizeof(unsigned long)`).

4   Experiments

The OpenSHMEM version of Graph 500 was executed on the Bazooka SGI cluster and on the Cray XK7 Chester cluster in the Oak Ridge Leadership Computing Facility. The default `edge_factor=16` (average vertex degree was 32) was used in all cases. Here the number of tasks is equivalent to the number of processing elements (pe) given by `shmem_npes`. The results are summarized in the following subsections.

4.1   SGI MPT

Bazooka is a 12-node SGI Altix XE1300 cluster. Each XE340 compute node has two 2.8 GHz/12 M/6.4 GT/s 95 W Six Core Xeon X5660 processors (total 12 physical cores, or 24 logical cores with Intel Hyper-Threading enabled), 48 GBytes of 1333 MHz registered DDR3 DRAM, and a Mellanox ConnectX

```
 1  void shmem_long_min (long *gvar, long value, int pe)
 2  {
 3    long cval = 0;
 4    long lval = 0;
 5    int is_done = 0;
 6
 7    assert( (0 <= pe) && (pe < shmem_n_pes()) );
 8
 9    lval = shmem_long_fadd( gvar, (long) 0, pe );
10    if (value < lval) {
11      do
12      {
13          cval = shmem_long_cswap (gvar, lval, MIN (lval, value), pe);
14          is_done = (cval == lval) || (cval <= value);
15          lval = cval;
16      }
17      while (!is_done);
18      };
19  }
```

Fig. 1. Atomic minimum for long integer implemented using CSWAP.

QDR Infiniband NIC. MPI-2 and SHMEM implementation are available in SGI MPT version 2.03.

Table 1 shows the times (in seconds) for random graph generation with `scale_factor=20`, conversion from edge list representation to compact sparse representation using MPI-2 one-sided and MPT version of OpenSHMEM as printed by the Graph 500 benchmark for different number of tasks on a single node. The graph generation time for OpenSHMEM and for MPI-2 are similar. The time for generation of compressed storage format for OpenSHMEM are lower than for MPI-2.

Table 2 shows the times for BFS using MPI-2 and OpenSHMEM. There was a general trend of decreasing time for OpenSHMEM BFS with increasing number of tasks. The minimum, median, and maximum times for BFS were consistently very similar. The highest performance was with 24 tasks at about 0.7 s.

There was a similar general trend of decreasing run-time for MPI-2 BFS with increasing number of tasks. The minimum, median, and maximum times were consistently very similar. The highest performance with MPI-2 one-sided with 24 tasks was about 1.3 s, which was nearly two times the time using OpenSHMEM (0.7 s).

A larger test case with `scale_factor=26` was attempted using 192 tasks over 8 nodes. However, the implementation with MPI-2 one-sided communication encountered an error about running out of request entries in `MPI_Win_fence` while performing the BFS. It is possible the error was related to too many outstanding requests. The OpenSHMEM implementation was able to complete the computations. For MPI-2, generation time was 13.1 s and construction time was 5.5 s. For OpenSHMEM, generation time was 13.1 s and construction time was 9.8 s. The minimum, median, and maximum times for BFS by OpenSHMEM was 796.5 s, 808.4 s and 818.1 s.

Graph 500 in OpenSHMEM   159

```
1   void shmem_ulong_bor(unsigned long *gvar, unsigned long value, int pe)
2   {
3     /*
4      * perform Bitwise OR
5      */
6     long cval = 0;
7     long lval = 0;
8     unsigned long ulval = 0;
9     unsigned long new_ulval = 0;
10    long new_lval = 0;
11    int is_done = 0;
12
13    assert( (0 <= pe) && (pe < shmem_n_pes()) );
14
15
16    lval = shmem_long_fadd( (long *) gvar, (long) 0, pe );
17
18    do
19      {
20
21        memcpy( &ulval, &lval, sizeof(ulval) );
22        new_ulval = ulval | value;
23        if (new_ulval == ulval) {
24          /* bits set already */
25          break;
26          };
27
28        memcpy( &new_lval, &new_ulval, sizeof(new_lval) );
29
30        cval = shmem_long_cswap ((long *) gvar, lval, new_lval, pe);
31        is_done = (cval == lval);
32        lval = cval;
33
34      }
35    while (!is_done);
36
37  }
```

Fig. 2. Atomic bit-wise OR for unsigned long integer implemented using CSWAP.

4.2 Cray XK7

The Cray XK7 Chester machine in the Oak Ridge Leadership Computing Facility (OLCF) consists of 96 compute nodes. Each compute node has 32 GBytes of memory, one 16-core AMD Opteron 6200 Interlagos processor and a NVidia K20X Kepler Graphics Processing Unit (GPU) with 6 GBytes of device memory. Each Interlagos processor has eight 256-bit floating point compute units shared by 16 integer cores. A variable number of MPI tasks can be spawned on each node. For example, 1 MPI task using all 16 cores and 32 GBytes, or 2 MPI tasks using 8 cores and 16 GBytes per task, upto 16 tasks on each node using 1 core and 2 GBytes per task. Two compute nodes are connected to a Cray Gemini network device (NIC) that has over 160 GBytes/sec of routing capacity. The global network is arranged as a three-dimensional (3D) torus. For this Graph 500 benchmark, only the CPU cores were used and the GPU was untouched.

Table 1. Runtimes (in seconds) for `scale_factor=20` over 1 node

	MPI-2 one-sided		OpenSHMEM	
Tasks	Generation	Construction	Generation	Construction
8	6.3	1.5	6.3	1.7
12	6.3	9.9	6.3	1.8
16	7.0	8.1	7.9	1.9
24	8.0	5.2	7.9	2.0

Table 2. Performance of BFS for `scale_factor=20` using MPI-2 one-sided and Open-SHMEM over 1 node

	MPI-2 BFS time (sec)			OpenSHMEM BFS time (sec)		
Tasks	Minimum	Median	Maximum	Minimum	Median	Maximum
8	2.7	2.7	2.8	1.3	1.3	1.8
12	2.2	2.2	2.2	1.1	1.1	1.2
16	1.8	1.8	1.8	0.9	1.0	1.0
24	1.3	1.3	1.4	0.7	0.7	0.7

Table 3. Runtimes (in seconds) for `scale_factor=20` over 16 Cray XK7 nodes

	MPI-2 one-sided		OpenSHMEM	
Tasks	Generation	Construction	Generation	Construction
64	14.4	2.0	14.9	1.8
128	15.1	2.2	14.9	2.0
256	19.1	3.0	20.5	2.5

The batch policy on Cray XK7 cannot guarantee allocation of contiguous nodes and this can lead to some variations in the communication performance. For example, two MPI tasks may be adjacent nodes on the 3D network in one batch run, but may require many hops across the network in another batch submission. The vendor provided Cray SHMEM and MPI implementation (module cray-shmem version 7.2.0) and Cray compiler was used to build the benchmark.

Table 3 shows the times for graph generation and compressed graph construction for `scale_factor=20` on 16 nodes. The generation and construction times were similar for MPI-2 one-sided and OpenSHMEM. Table 4 shows the performance of OpenSHMEM and MPI-2 one-sided implementation. Due to excessive run times, the performance for MPI-2 the validation phase was skipped by setting `export SKIP_VALIDATION=1` environment variable. BFS run-times for OpenSH-MEM were consistently lower compared to MPI-2 one-sided. As more tasks were used, the BFS time for both OpenSHMEM and MPI-2 BFS decreased. Note that `scale_factor=20` is a small graph with only $2^{20} = 1,048,576$ vertices that takes up about 16 MBytes per node.

Graph 500 in OpenSHMEM   161

Table 4. Performance of BFS for `scale_factor`=20 using MPI-2 one-sided communication and OpenSHMEM over 16 Cray XK7 nodes

	MPI-2 one-sided BFS time (sec)			OpenSHMEM BFS time (sec)		
Tasks	Minimum	Median	Maximum	Minimum	Median	Maximum
64	10.2	11.1	13.1	3.2	3.4	4.3
128	6.1	6.7	7.4	2.0	2.2	2.9
256	2.3	3.0	4.4	1.6	1.8	2.5

Table 5. Runtimes (in seconds) for `scale_factor`=24 over 16 Cray XK7 nodes

	MPI-2 one-sided		OpenSHMEM	
Tasks	Generation	Construction	Generation	Construction
64	18.1	3.9	18.4	4.4
128	18.6	3.2	19.0	4.1
256	24.6	3.8	26.8	4.6

Table 6. Performance of BFS for `scale_factor`=20 using OpenSHMEM over 16 Cray XK7 nodes

	OpenSHMEM BFS time (sec)		
Tasks	Minimum	Median	Maximum
64	42.9	44.1	45.9
128	22.7	23.4	25.7
256	14.9	15.6	17.4

Table 5 shows the times for graph generation and compressed graph construction for `scale_factor`=24 (16,777,216 vertices) on 16 compute nodes. The times for graph generation and construction were similar for MPI-2 one-sided and OpenSHMEM. For this size the MPI-2 one-sided implemented ran out of memory in the BFS computation. Table 6 shows the times for BFS processing by OpenSHMEM.

Table 7 shows the times for OpenSHMEM on 64 nodes on `scale`=28. Only 8 (instead of 64) BFS passes were used to reduce the runtimes. The times for BFS decrease as more tasks were used. Note problem size `scale`=28 is 4 times larger than `scale`=26 and 4 times as many nodes were used compared to the previous case. Table 8 show the times for OpenSHMEM on 64 nodes on `scale`=30, which is 4 times larger compared to `scale`=28. The execution times for Table 8 are roughly 4 times the data in Table 7. Thus, the data suggests the OpenSHMEM implementation is scalable to larger problem size and higher number of tasks.

Table 7. Performance of BFS for `scale_factor=28` using OpenSHMEM over 64 Cray XK7 nodes

Tasks	OpenSHMEM BFS time (sec)				
	Generation	Construction	Minimum	Median	Maximum
128	83.8	30.7	378.5	308.4	390.7
256	42.3	17.4	204.8	208.4	214.7
512	22.0	10.2	118.3	120.6	130.0
1024	31.6	10.4	76.9	79.4	85.0

Table 8. Performance of BFS for `scale_factor=30` using OpenSHMEM over 64 Cray XK7 nodes

Tasks	OpenSHMEM BFS time (sec)				
	Generation	Construction	Minimum	Median	Maximum
256	187.6	87.1	783.8	789.7	793.7
512	97.7	44.5	428.8	428.8	449.6

5   Summary

A prototype implementation of the Graph 500 benchmark has been implemented using OpenSHMEM based on the original MPI-2 one-sided implementation. The benchmark uses unsigned long integers that are not fully supported in OpenSH-MEM 1.0. OpenSHMEM operations for unsigned long integers have been implemented. New atomic capabilities such as atomic min, atomic binary OR have been implemented using atomic conditional swap. The OpenSHMEM benchmark has been tested on an SGI cluster and a Cray XK7 machine. The results suggest the OpenSHMEM implementation is competitive against the MPI-2 one-sided implementation. However, the MPI-2 one-sided implementation on SGI cluster and Cray XK7 encountered problems in `MPI_Win_fence` and was not able to complete BFS calculation for larger graphs.

Future work will consider performance profiling to further optimize the Open-SHMEM implementation and consider the performance on other graph generators such as R-MAT and BTER [6].

Acknowledgment. This work was supported by the United States Department of Defense (DoD) and used resources of the DoD-HPC Program at Oak Ridge National Laboratory. This research used resources of the National Center for Computational Sciences at Oak Ridge National Laboratory, which is supported by the Office of Science of the Department of Energy under Contract DE-AC05-00OR22725.

Graph 500 in OpenSHMEM   163

References

1. Chakrabarti, D., Zhan, Y., Faloutsos, C.: R-MAT: a recursive model for graph mining. In: SIAM Data Mining (2004). http://snap.stanford.edu/class/cs224w-readings/chakrabarti04rmat.pdf
2. Chamberlain, B., Callahan, D., Zima, H.: Parallel programmability and the Chapel language. Int. J. High Perform. Comput. Appl. **21**(3), 291–312 (2007). http://dx.doi.org/10.1177/1094342007078442
3. Chapman, B., Curtis, T., Pophale, S., Poole, S., Kuehn, J., Koelbel, C., Smith, L.: Introducing openSHMEM: SHMEM for the PGAS community. In: Proceedings of the Fourth Conference on Partitioned Global Address Space Programming Model, PGAS 2010, New York (2010)
4. El-Ghazawi, T., Carlson, W., Sterling, T., Yelick, K.: UPC: Distributed Shared-Memory Programming. Wiley-Interscience, Hoboken (2003)
5. Gropp, W., Lusk, E., Skjellum, A.: Using MPI: Portable Parallel Programming with the Message Passing Interface. MIT Press, Cambridge (1999)
6. Kolda, T.G., Pinar, A., Plantenga, T., Seshadhri, C.: A scalable generative graph model with community structure. SIAM J. Sci. Comput. **36**(5), C424–C452 (2014)
7. Forum, M.P.I.: MPI-2: a message passing interface standard. High Perform. Comput. Appl. **12**(1–2), 1–299 (1998)
8. Nieplocha, J., Carpenter, B.: ARMCI: a portable remote memory copy library for distributed array libraries and compiler run-time systems. In: Rolim, José D.P. (ed.) IPPS-WS 1999 and SPDP-WS 1999. LNCS, vol. 1586. Springer, Heidelberg (1999). http://dl.acm.org/citation.cfm?id=645611.662053
9. Numrich, R.W., Reid, J.: Co-array fortran for parallel programming. SIGPLAN Fortran Forum **17**(2), 1–31 (1998). http://doi.acm.org/10.1145/289918.289920
10. Poole, S.W., Hernandez, O., Kuehn, J.A., Shipman, G.M., Curtis, A., Feind, K.: OpenSHMEM - toward a unified RMA model. In: Padua, D. (ed.) Encyclopedia of Parallel Computing, pp. 1379–1391. Springer, Heidelberg (2011)
11. Pophale, S., Curtis, T., Chapman, B.: Improving performance of OpenSHMEM reference library by portable PE mapping techniques. In: Proceedings of the 27th International ACM Conference on International Conference on Supercomputing, pp. 485–486. ACM, New York (2013)
12. Pophale, S.S.: SRC: OpenSHMEM library development. In: Proceedings of the International Conference on Supercomputing, p. 374. ACM, New York (2011)
13. SGI: SGI MPI and SGI SHMEM User Guide. Technical report document number: 007–3773-026, SGI (2015). http://techpubs.sgi.com/library/tpl/cgi-bin/download.cgi?coll=linux&db=bks&docnumber=007-3773-026

Accelerating k-NN Algorithm with Hybrid MPI and OpenSHMEM

Jian Lin[1]($\boxtimes$), Khaled Hamidouche[1], Jie Zhang[1], Xiaoyi Lu[1],
Abhinav Vishnu[2], and Dhabaleswar Panda[1]

[1] Department of Computer Science and Engineering,
The Ohio State University, Columbus, USA
{linjia,hamidouc,zhanjie,luxi,panda}@cse.ohio-state.edu
[2] Pacific Northwest National Laboratory, Richland, USA
abhinav.vishnu@pnnl.gov

Abstract. Machine learning algorithms are benefiting from the continuous improvement of programming models, including MPI, MapReduce and PGAS. k-Nearest Neighbors (k-NN) algorithm is a widely used machine learning algorithm, applied to supervised learning tasks such as classification. Several parallel implementations of k-NN have been proposed in the literature and practice. However, on high-performance computing systems with high-speed interconnects, it is important to further accelerate existing designs of the k-NN algorithm through taking advantage of scalable programming models. To improve the performance of k-NN on large-scale environment with InfiniBand network, this paper proposes several alternative hybrid MPI+OpenSHMEM designs and performs a systemic evaluation and analysis on typical workloads. The hybrid designs leverage the one-sided memory access to better overlap communication with computation than the existing pure MPI design, and propose better schemes for efficient buffer management. The implementation based on k-NN program from MaTEx toolkit with MVAPICH2-X (Unified MPI+PGAS Communication Runtime over InfiniBand) shows up to 9.0 % time reduction for training KDD Cup 2010 workload over 512 cores, and 27.6 % time reduction for small workload with balanced communication and computation. Experiments of running with varied number of cores show that our design can maintain good scalability.

Keywords: MPI · OpenSHMEM · Hybrid programming model · Algorithm acceleration

1 Introduction

Machine learning algorithms are widely used in artificial intelligence, data analysis, and other application areas. To address the challenges of exascale computing and large volumes of data from Internet computing and other emerging scenes,

This research is supported in part by National Science Foundation grants #OCI-1148371, #CCF-1213084, #IIS-1447804 and #CNS-1419123.

© Springer International Publishing Switzerland 2015
M. Gorentla Venkata et al. (Eds.): OpenSHMEM 2015, LNCS 9397, pp. 164–177, 2015.
DOI: 10.1007/978-3-319-26428-8_11

parallelization and distribution are inevitable. MPI, MapReduce and PGAS programming models have been used in diverse machine learning libraries aiming at promoting performance and reducing costs [5, 9, 11, 15]. For example, the Apache Mahout project [3] implements a set of scalable machine learning algorithms based on the Hadoop [2] platform, and the MaTEx (Machine Learning Toolkit for Extreme Scale) project [19] from PNNL provides a group of typical machine learning and data mining algorithms parallelized with MPI or Global Arrays [18] for high-performance environment. It is important for the machine learning algorithms to leverage the semantics and paradigm of underlying middleware and computing frameworks, so that the capabilities of compute, storage, and network resources can be fully utilized.

1.1 k-NN Algorithm

k-Nearest Neighbors (k-NN) algorithm [1] is a popular supervised machine learning algorithm, which is used for classification and regression. It is referred as a lazy-learner approach, since the prediction for testing set (samples with unknown class labels) is done using the extracted features of training set (samples with known ground truth), unlike other algorithms such as Support Vector Machine and Deep Networks. For each testing sample, the algorithm finds k "nearest" neighbors using kernels such as the linear or Gaussian kernel. The parameter k is defined by user. The choice of k depends on data, and it determines the effect of noise and the distinctness of boundaries. In parallel implementations, the training set is usually communicated among processes, so that the kernel calculation can be executed iteratively over all the data.

1.2 PGAS Model and MVAPICH2-X

The Partitioned Global Address Space (PGAS) is a parallel programming model designed for scalable high-performance computing environment. It provides a global memory address space composed of symmetric memory portions in distributed processes. It supports remote memory access semantics as well as primitives for general communication patterns. Several PGAS implementations have been proposed, including language-based UPC [6], CAF [17], and library-based OpenSHMEM [8], etc. Comparing with two-sided message passing based communication, PGAS is productive and flexible when the communication patterns are irregular or unbalanced.

MVAPICH2-X [16] is a communication library supporting MPI, PGAS, and hybrid MPI+PGAS (OpenSHMEM, UPC, and CAF) programming models. It introduces a Unified Communication Runtime (UCR) that utilizes the communication capability of InfiniBand efficiently, and allows MPI and PGAS semantics running in a consistent behavior. Applications can benefit from the merits of both MPI and PGAS by using the hybrid model with MVAPICH2-X.

1.3   Research Objectives

As a popular PGAS library, OpenSHMEM has been used to accelerate a wide range of high-performance applications [12–14,20]. We are interested in whether it can benefit machine learning applications. This paper chooses the typical k-NN algorithm in machine learning, and focuses on accelerating k-NN with the hybrid MPI+ OpenSHMEM programming model. The following questions will be answered by this research.

1. What are the performance bottlenecks of the current MPI-based k-NN implementation?
2. Where and how to leverage the one-sided communication semantics to improve the performance of k-NN?
3. What are the benefits of performance and scalability by introducing hybrid MPI+ OpenSHMEM designs into k-NN?

The contribution of this paper is not only a high-performance design and implementation of k-NN algorithm based on MPI+OpenSHMEM, but also a general case for leveraging multiple alternative PGAS programming techniques in machine learning applications.

The rest contents of the paper are organized as follows: Sect. 2 analyzes the detailed research problem on accelerating k-NN. Section 3 proposes a group of alternative designs leveraging the hybrid MPI+OpenSHMEM programming models to accelerate k-NN. Section 4 presents the experimental results and discussion on them. Section 5 introduces some related work. Section 6 concludes this paper.

2   Problem Analysis

In order to identify the room for improving k-NN algorithm with hybrid MPI and OpenSHMEM, the features of the algorithm design and its implementation in MaTEx are analyzed, and the bottlenecks are investigated.

2.1   MPI-based k-NN Design in MaTEx

The k-NN program in MaTEx is written in C++, and uses MPI as communication library. It implements the supervised learning for classification, and supports input datasets in the LIBSVM [7] format. There are 3 main phases in one execution: (1) data loading, (2) training, and (3) testing. In the data loading phase, the process with rank 0 reads the input datasets from disk files, and distributes the partitioned datasets to other processes. In the training phase, each process iteratively transfers data to its right neighbor, and then performs local calculation, until all the input data being processed with all processes. In the testing phase, all the processes execute local calculation, and then summarize the results by collective communication. In this paper, we focus on the training phase, because it involves the most intensive part of communication and computation. In contrast, the data loading phase involves only simple I/O operations and a broadcast logic with little computation, which takes much less time comparing with training; the testing phase involves mainly local computation, which cannot benefit from communication oriented optimization. Based on the characteristics of the different phases, we believe that hybrid MPI+OpenSHMEM will bring the best of the both models, as stated in the Exascale Roadmap [10].

The timing relationship between communication and computation in the training phase is shown in Fig. 1. In each round of iteration, a process performs communication and computation in sequence. In order to allow concurrent read and write to the buffers at communication, a twin-buffer structure is designed as shown in Fig. 2. For each process, 2 buffers work as send and receive buffers alternatively in odd and even rounds, and the receive buffer in each round is used as the input of computation in the same round. The results of computation are saved locally, without participating the following communication.

In each process, 2 groups of twin-buffers are used respectively for original training samples (`samples`) and auxiliary row pointers (`row_ptr`). For workloads with a same schema, the approximate data size transferred and processed for each process in each round can be expressed as $s_i = a \cdot s_t/n$, where s_t is the total size of training dataset; n is the number of rounds, which is equal to the number of processes; a is a factor related to workload schema, and it is different

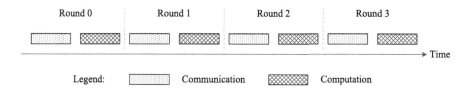

Fig. 1. The original timing relationship between communication and computation

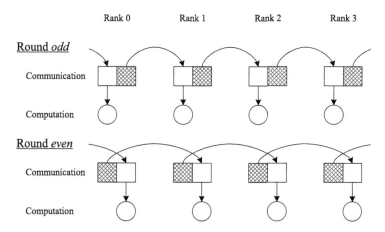

Fig. 2. The data process flow based on original twin-buffer structures

for `samples` and `row_ptr`. For certain a and s_t, the theoretical time overhead of communication for each process in each round can be expressed as $t_{comm} \propto s_i \propto 1/n$. According to the algorithm, the theoretical time overhead of computation for each process in each round can be expressed as $t_{comp} \propto s_i^2 \propto 1/n^2$.

2.2   Bottleneck Investigation

By exploring existing MPI-based k-NN design in MaTEx, we have the following observations: (1) For either intra-round or inter-round case, there is no overlap between communication and computation. It may restrain the performance. Since the computation results are not used for the following communication, there is potential to overlap communication with computation. (2) Each process will perform computation on the whole training dataset, but the twin-buffers only hold small parts of data at a certain moment. The amount of data prefetching is limited. Since each process will use the original dataset without modification, it is possible to cache more data in advance.

By further profiling the runtime characteristics of this program, we have the following observations: (1) For communication or computation with large data, the time overheads are consistent with theoretical estimation. For those with small data, the time overheads are heavier than the theoretical estimation and out of proportion. It is because of the inherent overheads of communication primitives and memory management, as well as the implementation overhead of auxiliary computation logics. (2) There are some variations for both communication and computation time across different rounds, especially for the cases of large workload and large number of processes. This is due to the differences of object distance distribution across different rounds, as well as some system-level variations caused by the intensive CPU, memory and I/O operations. These additional overheads will also restrain the performance of the k-NN program.

3   Design

Based on the analysis of the MPI-based k-NN program and its performance features, we propose a set of new designs leveraging the hybrid programming model in MVAPICH2-X to solve the observed bottlenecks.

3.1   Alternative Designs

The main ideas to accelerate the k-NN program in MaTEx are: (1) to overlap the time of communication and computation, and (2) to utilize the local memory for caching input datasets. We propose four alternative designs. The first one is to implement overlapping by reorganizing the logics in the original MPI design, which is referred as MPI_O in this paper. The other three employ Open-SHMEM as the communication library so that the communication buffers can be managed explicitly. With different optimization techniques, these designs are referred as OSH_OW, OSH_OM, and OSH_OC, respectively. They are hybrid

MPI+OpenSHMEM designs essentially, because MPI is still used for data loading and collective communication. The basic features of the alternative designs are shown in Table 1, and the concrete techniques in these designs are introduced in the following subsections. Note that the main reason why we propose the MPI_O design is for a fair comparison with the MPI+OpenSHMEM-based designs.

3.2   Overlapped Data Process Flow

The key to overlap communication with computation is using asynchronous data transfer. Since the input of computation in the original k-NN design depends on the receive buffer of communication in the same round, it is necessary to reorganize the logics. An overlapping communication mechanism is proposed as shown in Algorithm 1. Comparing with the original design, the start of data transfer in each round is moved to its previous round. For each process, it waits for the completion of communication launched in the previous round at first. After obtaining the data, it starts the data transfer for the next round asynchronously, and performs the computation of the current round immediately. To provide the input data for round 0, a special "round -1" is inserted, which involves only communication starting. Correspondingly, the last round will not start any data transfer.

The overlapped timing relationship between communication and computation in the training phase is shown in Fig. 3. Except for the communication finishing logic, the communication and computation can execute simultaneously. The percentage of overlapping depends on the time proportions of communication and computation, which are determined by the schema and size of workload, as well as the number of processes. For the typical cases that computation takes more time than communication, this mechanism can also hide the time variations of communication to a certain extent. The overlapping technique can be applied in both MPI- and OpenSHMEM-based designs. All the four new designs are using this mechanism.

Table 1. The alternative designs to accelerate the k-NN program

Name	Description
MPI	Original MPI-based design without overlapping
MPI_O	MPI-based design with overlapping
OSH_OW	MPI+OpenSHMEM-based design with overlapping and waiting
OSH_OM	MPI+OpenSHMEM-based design with overlapping and memory copy
OSH_OC	MPI+OpenSHMEM-based design with overlapping and circular-buffer

---

Algorithm 1. Overlapping communication for k-NN

---

1 **for** *round* ← −1 **to** *max_round* **do**
2 | **if** *round* ≠ −1 **then**
3 | | *wait_for_data(local_row_ptr)*
4 | | *wait_for_data(local_samples)*
5 | | *row_ptr_len* ← *get_length(local_row_ptr)*
6 | | *samples_len* ← *get_length(local_samples)*
7 | **end**
8 | **if** *round* ≠ *max_round* **then**
9 | | *async_transfer_data(local_row_ptr, remote_row_ptr, row_ptr_len)*
10 | | *async_transfer_data(local_samples, remote_samples, samples_len)*
11 | **end**
12 | **if** *round* ≠ −1 **then**
13 | | *do_computation(local_row_ptr, row_ptr_len, local_samples, samples_len)*
14 | **end**
15 **end**

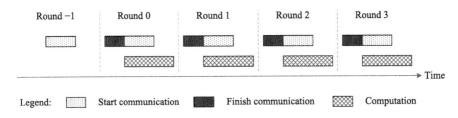

Fig. 3. The overlapped timing relationship between communication and computation

3.3   OpenSHMEM-Based One-Sided Data Transfer

The MPI and MPI_O designs of k-NN use the asynchronous MPI_Isend/MPI_Irecv and blocking MPI_Waitall for communication. In typical MPI libraries, a group of sophisticated logics for buffer management are implemented to handle the different timing orders of asynchronous primitive calls. These logics are useful for general cases, but they may introduce overhead for the simple and determined communication pattern in k-NN. The one-sided remote memory access operations in OpenSHMEM are employed in the OSH_OW, OSH_OM, and OSH_OC designs to handle the data transfer requirement between application buffers, which avoids the potential data copy between buffers of application and library. Although MPI-3 provides one-sided communication primitives as well, OpenSHMEM still has the advantage on programmability for this scene.

To achieve process synchronization and ensure data integrity, a light-weight package structure is designed for encapsulating the raw send/receive buffers. As shown in Fig. 4, the structure has a data length field and a head magic number before the data, and keeps a tail magic number after the data. All the new fields have fixed lengths. Meanwhile, a group of flags in the symmetric memory of each process are set for the notification from the destination process to the source process telling that the receive buffer is available. This design is called OSH_OW, where "W" means to wait. The source process performs shmem_wait_until on corresponding notification flag to wait for data transferring. Then it will transfer data with shmem_putmem. The destination process detects the location of head magic number to know that data transfer is started, so that the data length can be read. Then it detests the location of tail magic number to know that data transfer is done. Although the OpenSHMEM specification does not guarantee the completion order of each data block through one shmem_putmem, the InfiniBand-based implementation in MVAPICH2-X has a sequential assurance. It is a safe trick to avoid complex synchronous logics in this case. For general OpenSHMEM implementations, it is necessary to use communication channel dependent methods to know the data are available, but the overall logic is still feasible.

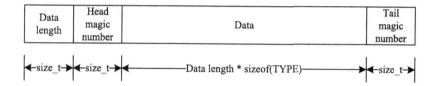

Fig. 4. The data package structure

3.4   Circular-buffer Structure Design

The notification flag in the OSH_OW design is still a limiting factor to the performance of k-NN training phase. It blocks communication on the source process if the computation or shmem_putmem issued by the destination process is not finished. In essence, it is a limitation derived from the twin-buffer structure. In order to alleviate this blocking issue, a memory copy based optimization is designed, which is called OSH_OM. In this design, the destination process will make a copy of the received data, using it as the input for local computation. The twin-buffers are marked as available as soon as the copy is done. Therefore, although the notification flag should still be waited, the blocking time on the source process side can be reduced. A time overhead for memory copy is introduced, but it is usually less than that of blocking on notification in real applications.

In order to completely break through the limitation derived from the twin-buffer structure, a circular-buffer structure is proposed. The design with this structure is called OSH_OC. This design aims at "trading space for time". As shown in Fig. 5, it introduces large contiguous buffers for samples and row_ptr in the symmetric memory that can be accessed as circular queues. Two pointers are set for each circular buffer to maintain the positions for reading and writing data. The blocking on notification will only occur if the whole buffer is full, which rarely happens if the buffer is large enough. Beyond this special case, the source process can always put data to the next available position in the circular buffer of destination, regardless of whether the current round is odd or even; the destination process can execute computation immediately without additional memory copy. This design allows caching more data in advance, and it further overlaps the communication and computation between rounds.

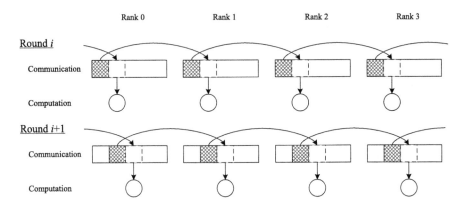

Fig. 5. The data process flow based on proposed circular-buffer structures

4   Evaluation

In order to evaluate the effects of the proposed designs for k-NN algorithm, a group of experiments are performed. The results and analysis are presented in this section.

4.1   Experimental Setup

We use a high-performance computing cluster at OSU for the performance and scalability evaluation. This cluster consists of computing nodes with Intel Westmere series of processors operating at 2.53 GHz. The memory on each node is 12 GB. All the nodes are equipped with MT26428 QDR ConnectX HCAs (32 Gbps data rate) with PCI-Ex Gen2 interfaces. The operating system is Red Hat Enterprise Linux Server release 6.5 with kernel version 2.6.32–431.el6.

The workload for the experiments comes from the LIBSVM project [7]. We use the KDD Cup 2010 dataset [21] as training workload. This dataset is designed for classification. It includes 8,407,752 records of 2 classes, and takes up 2.5 GB space. In the experiments, we use the parameter $k = 5$.

4.2   Small-Scale Performance Tests

To verify the effects of overlapping provided by the proposed designs, we execute a group of small-scale performance tests. The workload is a truncated version of KDD with 100,000 records (30 MB), which is referred as KDD-XS. The

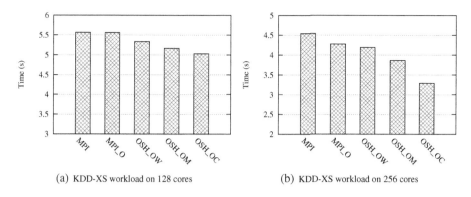

(a) KDD-XS workload on 128 cores   (b) KDD-XS workload on 256 cores

Fig. 6. The execution time for KDD-XS workload with different designs

testing scales are 128–256 cores. With this configuration, the time for communication and computation in each round has the same order of magnitude, so that overlapping can be highlighted. Figure 6 shows the experimental results. Taking the 256-core case as an example, the MPI_O design can save 5.9 % training time comparing with the original MPI design, and the OSH_OC design can save 27.6 % training time comparing with the original MPI design. Comparing with the cases of 128-core and 256-core, we find the scalability is limited for such small workload, because the overheads of communication primitives and memory management take up a large proportion in these cases.

4.3   Large-Scale Performance Tests

To verify the comprehensive effects of the proposed techniques in practical application scenarios, we execute a group of large-scale performance tests using the whole KDD workload. The testing scales are 512–1024 cores. With this configuration, the time for communication is universally shorter than the time for computation in each round, and there are some time variations among rounds under the intensive communication and computation. Figure 7 shows the experimental results. Taking the 512-core case as an example, the MPI_O, OSH_OW, OSH_OM and OSH_OC designs can save 2.7 %, 4.1 %, 7.6 %, and 9.0 % training time respectively comparing with the original MPI design. Comparing with the basic OSH_OW design, the memory copy based optimization in OSH_OM reduces 3.5 % time, and the circular-buffer structure based design in OSH_OC reduces 5.1 % time. The overlapping of communication and computation, the reduced memory copy between application and library, and the hidden variations contribute to the performance advantages.

4.4   Scalability Tests

Two groups of experiments are performed to evaluate the scalability of proposed designs, in which the OSH_OC design is used as a representative to compare

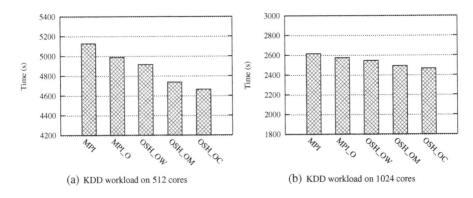

(a) KDD workload on 512 cores   (b) KDD workload on 1024 cores

Fig. 7. The execution time for KDD workload with different designs

with the original MPI-based design. The first group is for evaluating strong scalability. As shown in Fig. 8(a), we run the k-NN program with the whole KDD workloads on 256–1024 cores. The results show that the execution time of both MPI and OSH_OC are reduced with the increment of processes, which reflect good strong scalability. OSH_OC shows higher proportion of benefits for smaller scales, because their communication overheads take up higher proportion that can be overlapped with the proposed design. The second group is for evaluating weak scalability. As shown in Fig. 8(b), we run the k-NN program with different sizes of truncated KDD workload on 256–1024 cores (using 1,000,000 records as a unit for per 256 cores). The results show that the execution time of both MPI and OSH_OC increase slowly with the increment of processes, which is determined by the complexity of the k-NN algorithm. It shows that the MPI+OpenSHMEM design does not break the weak scalability.

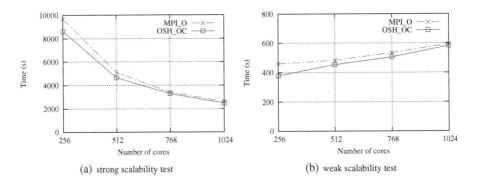

(a) strong scalability test   (b) weak scalability test

Fig. 8. The scalability test results with different configurations

5   Related Work

As a popular algorithm on machine learning, k-NN has been optimized by different parallel and distributed technologies. Arefin et al. [5] proposed an efficient parallel formulation of k-NN search problem, and implemented a software tool GPU-FS-kNN for CUDA enabled GPUs. Moon et al. [15] presented an MPI-based implementation, which allows clustering and nearest neighbor searches to be scaled to modern highly parallel platforms. Aparício et al. [4] described a parallel implementation of the k-NN algorithm in three levels: threads, MPI Processes and the Grid. Zhang et al. [22] proposed an exact and an approximate algorithm in MapReduce to perform efficient parallel k-NN joins on large data. Zhang et al. [23] presented an irregular partitioning method based k-NN algorithm using MapReduce, which can obtain high performance and guarantee a very efficient query when dealing with big data. Different from these studies, this paper aims at accelerating k-NN from the angle of hybrid programming model in high-performance computing environment.

Many studies have explored the adaption or reimplementation of high-performance applications with PGAS or hybrid MPI+PGAS programming models. Pophale et al. [20] presented an implementation of OpenSHMEM-based NAS Parallel Benchmarks that introduces effective methodologies for primitive-level adaption. Jose et al. [13] presented a hybrid MPI+OpenSHMEM version of the Graph500 benchmark leveraging the irregular nature of Graph500. Jose et al. [12] proposed a high-performance design of sorting using MPI with simple extensions to OpenSHMEM communication, which can alleviate the intensive overhead of two-sided communication. Li et al. [14] proposed a scalable MiniMD design with hybrid MPI+OpenSHMEM, which benefits from overlapped communication and efficient buffer management. All these studies show the advantages of performance, scalability and programmability to integrate the merits of different high-performance programming models. This paper extends the methodologies, and brings the merits to a new application area.

6   Conclusion

The PGAS programming models represented by OpenSHMEM have shown their advantages of performance, functionality and programmability on many applications in the high-performance and distributed computing areas. In this paper, the potential of using PGAS and hybrid programming models in k-NN, a widely used machine learning algorithm in the emerging Internet computing environment, is explored. We analyze the design and runtime features of current MPI-based k-NN implementation in MaTEx, and locate the bottlenecks in the training phase. Several techniques are proposed, including overlapped data process flow, memory copy based optimization, circular-buffer structure, etc. They aim at overlapping the communication with computation, and utilizing the local memory resource. Integrating these techniques, a group of new designs of k-NN are constructed on MVAPICH2-X, a unified MPI+PGAS communication runtime over InfiniBand.

The experiments show that our new designs save up to 9.0 % time for training typical KDD Cup 2010 workload over 512 cores, and up to 27.6 % time for small workload with balanced communication and computation. It also keeps good strong scalability as the original MPI design does. This work provides a general case for leveraging multiple PGAS programming techniques in machine learning applications.

The future improving directions include further decoupling communication and computation by adjusting data placement, accelerating data loading by efficient data distribution algorithm, etc. On the implementation side, it will be helpful to propose a portable version for different OpenSHMEM runtime. We are also interested in accelerating other popular algorithms from machine learning and deep learning with the hybrid MPI+PGAS technology.

References

1. Altman, N.: An introduction to kernel and nearest-neighbor nonparametric regression. Am. Stat. **46**(3), 175–185 (1992)
2. Apache Software Foundation: Apache Hadoop. http://hadoop.apache.org/
3. Apache Software Foundation: Apache Mahout. http://mahout.apache.org/
4. Aparício, G., Blanquer, I., Hernández, V.: A parallel implementation of the K nearest neighbours classifier in three levels: threads, MPI processes and the grid. In: Daydé, M., Palma, J.M.L.M., Coutinho, Á.L.G.A., Pacitti, E., Lopes, J.C. (eds.) VECPAR 2006. LNCS, vol. 4395, pp. 225–235. Springer, Heidelberg (2007)
5. Arefin, A.S., Riveros, C., Berretta, R., Moscato, P.: GPU-FS-kNN: a software tool for fast and scalable kNN computation using GPUs. PLoS ONE **7**, e44000 (2012)
6. Carlson, W., Draper, J., Culler, D., Yelick, K., Brooks, E., Warren, K.: Introduction to UPC and Language Specification. Center for Computing Sciences, Institute for Defense Analyses (1999)
7. Chang, C.C., Lin, C.J.: LIBSVM: a library for support vector machines. ACM Trans. Intell. Syst. Technol. **2**(3), 27:1–27:27 (2011)
8. Chapman, B., Curtis, T., Pophale, S., Poole, S., Kuehn, J., Koelbel, C., Smith, L.: Introducing openSHMEM: SHMEM for the PGAS community. In: Proceedings of the 4th Conference on Partitioned Global Address Space Programming Model, p. 2 (2010)
9. Chu, C.T., Kim, S., Lin, Y.a., Yu, Y., Bradski, G., Olukotun, K., Ng, A.: Mapreduce for machine learning on multicore. In: Advances in Neural Information Processing Systems, vol. 19 (2007)
10. Dongarra, J., Beckman, P., Moore, T., Aerts, P., et al.: The international exascale software project roadmap. Int. J. High Perform. Comput. Appl. **25**(1), 3–60 (2011)
11. Ghoting, A., Krishnamurthy, R., Pednault, E., Reinwald, B., Sindhwani, V., Tatikonda, S., Tian, Y., Vaithyanathan, S.: SystemML: declarative machine learning on mapreduce. In: Proceedings of IEEE 27th International Conference on Data Engineering (2011)
12. Jose, J., Potluri, S., Subramoni, H., Lu, X., Hamidouche, K., Schulz, K., Sundar, H., Panda, D.K.: Designing scalable out-of-core sorting with hybrid MPI+PGAS programming models. In: Proceedings of the 8th International Conference on Partitioned Global Address Space Programming Models (2014)

13. Jose, J., Potluri, S., Tomko, K., Panda, D.K.: Designing scalable graph500 benchmark with hybrid MPI+OpenSHMEM programming models. In: Kunkel, J.M., Ludwig, T., Meuer, H.W. (eds.) ISC 2013. LNCS, vol. 7905, pp. 109–124. Springer, Heidelberg (2013)
14. Li, M., Lin, J., Lu, X., Hamidouche, K., Tomko, K., Panda, D.K.: Scalable MiniMD design with hybrid MPI and OpenSHMEM. In: Proceedings of the 8th International Conference on Partitioned Global Address Space Programming Models, p. 24 (2014)
15. Moon, L., Long, D., Joshi, S., Tripathi, V., Xiao, B., Biros, G.: Parallel algorithms for clustering and nearest neighbor search problems in high dimensions. In: Proceedings of the 2011 ACM/IEEE Conference on Supercomputing (2011)
16. Network Based Computing Lab, The Ohio State University: MVAPICH2-X: Unified MPI+PGAS Communication Runtime over OpenFabrics/Gen2 for Exascale Systems. http://mvapich.cse.ohio-state.edu/
17. Numrich, R., Reid, J.: Co-Array Fortran for Parallel Programming. Technical Report RAL-TR-1998-060, Rutheford Appleton Laboratory (1998)
18. Pacific Northwest National Laboratory: Global Arrays Programming Models. http://hpc.pnl.gov/globalarrays/
19. Pacific Northwest National Laboratory: MaTEx: Machine Learning Toolkit for Extreme Scale. http://hpc.pnl.gov/matex/
20. Pophale, S., Jin, H., Poole, S., Kuehn, J.: OpenSHMEM performance and potential: A NPB experimental study. In: Proceedings of the 1st Workshop on OpenSHMEM (2013)
21. Yu, H.F., Lo, H.Y., Hsieh, H.P., Lou, J.K., Mckenzie, T.G., Chou, J.W., Chung, P.H., Ho, C.H., Chang, C.F., Weng, J.Y., et al.: Feature engineering and classifier ensemble for KDD cup 2010. In: JMLR Workshop and Conference Proceedings (2011)
22. Zhang, C., Li, F., Jestes, J.: Efficient parallel kNN joins for large data in MapReduce. In: Proceedings the 15th International Conference on Extending Database Technology (2012)
23. Zhang, Q., Li, C., He, P., Li, X., Zou, H.: Irregular partitioning method based K-nearest neighbor query algorithm using mapreduce. In: Proceedings of 2015 International Symposium on Computers & Informatics (2015)

Parallelizing the Smith-Waterman Algorithm Using OpenSHMEM and MPI-3 One-Sided Interfaces

Matthew Baker[✉], Aaron Welch, and Manjunath Gorentla Venkata

Oak Ridge National Laboratory, Oak Ridge, USA
bakermb@ornl.gov

Abstract. The *Smith-Waterman* algorithm is used for determining the similarity between two very long data streams. A popular application of the *Smith-Waterman* algorithm is for sequence alignment in DNA sequences. Like many computational algorithms, the *Smith-Waterman* algorithm is constrained by the memory resources and the computational capacity of the system. As such, it can be accelerated and run at larger scales by parallelizing the implementation, allowing the work to be distributed to exploit HPC systems. A central part of the algorithm is computing the similarity matrix which is the mechanism that evaluates the quality of the matching sequences. This access pattern to the matrix to compute the similarity is non-uniform; as such, it better suits the Partioned Global Address Space (PGAS) programming model. In this paper, we explore parallelizing the *Smith-Waterman* algorithm using the *OpenSHMEM* model and interfaces in *OpenSHMEM* 1.2 as well as the one-sided communication interfaces in *MPI-3*. Further, we also explore the advantages of using non-blocking communication interfaces, which are proposed as extensions for a future *OpenSHMEM* specification. We evaluate the parallel implementation on Titan, a Cray XK7 system at the *Oak Ridge Leadership Computing Facility* (OLCF). Our results demonstrate good weak and strong scaling characteristics for both of the *OpenSHMEM* and *MPI-3* implementations.

Keywords: OpenSHMEM · MPI-3 · Smith-Waterman

© Springer International Publishing Switzerland 2015
M. Gorentla Venkata et al. (Eds.): OpenSHMEM 2015, LNCS 9397, pp. 178–191, 2015.
DOI: 10.1007/978-3-319-26428-8_12

1   Introduction

The sequence alignment is the central functionality of genetic analysis and many other Bioinformatics applications. It infers the structural and functional relationship between the DNA/RNA or protein sequences, and finds similarity between the query and reference sequences. The sequence matching functionality, essentially a pattern matching function, has wider applications besides Bioinformatics. One of the most popular algorithms for sequence matching is the *Smith-Waterman* algorithm, which employs a dynamic programming approach to find local alignment, which finds local regions with high levels of similarity. Given the importance of this algorithm and its wider application, it is included in many benchmark suites including Scalable Synthetic Compact Applications 1 (SSCA1) [1] and BioParallel [2], and is used in tools for analyzing next generation sequencing data such as SNPTools [3].

Like many scientific simulations and workloads, the *Smith-Waterman* algorithm execution is constrained by the availability of resources. The algorithm complexity is bounded by $\mathcal{O}(mn)$, where m and n are the lengths of the sequences. Given the importance of the algorithm and the asymptotic runtime of the algorithm, there are various parallelization and optimization strategies to address the resource problem. Researchers have parallelized the *Smith-Waterman* algorithm by implementing the algorithm using parallel programming models such as MPI and BSP models and use distributed memory systems for execution [4,5]. For multicore systems, it has been optimized using hybrid programming paradigms such as MPI+OpenMP [6]. With GPUs providing more performance per watt, the GPU based distributed memory systems have become ubiquitous. To take advantage of this computing architecture, researchers have developed a parallelized implementation of the *Smith-Waterman* algorithm for many thread systems such as GPUs [7].

A typical implementation of the *Smith-Waterman* algorithm involves generating a similarity matrix, tracing back the sequences for a suitable alignment, and finding the optimal alignment. Parallelizing this algorithm results in communication that is not uniform. Further, the pattern to find the optimal sequence or tracing back the sequence is rather irregular, i.e. one cannot predict where the beginning of an optimal sequence is. Using a two-sided model such as MPI for parallelizing this algorithm means that one has to predict the sequence and post the receives appropriately. If the prediction is wrong, the receives have to be cancelled, which is awkward and can give unpredictable performance behavior.

To overcome this programming drawback, we explore the advantages of using one-sided communication interfaces provided by *OpenSHMEM* [8] and *MPI-3* [9] for parallelizing the *Smith-Waterman* algorithm. In the one-sided communication model, the sender of data is aware of not just a source buffer address but also the destination buffer address. As a consequence, only the sender of data actively participates in the execution of basic communication operations, while the receiving side stays passive. While implementing using these models, we explore two approaches. First, using blocking one-sided communication interfaces, and second using non-blocking one-sided communication interfaces. The non-blocking communication interfaces enables asynchronous progress of communication, enabling the ability to overlap communication and computation.

The rest of the paper is organized as follows: Sect. 2 provides background details of the *Smith-Waterman* algorithm, *OpenSHMEM* and *MPI-3* interfaces, and extensions to *OpenSHMEM* interfaces. Section 3 provides details of the *OpenSHMEM* and *MPI-3* implementations of the *Smith-Waterman* algorithm. Section 4 provides details of the evaluation of the implementation on Titan, a Cray XK7 system. Finally, Sect. 5 provides a summary of the paper's findings.

2 Background

OpenSHMEM is an API for programming in the PGAS model, and provides low level interfaces for communication and synchronization between the many processing elements (PEs) in the system. *OpenSHMEM* is primarily focused on one-sided communication, and one of its distinguishing factors is its memory model. The *OpenSHMEM* memory model uses the concept of symmetric data objects, which are variables that are allocated with the same type, size, and offset on all PEs for easy access to and simple partitioning of memory. *OpenSHMEM* includes a set of interfaces for Remote Memory Access (RMA) operations, atomic memory operations, synchronization operations, collective communication operations, distributed lock operations, and operations for querying process and data availability, and is available for C and Fortran.

2.1 *Smith-Waterman* Algorithm

The *Smith-Waterman* algorithm looks for sequence subsets that best match in two large sequences. This algorithm will execute in $\mathcal{O}(mn)$ time where m is the length of the main sequence while n is the length of the match sequence. We fix the length of the main and match sequences to be the same, so the algorithm effectively runs in $\mathcal{O}(n^2)$ time.

The first step is to generate a similarity matrix. This similarity matrix decides if a pair of codons, a triplet of adjacent DNA nucleotides that code for proteins, are either exact matches, similar matches that are distinct but serve the same function, or dissimilar matches. This can be generalized as a function $sim(a, b)$ that will return an exact match score, a similar score, or a no match score.

This algorithm works with a dynamic programming matrix A. This matrix is formed for each element A_{ij} by comparing element i in the main sequence and j in the match sequence using the $sim(a, b)$ function to derive a score that is added to element $A_{(i-1)(j-1)}$ of the score matrix representing the score if the current sequence were matched. A score is derived for a gap in the main sequence by subtracting a gap penalty from element $A_{i(j-1)}$ in the score matrix. A score for a gap in the match sequence is also derived by taking element $A_{(i-1)j}$ and subtracting the gap penalty. These scores, for the gap in main, the gap in match, and a similarity value between main and a match, are all compared and the highest score is the score used for element A_{ij} in the matrix to a minimum score of 0.

Additionally, our implementation used the Gotoh improvements [10], which keeps a pair of additional arrays to map a changing gap penalty to penalize small gaps over large gaps. This is done using an additional array where the previous match against the main sequence is penalized with a gap start penalty, while the previous gap penalty, represented by $E_{(i-1)}$ is penalized with a gap extension value. Match has a similar array where previous gap penalties in the match sequence are located in $F_{(j-1)}$. These gap values are compared against the matching value rather than a fixed gap penalty. This is done on the observation that in nature a genome usually sees larger gaps rather than smaller gaps.

2.2   *OpenSHMEM* Non-blocking Extensions

The proposed *OpenSHMEM* non-blocking extensions include four core components: data transfer operations (put/get), atomic operations, collectives, and functions to test for completion. The new operations for non-blocking remote memory access highlight one of the important differences with the proposed API, particularly concerning put operations. Put operations have often been considered as non-blocking already, since the calls return before remote completion is guaranteed. However, the key consideration concerns how completion itself is defined, which can have many different levels ranging from virtually no completion to remote completion. These differing definitions of completion semantics include, in progressive order from early to late in the operation: when local buffers can be reused, local completion, and finally remote completion. The old put operations returned after local buffers could be reused, but did not necessarily guarantee local completion, and guaranteeing remote completion required the use of a quiet operation. The newly proposed non-blocking put instead returns even earlier, before local buffers can safely be reused, and requires an extra operation to either test or wait for the completion equivalent to the older blocking form. This same change in semantics carries over to all the other non-blocking operations, including get, atomic, and collective operations.

In order to properly take advantage of these new functions and test for completion, all non-blocking calls return an opaque request handle shmemx_request_handle_t that can later be used with either of two new functions to query completion status. The first of these functions is shmemx_wait_req(), which simply blocks until the non-blocking call is complete (as according to the appropriate blocking call's original semantics). The second of these is shmemx_test_req(), which checks and immediately returns the current status of the operation so that further work may be done in the event that it is not yet complete.

The current proposal makes no mention of how these non-blocking operations interact with synchronization functions such as shmem_fence() and shmem_quiet(). Instead, the proposal explicitly says that a conformant *OpenSH-MEM* implementation can progress non-blocking operations however it sees fit.

2.3   Cray Non-blocking Extensions

The Cray non-blocking extensions are incomplete with respect to the *OpenSHMEM* proposed extensions. In particular, rather then implement shmemx_wait_req() and shmemx_test_req(), the Cray SHMEM library requires the use of shmem_quiet() to ensure the completion of non-blocking routines. This can produce unnecessary overhead if the algorithm in use does updates with shmem_put() and does prefetching with non-blocking shmem_get() operations as in the case of this paper's implementation of the *Smith-Waterman* algorithm. The Cray API still has request handles as parameters, but they are both of a different type and are currently unused in the implementation, and may be passed in as NULL [11].

3   *Smith-Waterman* Implementation

Among all kernels in the SSCA1 benchmark suite [12], the *Smith-Waterman* algorithm is the most difficult to parallelize and runs in $\mathcal{O}(n^2)$ time. The only input provided to the algorithm is a SCALE number. The size of the score matrix is determined by SCALE, with each increment roughly doubling the number of elements in the score matrix, effectively doubling the length of the computation. Pseudo code is shown in Listing 1.1.

To make the *Smith-Waterman* algorithm parallel, this implementation is set up to be data parallel on the score matrix's anti-diagonal. This is based on the observation that a particular entry in the score matrix is only dependent on the values at $A_{(i-1)(j-1)}$, $A_{i(j-1)}$, and $A_{(i-1)j}$ as seen in Fig. 1. This will require $2n$ iterations to complete, forming the outer loop started on line 10. The algorithm as a whole is still $\mathcal{O}(n^2)$ since in addition to the outer iterations there will be, at most, n values to compute in the inner loop started on line 26.

In a naive implementation the benchmark will allocate a matrix of n^2 elements and compute all of the values. The benchmark can compute values for each A_{ij} on an anti-diagonal independently. The data will only depend on the

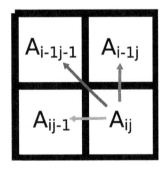

Fig. 1. Computing a dynamic programming matrix entry using two immediate neighbors at $i-1, j$ and $i, j-1$ and the diagonal element, $i-1, j-1$.

previous two anti-diagonals. This naive implementation would fill in the entire dynamic programming matrix A before scanning for potential good matches.

Additionally, there are two arrays for the current gap penalty. The gap penalty is based on the previous iteration of the benchmark and whether the penalty for continuing a previous gap is larger then the penalty for starting a new gap. These arrays require an additional $2n$ amount of memory, since each array must be n values long and an array must be made for the main sequence and the match sequence.

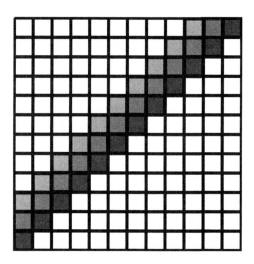

Fig. 2. Computation of the Score Matrix: the black anti-diagonal is calculated using two light shaded anti-diagonals

A key observation is that each anti-diagonal is only dependent on the previous two anti-diagonals; the previous ones are unneeded to compute a particular A_{ij}. This can be seen in Fig. 2. This means that the score matrix can be reduced to a three row matrix of n elements with each row representing an anti-diagonal. The memory requirement for the diagonal can thus be reduced from n^2 to $3n$ and caching behavior is improved because writes are done in adjacent localities independent of the reads as can be seen in Fig. 3. It is important to note that each row in Fig. 3 corresponds to the same colored row in Fig. 3.

Discarding previous diagonals means that you cannot wait until the end to scan for good matches. During the compute portion a score is evaluated based on a minimum score, the adjacency of other stored ends, and if the next match will produce a better score to decide if it should store a pair of well scoring end points.

In total, with all of the gap arrays, the score matrix, and sequence data, the *Smith-Waterman* algorithm will require, at most, $5j + 2k$ space in memory, where j is the size of an entry in the score matrix and k is the size of a codon.

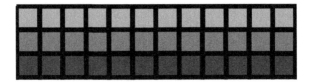

Fig. 3. In this implementation of the *Smith-Waterman* algorithm, the entire score matrix is transformed into three rows. Each row of the same color is equal to the same color anti-diagonal in Fig. 2.

Using the anti-diagonals as matrix rows, the indices for the elements to compare are no longer the same as described in the basic *Smith-Waterman* algorithm. The main gap is still at $A_{(i-1)j}$, but now the match gap is at $A_{(i-1)(j-1)}$ while the match is at index $A_{(i-2)(j-1)}$. Figure 4 shows the new dependency layout, where the colored arrows as the same as in Fig. 1

This implementation allows for dense memory access and use, but requires inline analysis of the score results. Either each row is scanned for the highest score to find only the best match, or a list of scores must be retained for comparison if multiple sub sequences are to be analyzed.

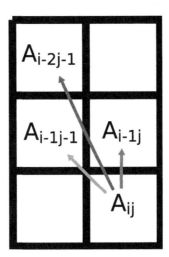

Fig. 4. The score matrix after transformation and the entries involved in computing a score matrix entry

Once the gap arrays and the score matrix are arranged in a loop independent way, distributing the elements across PEs becomes straightforward. Each PE gets an equal number of codons and since the gap and score matrices are based on codon length, these matrices can be distributed in the same manner. This locality will also minimize distributed memory access. This layout is illustrated in Fig. 5.

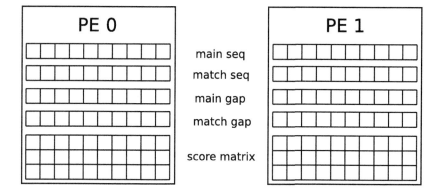

Fig. 5. Symmetric Heap with a ten codon main sequence and ten codon match sequence

The end result of these changes is that the benchmark runs in $2n$ iterations that can be parallelized within each iteration. This is most helpful in the middle iterations where there can be as many as n elements to be processed.

```
 1  local_align(main_codon_seq, match_codon_seq){
 2  /* A is the score Matrix */
 3    A[len(main_codon)][len(match_codon)];
 4  /* E is the main gap matrix */
 5    E[len(main_codon)][len(match_codon)];
 6  /* F is the match gap matrix */
 7    F[len(main_codon)][len(match_codon)];

 9    /* outer loop */
10    for(outer=0; outer < 2 * length(main_codon_seq)){
11      wait_for_puts();
12      barrier_all();
13      start = compute_local_start_index(outer);
14      end = compute_local_end_index(outer);

16      /* prestage non-blocking operations */
17      if(non_blocking_enabled){
18        nb_previous_match = get_nb(A, i-1, j-1)
19        nb_main_codon = get_nb(main_codon_seq,i);
20        nb_match_codon = get_nb(match_codon_seq,j);
21        nb_gap_main = get_nb(E,i-1,j);
22        nb_gap_match = get_nb(F,i,j-1);
23      }

25      /* inner loop */
26      for(inner = start; inner < end){
27        i = compute_main_index(outer, inner);
28        j = compute_match_index(outer, inner);

30        if(non_blocking_enabled){ /* non-blocking gets */
31          nb_i = compute_next_main_index(outer, inner);
32          nb_j = compute_next_match_index(outer, inner);

34          wait_for_previous_gets();
35          previous_match = nb_previous_match;
36          main_codon = nb_main_codon;
37          match_codon = nb_match_codon;
38          gap_main = nb_gap_main;
39          gap_match = nb_gap_match;

41          nb_previous_match = get_nb(A, nb_i-1, nb_j-1);
```

```
42          nb_main_codon =get_nb(main_codon_seq,nb_i);
43          nb_match_codon = get_nb(match_codon_seq,nb_j);
44          nb_gap_main = get_nb(E,nb_i-1,nb_j);
45          nb_gap_match = get_nb(F,nb_i,nb_j-1);
46        } else { /* blocking gets */
47          previous_match = get(A, i-1, j-1);
48          main_codon = get(main_codon_seq,i);
49          match_codon = get(match_codon_seq,j);
50          gap_main = get(E,i-1,j);
51          gap_match = get(F,i,j-1);
52        }

54        new_match = sim(main,codon);
55        new_score = max(new_match, gap_main, gap_match, 0);

57        if(is_score_good(new_score)){
58          add_new_pair(new_score, i, j);
59        }

61        new_gap_score = new_match - new_gap_penalty;
62        extend_main_gap = gap_main - extend_gap_penalty;
63        extend_match_gap = gap_match - extend_gap_penalty;

65        put(A,i,j,new_score);
66        put(E,i,j,max(new_gap_score,extend_main_gap));
67        put(F,i,j,max(new_gap_score,extend_match_gap));
68      }
69    }
70  }
```

Listing 1.1. Pseudo code for the implementation of the main loops for the *Smith-Waterman* algorithm

3.1   *Smith-Waterman* Implementation Using Blocking and Non-blocking *OpenSHMEM* Operations

In the *OpenSHMEM* version of the *Smith-Waterman* algorithm, the sequence of length n is split up across the p PEs, where each PE gets n/p codons. Each PE will fill out the matrix A for each element it has in the main sequence, ensuring that access for the score matrix, the main gap matrix, and main sequence are all local, leaving remote access for the match sequence and the match gap array.

An additional optimization to the *OpenSHMEM* version of *Smith-Waterman* algorithm is the option for prefetching data. On a particular PE it is easy to compute which codons will be needed next and which element of the score matrix will be needed next. Therefore, it is easy to issue the fetches for the next loop iteration at the beginning of the current inner loop using the code path at line 30 in Listing 1.1.

The communications in the inner loop are completed by shmem_quiet(). At the very end of the inner loop, at line 65, the algorithm will issue blocking put operations to write the new results for scores and gaps. The algorithm does not need these values until the next iteration of the outermost loop. This means that each inner loop will wait on the put operations as well as the non-blocking get operations on line 34.

In the future, we will extend the implementation to include non-blocking bulk get operations to process indices that are expected to be local to the calling PE.

This may help get additional overlap by reducing the network overhead. It should be easy to compute which indices will be needed on the next iteration and do a non-blocking bulk get on the entire index range.

3.2 *Smith-Waterman* Implementation Using *MPI-3* One-sided Operations

In the *Smith-Waterman* version that uses *MPI-3* one-sided interfaces, the sequence length is split evenly across the Message Passing Interface (MPI) processes. A single block of memory on each process was allocated to store all the necessary information, and it was associated with a window. The window was synchronized with the *MPI_Win_lock_all()* and *MPI_Win_unlock_all()* interfaces.

For communication, we used one-sided *put* and *get* interfaces, and we explored both blocking and non-blocking communication operations. The communication interfaces were mostly used for retrieving and setting data for the parts of the sequence that were located on other ranks. This was done using two approaches, with one version that simply retreived remote data as it was needed, and another that was optimized to prefetch data for future iterations by exploiting non-blocking operations. In this way, the two versions can be directly compared to the blocking and non-blocking *OpenSHMEM* versions, respectively. Since these operations are always non-blocking in nature (to the extent that local buffers can't be reused), MPI_Rget() was used in place of blocking routines, so that the associated request handle could be waited on for completion before the results are needed without having to flush out all other pending operations as well. When prefetching future data in the optimized version, MPI_Get() was simply used instead, and a flush was performed on a future iteration before the results were needed.

The performance of both *MPI-3* implementations was worse than the *OpenSHMEM* implementation as you can observe from Fig. 6. When trying to improve upon them, all the MPI_Rget() calls were replaced with MPI_Get(), and instead of waiting on a request handle, additional flushes had to be issued for each time the result was about to be used. This inevitably caused a lot of unnecessary flushing and noticeably negated the potential improvement for the "non-blocking" prefetch version since those operations still had to be flushed out early due to future "blocking" calls. However, this actually resulted in a significant performance boost, though it was still noticeably slower than the *OpenSHMEM* runs, which may be attributed to the excessive flushing. Why the use of MPI_Rget() resulted in such a large drop in performance is unclear, though may simply be an implementation quirk due to the relatively young age of the new one-sided API.

4 Evaluation

This section presents the evaluation and performance characteristics of the *Smith-Waterman OpenSHMEM* and *MPI-3* implementations.

4.1   Testbed

The experiments were conducted on Titan, housed at OLCF. It contains 18,688 compute nodes, each of which includes one 16-core 2.2 GHz AMD Opteron 6274 (Interlagos) processor with 32 GB of RAM and an NVIDIA Kepler GPU with 6 GB of DDR5 memory. It uses a 3D torus network built from Gemini application- specific integrated circuits (ASICs).

For our experiments, the *OpenSHMEM* implementation of the benchmark uses Cray SHMEM, and the *MPI-3* implementation uses Cray MPI.

4.2   Performance of Strongly Scaling *Smith-Waterman* Implementation - *OpenSHMEM* and *MPI-3*

Figure 6 shows the completion time in seconds for the *OpenSHMEM* implementation and *MPI-3* while keeping the matrix size sequence size constant at sequence size 65536 for a score matrix size 65536^2 (SCALE=32), and increasing the number of the nodes. For this experiment, the problem was launched with one PE per node. The benchmark was run for two iterations and we are presenting the average runtime. The green bar is the completion time of the *OpenSHMEM* implementation when using blocking *put* and *get* interfaces, while the yellow bar is the completion time of the *OpenSHMEM* implementation when using non-blocking *get* interfaces. The red bar is the completion time of the *MPI-3*

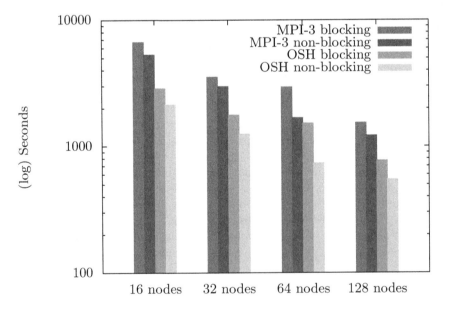

Fig. 6. The completion times of the *OpenSHMEM* and *MPI-3 Smith-Waterman* implementations, while the problem size is kept constant and the number of nodes is increased (Color figure online)

implementation when using blocking *put* and *get* interfaces, while the blue bar is the completion time of the *MPI-3* implementation when using non-blocking *get* interfaces.

OpenSHMEM Strong Scaling: From Fig. 6, we can observe that the implementation has good strong scaling, i.e. as we increase the resources (nodes) to the solve the problem, the completion time decreases. For 16 PEs and nodes, the completion time is 2877.5 s, and for 128 PEs and nodes, the completion time decreases to 770 s.

The results also show that the *Smith-Waterman* algorithm implementation with non-blocking operations performs better than the implementation with blocking operations. It is 34 % better when using 16 PEs, and 41 % better when using 128 PEs. This makes sense as we can achieve an overlap of communication and computation when using non-blocking operations. The innermost loop can issue a non-blocking *get* at the top of its loop for the next iteration. The loop then waits for the completion of the non-blocking *get* before starting the next iteration of the inner loop.

Performance Comparision of *MPI-3* and *OpenSHMEM* Implementations: Fig. 6 clearly shows that the *OpenSHMEM* implementation runs considerably faster than the *MPI-3* implementation. At 128 nodes the *OpenSHMEM* implementation completes in 546.5 s while the *MPI-3* implementation completes in 1220 s, a 123 % improvement.

At 16 nodes the *MPI-3* implementation completes in 5318 s while the *OpenSHMEM* implementation completes in 2142 s, a 148 % improvement. At 64 nodes the *OpenSHMEM* implementation was 129 % faster and at 32 nodes it was 138 % faster then the *MPI-3* implementation. In all cases the *OpenSHMEM* implementation was over 100 % faster.

There is an interesting performance anomaly at 64 nodes, where going from 32 nodes to 64 nodes in the blocking implementations of both *MPI-3* and *Open-SHMEM* did not get the expected speed ups. There was only a 22 % speed up instead of the 67 % speed up seen in the non-blocking implementations and the 61 % speed up seen going from 16 nodes to 32 nodes in the blocking implementation. This anomaly seems to be Titan specific, since it is not reproducible on other test systems at similar scales.

4.3   Performance of Weakly Scaling *Smith-Waterman* - *OpenSHMEM* Implementation

Figure 7 shows the completion time in seconds for *OpenSHMEM*, while the problem is scaled logarithmically and the number of nodes is doubled. For 16 nodes, the completion time is 263 s, and the problem size is 29 in the non-blocking version.

The *OpenSHMEM* implementation using non-blocking interfaces performs better than the implementation using blocking interfaces. This is similar to the

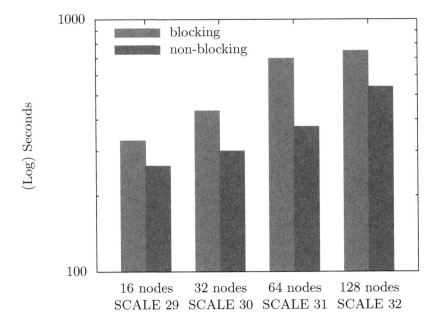

Fig. 7. The completion times of the *OpenSHMEM* and *MPI-3 Smith-Waterman* implementations, while the problem size and the number of nodes is increased

results that we observed for the strong scaling case. For 128 nodes, the non-blocking version performs 39 % better than the blocking version.

5   Conclusion

This paper presented two approaches to parallelize the *Smith-Waterman* algorithm for distributed memory systems using one-sided semantics provided by *OpenSHMEM* and *MPI-3*. The results show the advantages of parallelization for both strong and weak scaling experiments. Our experience and results show that though both programming models provide interfaces and semantics to implement the algorithm, the performance characteristics of the *OpenSHMEM* implementation were better than the *MPI-3* implementation. Due to the preliminary nature of the comparison analysis, these performance advantages may be more of a consequence of implementation rather than semantics. The code is available on the web site gitlab, and we plan to open source the implementation and make it available publicly.

Acknowledgments. This work is supported by the United States Department of Defense and used the resources of the Extreme Scale Systems Center (ESSC) located at the Oak Ridge National Laboratory (ORNL).

References

1. Smith, T.F., Waterman, M.S.: Identification of common molecular subsequences. J. Mol. Biol. **147**, 195–197 (1981)
2. Jaleel, A., Mattina, M., Jacob, B.: Last level cache (llc) performance of data mining workloads on a CMP - a case study of parallel bioinformatics workloads. In: 2014 IEEE 20th International Symposium on High Performance Computer Architecture (HPCA), pp. 88–98 (2006)
3. Wang, Y., Lu, J., Yu, J., Gibbs, R.A., Yu, F.: An integrative variant analysis pipeline for accurate genotype/haplotype inference in population NGS data. Genome Res. **23**, 833–842 (2013)
4. El-Saghir, Z., Kelash, H., Elnazly, S., Faheem, H.: Parallel implementation of smith-waterman algorithm using MPI, openmp and hybrid model. Int. J. Innovative Technol. Exploring Eng. **4**, 1–5 (2014)
5. Hamidouche, K., Mendonca, F., Falcou, J., de Melo, A., Etiemble, D.: Parallel smith-waterman comparison on multicore and manycore computing platforms with BSP++. Int. J. Parallel Prog. **41**, 111–136 (2013)
6. Noorian, M., Pooshfam, H., Noorian, Z., Abdullah, R.: Performance enhancement of smith-waterman algorithm using hybrid model: Comparing the mpi and hybrid programming paradigm on smp clusters. In: SMC 2009, IEEE International Conference on Systems, Man and Cybernetics, pp. 492–497 (2009)
7. Khajeh-Saeed, A., Poole, S., Perot, J.B.: Acceleration of the smith-waterman algorithm using single and multiple graphics processors. J. Comput. Phys. **229**, 4247–4258 (2010)
8. OpenSHMEM Org.: OpenSHMEM Specification (2015). http://openshmem.org/
9. The MPI Forum: MPI: A Message Passing Interface. Technical report, Version 3.0 (2012)
10. Gotoh, O.: An improved algorithm for matching biological sequences. J. Mol. Biol. **162**, 705–708 (1982)
11. ten Bruggencate, M.: Cray shmem update. Presentation regarding extensions to OpenSHMEM by Cray (2014). Accessed 23 June 2015
12. Bader, D., Madduri, K., Gilbert, J., Shah, V., Kepner, J., Meuse, T., Krishnamurthy, A.: Designing scalable synthetic compact applications for benchmarking high productivity computing systems. Cyberinfrastructure Tech. Watch **2**, 1–10 (2006)

Poster

Toward an OpenSHMEM Teams Extension to Enable Topology-Aware Parallel Programming

Ulf R. Hanebutte, James Dinan, and Joseph Robichaux

Intel Corporation, Seattle, USA

Abstract. The quest to reach exascale performance and beyond, requires holistic, system wide optimizations, including techniques to achieve more effective mappings of applications to the evolving system topology. Presently, the OpenSHMEM [3] standardization group is defining a new Processing Element (PE) teams API. Teams have conventionally been used in, e.g. MPI communicators [2], to define communication groups. In this work, we consider expanding upon this usage model by defining a teams interface that can be used to expose detailed system topology information to application developers. In addition to supporting conventional communication groups, the proposed teams API can be used to dynamically expose evolving network topology as well as heterogeneous node architecture and characteristics.

Keywords: OpenSHMEM standard · Exascale computing · TEAM concept · Platform topologies · Optimization

1 Proposed Teams API

Recently, Cray proposed an OpenSHMEM Teams extension [1] as a flexible way to manage PE subsets and they have provided an implementation in version 6.2.1 of the Cray Message Passing Toolkit (MPT). The proposed teams concept takes a PE-centric viewpoint that is intended to support intra-team communication, and we utilize this proposed interface as a foundation upon which to add additional enhancements.

The foundational teams API defines two baseline teams, `SHMEM_TEAM_WORLD`, which comprises all PEs, and `SHMEM_TEAM_NODE`, which comprises all PEs that share a processing node. Team creation is a collective operation that is carried out by all PEs belonging to the parent team. Creation is achieved through a collective call to the `shmem_team_split` routine, which groups PEs into new teams based on the value supplied in the `color` argument. It is the application's responsibility to set the color value and to track it, if needed. The proposed API provides information only about the group in which the given PE is a member; it does not provide query functions to obtain the number of groups that resulted from the split or the size of the groups produced. In addition, the `shmem_team_t` object that is returned is opaque and valid only on the PE at which it was produced.

© Springer International Publishing Switzerland 2015
M. Gorentla Venkata et al. (Eds.): OpenSHMEM 2015, LNCS 9397, pp. 195–197, 2015.
DOI: 10.1007/978-3-319-26428-8

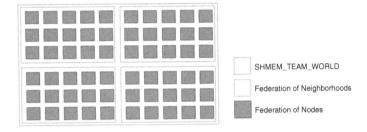

☐	SHMEM_TEAM_WORLD
☐	Federation of Neighborhoods
■	Federation of Nodes

Fig. 1. Graphical Depiction of two Federations created by Split Operations performed on SHMEM_TEAM_WORLD.

1.1 Federations — A System-Centric View

Extreme scale computing systems are increasingly comprised of hierarchical building blocks connected by scalable fabric topologies, including nodes with non-uniform memory access (NUMA) characteristics and hierarchical interconnection networking topologies, such as fat trees and dragonflies. Knowledge of the teams to which a given PE belongs can be provided through the foundational teams API, and this information can be used to accomplish many important tasks, such as topology-aware parallel decomposition. However, additional information about the broader system topology of the nodes allocated to a running job may open new opportunities in optimizing data distribution, work distribution, and communication planning.

In this work, we propose a two-stage approach to extending OpenSHMEM, where foundational team APIs are defined for the OpenSHMEM standard, and a reference user-level library is created to demonstrate a proposed, rich set of APIs that expose a greater degree of information to the application through a federations interface. System topology information can be gathered using existing efforts, such as netloc, hwloc and PIMx, and exposed through the proposed federations interface.

While OpenSHMEM Teams take a PE centric view, a system centric view is required to express topologies and to define inter-team operations. We capture this system-centric view through *federations*, which are represented in OpenSHMEM using a new shmem_federation_t type. Federations are created similarly to teams, through a split operation. However the resulting federation contains the set of all teams that were created as the result of split operation, as shown in Figure 1. We further define split keys, similarly to those used in the MPI_Comm_split_type operation, that can be used to generate federations that are derived from system topology.

In Figure 1, we show an example where SHMEM_TEAM_WORLD is split into a federation comprised of four teams. These teams correspond to neighborhoods in the system, for example all-to-all connected subgroups in a dragonfly network. We further show a second federation where SHMEM_TEAM_WORLD is split into a federation that contains all node teams. In both cases, the federation can be used to facilitate mapping of computation and data, and also to facilitate communication between PEs located in different topological groupings within the system. By defining API to generate federations based on system topology, PEs gain the capability to see a complete picture of how the given job maps to the system topology and adjust data, computation, and communication patterns to optimize for the given system.

References

1. ten Bruggencate, M.: Cray SHMEM update. Presented to OpenSHMEM Workshop, March 2014, http://www.csm.ornl.gov/workshops/openshmem2013/documents/presentations_and_tutorials/tenBruggencate_Cray_SHMEM_Update.pdf
2. Message Passing Interface Forum: MPI: A message-passing interface standard version 3.1. Technical report, University of Tennessee, Knoxville June 2015
3. OpenSHMEM Community: OpenSHMEM application programming interface, version 1.2. Technical report, (2015)

Author Index

Printed in the United States
By Bookmasters